History of the Late war Between the United States and Great Britain

HISTORY

OF

THE LATE WAR

BETWEEN THE

UNITED STATES AND GREAT BRITAIN:

COMPRISING

A MINUTE ACCOUNT OF THE VARIOUS

MILITARY AND NAVAL OPERATIONS.

BY H. M. BRACKENRIDGE.

Battle of the Wasp and Frolic.—Page 49.

Sixth Edition, improved and revised by the Author.

PHILADELPHIA:
JAMES KAY, JUN. & BROTHER, 122 CHESTNUT STREET.
PITTSBURGH: JOHN I. KAY & CO.
1836.

2644

Printed and Bound by
JAMES KAY, JUN. & BROTHER,
Philadelphia

PREFACE.

THE work now presented to the public, after passing
through five large editions, has been for many years entirely out of circulation, and it was with much difficulty
that a copy of it could be procured by the publishers. At
the time of its publication it was the only one calculated
for general use, and none has yet appeared comprising in
so small a compass so many details of the events of the
last war between Great Britain and the United States.
The frequent demands for the work have induced the
publishers to prevail on the author to revise and prepare it
for a new edition with great care. This is now offered to
the public.

As to the merit of the work, the reader must judge for
himself. Its *general accuracy* has received the approbation
of those most capable of judging. It has been translated
by a French writer, M. Dalmas, who speaks in high terms
of the energy of the style, and the clearness of the narrative. It has also been translated by an Italian writer of
celebrity.

The design of the work was not *a history of the times,*
embracing the legislative, diplomatic and statistical subjects connected with the war. These are occasionally
glanced at. But it was the intention of the author to
bring within one narrative, as far as it was practicable,
all the campaigns, battles, skirmishes and incidents which
may properly be considered as constituting the *events of the
war.* In a popular government like that of the United
States, where every individual occupies an important station in society, a war necessarily assumes a certain cast

of individuality; hence the necessity of introducing the names of so great a number of persons as we find in this work.

It was difficult, if not impossible, to weave all these materials into one connected story, especially when we consider that the war was carried on at so many different points having no connection with each other. There was the war of the south, that of the north-west, that on the Niagara, that along the seabord at various points; and there was the maritime contest, which was entirely distinct from that on the land. On the Niagara frontier there was much hard fighting; but every campaign opened under a new general, and sometimes before its close that general was superseded. After the fall of general PIKE, the war in that quarter was carried on without any settled plan or object, and it ended without accomplishing any thing, except to afford opportunity to a number of officers to distinguish themselves for their military talents and intrepidity : of these, generals BROWN, SCOTT, JESUP, MILLER, RIPLEY, TOWSON, are among those most deservedly eminent. To the north-west our military affairs were conducted on a different plan, and under a commander who was completely successful in what he undertook : in the south, the war was also confided to a single individual, who was found fully competent to the duties assigned him. HARRISON and JACKSON are therefore the only generals who can be said to have conducted entire plans of operation to a successful issue ; and their names are decidedly the most conspicuous in the history of the war.

CONTENTS.

CHAPTER I.

CHAPTER II.

CHAPTER III.

CHAPTER IV.

CHAPTER V.

A*

CHAPTER VI.

CHAPTER VII.

CHAPTER VIII.

CHAPTER IX.

CHAPTER X.

CONTENTS.

CHAPTER XI.

CHAPTER XII.

CHAPTER XIII.

CHAPTER XIV.

CHAPTER XV.

CHAPTER XVI.

CONTENTS. ix

CHAPTER XIX.

CHAPTER XX.

ERRATUM.—*At line 3 of page* 43, *and line* 1 *of page* 44, *for* captures *read* chases

BRACKENRIDGE'S

HISTORY OF THE WAR.

CHAPTER I.

Causes of the War with Great Britain—Rule of 1756—British Impressment of American Seamen—Attack on the Chesapeake—Differences with France—French Decrees—Embargo—Non-Intercourse—Indian Hostilities—Tecumseh—General Harrison—Battle of Tippecanoe—War with Great Britain inevitable.

THE perseverance of the British nation in attempting to exercise a power without right, over her American brethren, first broke the ties of dependence, which it was so much her interest to preserve; and her subsequent illiberal policy tended to weaken the influence of affinity, which a true wisdom would have taught her to cherish. Why is it that the enmity of those, between whom there are by nature the most numerous bonds of friendship, is the most bitter? It is because each of these is a distinct cord which may vibrate to the feelings of hatred, as well as of love. With China, with Turkey, with France, we may be governed by temporary and varying policy; but towards England we can never feel indifference. There always have been, and there still are numerous ties to attach us to Britain, which nothing but an ungenerous and unnatural policy can weaken or destroy.

With the acknowledgement of our independence, Great Britain did not renounce her designs of subjugation. Force had been found unavailing, she next resolved to try what might be done by insidious means. For many years after the peace of 1783, our affairs wore no promising appearance. The confederation which bound the states during their struggle against a common enemy, was too feeble to hold them together in a time of peace. The cement of our union being thus eaten

B

away, England foresaw what we had to encounter, and pro-
phesying according to her wishes, solaced herself with the
hope of seeing us divided, and engaged in civil broils. The
seeds of dissension had been abundantly sown; our state of
finance was deplorably defective; it might almost be said, that
the nation was at an end, for so many jarring interests discovered themselves in the states, as almost to preclude the hope
of reducing these discordant elements to harmony and order.
A state of anarchy and civil war might restore us to Great
Britain. Happily for America, she possessed at this moment,
a galaxy of sages and patriots, who maintained a powerful influence over the minds of their fellow-citizens. By their exertions, a spirit of compromise and accommodation was introduced,
which terminated in our present glorious compact—a second
revolution which secured to us the benefits of the first.

By this event Great Britain lost, for a time, the opportunity
of tampering with the individual states, of fomenting jealousies,
and of governing by division. Her policy was changed; it
became a favourite idea, that our growth should be repressed,
and so many impediments thrown in our way, as to convince
us, that we had gained nothing in becoming free. We soon
experienced the effects of her disappointment. Contrary to
express stipulation, she refused to surrender the military posts
on our western frontier, and, at the same time, secretly instiga-
ted the savages to murder the frontier settlers. Spain was, at
this very moment, practising her intrigues to draw off the western states from the confederacy, of which there is little doubt
England would soon have taken advantage.

But we also came in contact with Britain on the ocean: our
commerce began to flourish; and on the breaking out of the
French war, she found in us formidable rivals. In order to
put a stop to our competition, she called into life the odious,
and almost obsolete rule of 1756, which is in palpable violation
of the law of nations. The spirit of this rule is to prevent the
neutral from enjoying any commerce, which would not, at the
same time, be open to the belligerent; in other words, to permit no neutral. In practice it was carried to the full extent.
The orders in council of the 8th of January 1793, became the
source of a thousand vexations to American commerce; and yet
they were in a manner tolerable. compared to those of the 6th
of November, which were secretly circulated among the British
cruisers, authorising them to capture " all vessels laden with
the produce of any of the colonies of France, or carrying provisions or supplies to the said colony." The greater part of
our commerce was at once swept from the ocean. On this

occasion, our mercantile communities came forward, unbiassed by party divisions. They expressed themselves in the strongest terms against this treacherous and wicked procedure. The war of the revolution had not been forgotten ; that with the savages still raged : it was not by such acts, we could be induced to entertain a friendly feeling towards England. There prevailed a universal clamour for war, among the merchants particularly, and which it required all the firmness of Washington to withstand. This great man had marked out to himself the wise policy, of keeping aloof from European politics, and of avoiding all entanglements in their wars. Mr Jay was despatched as a special messenger, with orders to remonstrate in a manly tone. This mission terminated in the celebrated treaty of 1794 ; which was sanctioned by the nation, although not without great reluctance. It appeared in the sequel, that we had merely evaded a war, in order to recommence disputes concerning the same causes.

The British did little more than modify their orders in council, by those issued in 1795 and 1798. In fact, down to the peace of Amiens, the same vexations and abuses furnished a constant theme of remonstrance. Neither General Washington, nor Mr Adams, was able to arrange our differences with England, or induce her to consult her own true interests, by a just and liberal policy towards us. From this we may fairly infer, that no administration of our government could have succeeded in accommodating our differences upon just and equitable principles.

Another cause of complaint accompanied with equal step the violations of our commercial and maritime rights, and was of a nature still more vexatious. It is one upon which American feeling has always been much alive. Great Britain is the only modern nation, within the pale of civilization, at least of those who recognise the general maritime law, who does not consider the flag as protecting the person who sails under it; and we are the only people who, during peace, have been dragged from our ships on the high seas, by Christian nations, and condemned to servitude. This intolerable outrage grew up from a small beginning, by imprudent acquiescence on our part ; perhaps not conceiving it possible, that it could ever assume so hideous a front. At first, it was a claim to search our merchant vessels for deserters from the public service of Britain ; next, it became a right to impress English seamen, who had engaged themselves in American ships ; finally, every person who could not prove on the spot, to the satisfaction of the boarding officer, that he was an American, was carried away into a most hateful bondage. England had gone far, in asserting the right to search a neutral vessel, for enemy's goods ; but this pretended exception to the general rule that a ship on the high seas is as inviolable as the territory of the nation at peace, had been opposed by every power in Europe, excepting the one which happened for the time to be mistress of the seas ; a strong proof that it was not a right, but an abuse. The claim set up of a right to search neutral ships *for men*, is unsupported by any writer on the public law, or by one sound reason. She had no more right to claim her subjects from our ships, than from our territory. Whatever right she might have, to prevent them from quitting their country, at times when their services were required ; or of punishing them for doing so : she had no right to pursue them into our country, or demand them from us, unless sustained in doing so by express stipulation. But what she had no right to demand, she had a right to take by force! When closely pressed, she deigned at last to give some reasons in support of her practice :—she must have men to man her thousand ships—she was contending for her existence—we had no right to employ her seamen—our flag had no regard to her interests—our employment of foreign seamen was not regulated—our sufferings were the consequences of our own imprudence.—These were the only arguments that could be used in support of such a practice. If England said she must have men, we answered that we must have men also. We also were contending for our existence, but did not think it justifiable on that account to plunder our neighbours, or make them slaves. She said that we had no right to employ her seamen— we could answer that she had no right to employ ours. We were no more bound to consult her interest, than she considered herself bound to consult ours. The fact is, that no nation in the world employs a greater number of foreign seamen than Great Britain, in her immense commerce, and in her immense navy ; *and she has a right to employ them*, not for the reason she then assigned, to wit, that she was contending for her existence, or fighting the battles of the world, but because the thing was lawful in itself. So far from restricting herself, or *regulating* the practice, or consulting the *interests* of others, she consulted only her own interests, and held out enticements to foreign seamen, which no other nation did. Here, then, was a simple question ; how came that to be unlawful in America, which was lawful in Britain ? Would not Great Britain protect an American seaman, who has been made an Englishman by being two years in her service ? But were we to blame because her seamen preferred our service ? There was, in fact, nothing in the American practice to justify reprisals. The employment of English seamen, who voluntarily tendered their services, was lawful, however disagreeable it might be to England. How far a friendly feeling towards that country, might induce us to consult her convenience and interests, or how far our own weakness, or interest, might require us to waive our rights, was another matter.

This is placing the subject in the least reprehensible view, as respects England. But when we come to examine the manner in which this pretended right was exercised by her, it cannot be doubted for a moment, that the whole was a mere pretext to vex our commerce, and recruit for her navy, from American ships. This is evident, from the uniform practice of impressing men of all nations, found in them : Spaniards, Portuguese, Danes, Russians, Hollanders, and even Negroes. It was, in fact, an insult to every nation in the civilized world. *Tros Tyriusque nullo,* was the motto, although not in the friendly sense in which it was used by the Queen of Carthage. The British practice amounted to subjecting the crew of every American vessel, to be drawn up before a lieutenant of the navy, that he might choose out such as suited his purpose. The good sailor was uniformly an Englishman, and the lubber an American. It has been said, that the number of impressed Americans was exaggerated; was there no exaggeration as to the number of Englishmen in the American service ? Was it then of more importance, that Great Britain should prevent a few of her seamen from escaping into a foreign service, than it was to us, that free Americans should be doomed to the worst of slavery ?

England has never known the full extent of the sensations produced in America, by her practice of impressment. The influence of party spirit has contributed to deceive her. The great body of Americans have always felt this outrage to their persons, with the keenest indignation ; no American administration would ever express a different sentiment. She was much mistaken, if she supposed, that the outcry against her conduct was a mere party trick : it was deeply felt as an egregious insult. She did not know that the American seamen were, in general, of a class superior to her own ; that is, more decently brought up, of more reputable connexions, of better morals and education, and many of them looking forward, after the expiration of their apprenticeships, to be mates and captains of vessels ; or rather she knew it well, and therefore gave them her baleful preference. But mark the retribution which follows the steps of injustice. When any of these men were so fortunate as to escape from seven or ten years servitude on board a

B*

British man of war, they breathed nothing but revenge, and
imparted the same feeling to their countrymen. It was pie-
dicted, that these men who had *wrongs of their own*, would
be found, in case of war with England, no common foes. War
came, and Britain may read in our naval combats, a commen-
tary on her practice of impressment, and her tyranny on the
ocean.

As early as the year 1793, it was declared by the American
minister at London, that the practice of impressment had produced great irritation in America, and that it was difficult to
avoid making reprisals on the British seamen in the United
States. It is perhaps to be regretted, that General Washington's threat was not carried into execution, as it might have
brought the affair to issue at once. The practice had grown
so vexatious after the treaty of 1794, that the British government was told in plain terms, that unless a remedy was applied,
war would be inevitable. It was said to be of such a nature,
as no American could bear; "that they might as well rob the
American vessels of their goods, as drag the American seamen from their ships, in the manner practised by them." Certainly the offence would have been as much less, as a bale of
goods is of less value than a man. It was stated, that as many
as two hundred and seventy Americans were then actually in
the British service. the greater part of whom persisted in refusing pay and bounty. They were told, that if they had any
regard for the friendship of this country, they would facilitate the
means of relieving those of our oppressed fellow-citizens. That
the excuse alleged by Great Britain, of not being able to distinguish between her subjects, and the citizens of America,
was without foundation, inasmuch as foreigners who could not
be mistaken, were equally liable to impressment. The honour of the nation, it was said, was deeply concerned, and unless the practice should be discontinued, it must ultimately lead
to open rupture. This was the language uniformly held forth,
by every successive administration of the American government.
It was the theme of reprobation, and remonstrance, of every
distinguished statesman of this country. On this subject we
find Washington, Adams, Jefferson, Madison, Monroe, Marshall, Jay, Pickering, King, and many others, in their official
correspondence, fully and uniformly concurring. In fact, these
complaints continued until the last hour, in consequence of our
impolitic submission.

This shocking outrage was at length carried to such extent,
that voyages were often broken up, and the safety of vessels
endangered, by not leaving a sufficient number of mariners on

board to navigate them. It was estimated, that at least *seven thousand Americans* were at one time in the British service, against their will. Even as respects her own subjects, the practice of impressment is one of the most cruel and unjust; in direct opposition to the general freedom of her constitution, and only covered by the most miserable sophistry; but to America, who would not endure a single one of her citizens to be impressed into her own service, it is not surprising that it should appear detestable. The tribute of Minos, or of Montezuma, of the youth doomed as a sacrifice to infernal idols, was not more hateful. The American was compelled to stoop to the humiliation of carrying about him, on the high seas, the certificate of his nativity; and this was soon found unavailing, it was torn to pieces by the tyrant, and its fragments scattered to the winds. She boldly asserted the right of dragging from underneath our flag, *every one who could not prove on the spot, that he was not a British subject.* Every foreigner, no matter of what country, was, in consequence, excluded from our merchant service. On the part of the United States, every possible effort was made to compromise the matter, but in vain. No offer was ever made by Great Britian, which presented any prospect of putting an end to these abuses; while the most fair and rational on our part, were rejected. About the year 1800, a proposal was made for the mutual exchange of deserters, but this was rejected by Mr Adams, for the same reason that the President rejected the treaty of 1806—because it was thought better to have no provision, than one which did not sufficiently provide against the abuses of impressment. England offered to make it penal, for any of her naval officers to impress our seamen, provided we discontinued our practice of *naturalizing her subjects.* The mockery of such a proposition, alone fully proves her fixed mind. No plan could be devised so suitable to her wishes, as that of subjecting the liberty, life, and happiness of an American citizen, to the caprice of every petty lieutenant of her navy : otherwise, she would have been contented, with the exclusion of her subjects from all American vessels, a thing which she had no right to ask, but which we were willing to grant for the sake of peace.

The climax of this extraordinary humiliation, and which, a century hence, will scarcely be credited, was still wanting; the attack on the Chesapeake occurred, and, for the moment, convulsed the nation. This vessel was suddenly attacked within our waters in profound peace, compelled to surrender, and several seamen, alleged to be British, were then forcibly taken from her. The burst of indignation which followed, was even more

violent than that which was produced by the orders in council
of 1793. Party animosity was suspended, meetings were assembled in every village, the newspapers were filled with formal
addresses, volunteer companies were every where set on foot,
and, in the first phrensy of the moment, the universal cry was
for immediate war. Although hostilities were not declared,
the feelings of America were from that day at war with England: a greater attention was paid to the discipline of our
militia, and the formation of volunteer corps; and the government was continually making appropriations for our national
defence. We still resorted to negotiation; and the aggressors,
thinking that we might now possibly be in earnest, were willing
to avoid war by a sacrifice of pride. They yielded to the humiliation of surrendering the American citizens, upon the very
deck from which they had been forced; but, at the same time,
rewarded the officer by whom the violence had been offered.
In excusing her conduct, England condescended to tell us,
with a serious face, *that she never pretended to the right of
impressing American citizens*, and this, she seemed to consider,
rather as a magnanimous acknowledgement. Humiliating indeed, to be seriously told, that she did not regard our citizens
as her property! Nothing can furnish stronger proof of the
extent of the abuse, and the bad policy of our pacific course of
remonstrance. Our sacred duty to our fellow-citizens, as well
as a regard to our national character, forbade such an acquiescence.

From this review of the subject of impressment, we return
to the other principal branch of our national differences. It
must be evident to the reader, that nothing was to be expected
from any temporary arrangement on the part of our enemy:
that nothing short of a change in her general policy and temper,
would suffice, and nothing but a war could effect this change.
Whatever disputes we may have had with other nations, they
were of little moment, compared to our differences with England.
To settle the terms on which we were to be with her, was of
the first importance; our mutual intercourse and trade were of
vast extent; she occupied the highway to other nations, which
she could interrupt when she pleased; it was of little consequence on what terms we were with others, so long as our
relations with England were not properly adjusted. Our intercourse with France was comparatively of but little moment.
She had not recovered from the phrensies of her revolution; her
deportment was eccentric, lawless, and unstable; she was a
comet, threatening all nations. Our true wisdom was to keep
out of her way. On the ocean she was but little to be dreaded,

and was in no condition to execute her threats. But notwithstanding the power of England to sweep our commerce from
the ocean, and to seal our ports, we still expected something
from her good sense, her justice, or her interest. Yet scarcely
was the flame of war once more lighted up on the continent, than
both the belligerents began, under various pretexts, to prey upon
our commerce. On the part of England, the rule of 1756 was revived, and applied in a manner more intolerable than ever. The
sufferings of the American merchants were such, as to cause
them to call loudly on the government for protection; and a
war with England, at this time, was by many thought inevitable. It appeared to be her fixed determination, that neutrals
should enjoy no trade without her special license and permission. By some it was thought, that if we should enter into
her views, and declare war against France, she would amicably
arrange the points in dispute between us. This, however, was
very doubtful; it would only have encouraged her to make still
further claims. Such a thing was, besides, impossible. The
American people, still smarting under so many wrongs unre-
dressed, could not be induced to do what would amount almost
to a return to subjection.

In May 1806 Great Britain commenced her system of paper
blockade, by interdicting all intercourse with a great part of
France and her dependencies. This operated exclusively on
the United States, who were the only remaining neutrals. The
decrees of the French emperor of the 6th of November followed, and were immediately made known to our minister at London by the British government, with a threat, that if they were
put in execution (although the British minister well knew, that
it could be nothing more than a bravado) similar measures
would be adopted. But without waiting the result, in fact before the lapse of a fortnight, the British government issued the
orders in council of the 7th of January 1806, which went the full
length of declaring, that no vessel should be at liberty to trade
from one port of France to another, or from a port under her
control, and from which the English were excluded. Napoleon's Milan decrees succeeded, which were little more than
nominal to the neutral who did not place himself in his power;
they affected us, not England. We were the only sufferers in
this system of retaliation, which was, in fact, a gross violation
of neutral rights on the part of both. England was apparently
benefited, inasmuch as it struck a blow at our commerce, and
rendered it impossible for us to spread a sail without her permission. The belligerents presented the spectacle of two

highwaymen, robbing a passenger and then quarrelling for the
spoil; and yet this was called retaliation!

The United States sincerely wished to be at peace.   Each
of the belligerents accused us of partiality: and wherein was
that partiality?   Simply in this: France declared that we suffered the depredations of England with more patience, than her
own; and England, that she alone had a right to plunder us!
Each seemed to consider it as a previous condition of rendering
us justice, that we should compel her adversary to respect our
rights.   In this singular situation, it appeared the wisest course
to withdraw entirely from the ocean.   Experience soon taught
us that our embargo system could not be carried into effect, for
reasons which it is unnecessary to repeat.   The restrictive system was substituted; we placed it in the power of either of the
wrong'doers, to make us the open enemy of the other, unless
that other renounced his practices.   Napoleon was the first to
announce " a sense of returning justice;" our government, the
suffering party, declared itself satisfied.   *England had shown
no such sense of returning justice*, on this occasion; she had
promised to repeal her orders, provided the French decrees
were rescinded; but refused to take the official declaration of
the French minister, although we had, in a similar case before,
accepted her own, and positively refused to repeal the orders
in council, in default of evidence *that the French were disposed
to do us justice!*   It were useless to discuss the question of our
partiality to France or to England, while we were complaining
of the aggressions of both.   The meaning of both was obvious
enough; it was that we should take part in the affairs of Europe.   England supposed that we could do her service, and
Napoleon thought that we could injure England.

In the meantime, the loss of American property by the depredations of the belligerents, had been immense.   The vexations practised by the British cruisers off our coast, who made
it a point to harass the issuing and returning commerce of the
United States, kept the public mind continually inflamed.   Our
citizens were distracted amid these surrounding difficulties.   It
was agreed that we had ample cause of hostility against both
belligerents, but the administration was accused of undue lean-
ing towards France, and a disposition not sufficiently conciliatory towards England.   The friends of the administration declared, that the efforts to obtain redress from England were
weakened by a powerful British influence, which had grown
up of late years, in the Eastern States and in the commercial
cities.

While the public mind was in this state of ferment, from

our disputes with England and France, our frontiers were threatened with an Indian war, which, as usual, was attributed to the instigations of the former. The United States have frequently been charged with cruel violence and injustice to the Indians. That we have encroached upon their hunting grounds, cannot be denied, but this was the necessary consequence of the increase in our population: but the great difference between us and other nations, in relation to the Indian lands, is, that instead of taking them without ever acknowledging the right of the Indians, we have endeavoured to obtain them by fair purchase. The United States were the first to respect the Indian territorial right, as they were the first to abolish the slave trade.

There was, at this time, a celebrated Indian warrior, who had been always remarkable for his enmity to the whites, and who, like Pontiac, had formed the design of uniting all the different tribes, in order to oppose an effectual barrier to the further extension of the settlements. Tecumseh was a formidable enemy; he resorted to every artifice to stir up the minds of the Indians against us. Of an active and restless character, he visited the most distant nations, and endeavoured to rouse them by his powerful eloquence. He also assailed the superstitious minds of his countrymen, by means of his brother, a kind of conjuror, called "the Prophet." He had received assurances from the British of such assistance as would enable him to carry his plans into execution. In the year 1811, a council was held by governor Harrison, of the territory of Indiana, at Vincennes, and at which Tecumseh attended, to remonstrate against a purchase lately made from the Kickapoos and some other tribes. In a strain of native eloquence, the orator inveighed against the encroachments of the Americans, gave a history of the progress of the settlements, from the first commencement on the Delaware, to the moment at which he spoke, insisting that the lands were bestowed by the Great Spirit upon all the Indians in common, and that no portion could be disposed of without the consent of all. When Harrison replied to this extravagant pretension, he grasped his tomahawk, in a fit of phrensy, and boldly charged the American governor with having uttered what was false, while the warriors who attended him, twenty or thirty in number, followed his example: but Harrison had fortunately posted a guard of soldiers near, who put a stop to their fury. The council was, however, broken up, and nothing short of war was expected to result.

Towards the close of the year, the frontier settlers had become seriously alarmed; every thing on the part of the Indians appeared to indicate approaching hostilities. Governor Harrison resolved to move towards the Prophet's town, with a body of Kentucky and Indiana militia, and the Fourth United States regiment, under colonel Boyd, to demand satisfaction of the Indians, and to put a stop to their hostile designs.

On the 6th of November 1811, the army approached the Prophet's town; the Indians during the day manifesting every hostile disposition, excepting that of actually attacking, which they were not likely to do without having a decided advantage. Several attempts had been made, on the part of the governor, to bring them to a parley, which they sullenly rejected, until he approached within a mile of the town, when becoming alarmed for their own safety, they at length sent a deputation to make their excuse, and to profess their willingness to meet in council. The governor, in obedience to his instructions to avoid hostilities as long as it was possible, had been unwilling to attack their town until compelled by necessity, and now acceded to their proposals of holding a treaty the next morning. But distrusting these savages, with whose wily arts he was well acquainted, he cautiously looked out a place of encampment. He chose an elevated piece of ground, in the open prairie, after a careful reconnoissance by majors Taylor and Clark. The two columns of infantry occupied the front and rear. The right flank was occupied by captain Spencer's company; the left flank by three companies commanded by general Wells as major. The front line was composed of one battalion of United States infantry under major Floyd, and a regiment of Indiana militia under colonel Bartholomew. The rear line consisted of a battalion of United States infantry under captain Baen, commanding as major, and four companies of Indiana volunteers under lieutenant colonel Decker. The right flank was composed of Spencer's company of Indiana volunteer riflemen; the left of Robb's company of Indiana volunteers, and Guiger's, a mixed company of Kentucky and Indiana volunteers; a portion of United States troops turning the left front and left rear angles respectively. The cavalry under major Davies were encamped in the rear of the front line and left flank, and held in reserve as a disposable force. The army thus judiciously posted, was not more than a mile from the town.

The order given to the army in the event of a night attack, was for each corps to maintain its position until relieved. The dragoons were directed in such case, to parade dismounted, with their swords and pistols, and to wait for orders. The guard for the night consisted of two captain's commands of twenty-four men, and four non-commissioned officers; and two subaltern's guards of twenty men and non-commissioned officers; the whole under the command of a field officer of the day.

On the night of the 6th, the troops lay under arms, and the commander-in-chief was ready to mount his horse at a moment's warning. On the morning of the 7th, about four o'clock, he arose, and sat by the fire conversing with some of his family; orders had been given to beat the reveillé; the moon had risen, but overshadowed with clouds, which occasionally discharged a drizzling rain. At this moment the attack commenced. The Indians, in their usual stealthy manner, had crept up to the sentinels, intending to rush upon them, and kill them before they could fire; but being discovered, and the alarm given, they raised their yell, and made a furious charge upon the left flank. The guard in that quarter, being struck with panic, gave way, and the first onset was received by captain Barton's company of regulars, and captain Guiger's company of mounted riflemen, forming the left angle of the rear line. The fire there was severe; but the troops being already prepared, were soon formed, and gallantly opposed the fury of their assailants. The fires of the camp were instantly extinguished, excepting in front of Barton's and Guiger's companies, where the suddenness of the attack prevented this from being done. The governor, having no time to wait, mounted the first horse that could be brought to him, a fortunate circumstance, as his own, a fine grey, was known to the Indians, and became the object of their search. Finding the line weakened at the first point attacked, he ordered two companies from the centre of the rear line, to march up, and form across the angle in the rear of Barton and Guiger's companies. In passing through the camp, towards the left of the front line, he met major Daviess, who informed him that the Indians, concealed behind some trees near the line, were annoying the troops very severely, and requested permission to dislodge them. In attempting this, he fell mortally wounded, as did colonel White of Indiana.

In the mean time, a fierce attack was made on Spencer's and Warwick's companies on the right. Captain Spencer and his lieutenants were all killed, and captain Warwick was mortally wounded. The governor, in passing towards that flank, found captain Robb's company near the centre of the camp. They had been driven from their post, or rather had fallen back. He led them to the aid of captain Spencer, where they fought bravely during the remainder of the action: while in this act, his aid, colonel Owen, was killed at his side; this officer was

c

mounted on a white horse, and as the governor had ridden a grey the day before, it is probable that Owen was mistaken for him, by one of those Indians who had devoted themselves to certain destruction, in order to insure victory by killing the commander-in-chief.

Captain Prescott's company of United States infantry had filled up the vacancy caused by the retreat of Robb's company. Soon after Daviess was wounded, captain Snelling, by order of the governor, charged upon the same Indians, and dislodged them with considerable loss. The battle was now maintained on all sides with desperate valour. The Indians advanced and retreated, by a rattling noise made with deer hoofs, and fought with a degree of desperation seldom equalled. When the day dawned, captain Snelling's company, captain Posey's, under lieutenant Albright, captain Scott's and captain Wilson's, were drawn from the rear, and formed on the left flank; while Cook's and Baen's companies were ordered to the right. General Wells was ordered to take command of the corps formed on the left, and with the aid of some dragoons, who were now mounted, and commanded by lieutenant Wallace, to charge the enemy in that direction, which he did successfully, driving them into a swamp where the cavalry could not follow them. At the same time, Cook's and Larrabee's companies, with the aid of the riflemen and militia, on the right flank, charged the Indians and put them to flight in that quarter, which terminated the battle.

This is one of the most desperate battles ever fought with the Indians, and but for the caution and efficiency of the commander-in-chief, might have terminated like the night attack on general Sinclair. The army, with the exception of the regular troops under general Boyd, was chiefly composed of militia and volunteers, who had never been in battle before. Resolutions were passed by the legislatures of Kentucky and Indiana, highly complimentary of governor Harrison, and the officers and troops under his command; and the reputation of the commander-in-chief, as an able and prudent general, was established on the most solid foundation.

The battle of Tippecanoe contributed to inflame the temper of the country, already calling for war. A naval incident which occurred some time afterwards, did not serve to allay it. Off the American coast, commodore Rodgers, during the night, fell in with a British frigate, which afterwards proved to be the Little Belt; being hailed by the commodore, the commander merely repeated the question, and, after some minutes, actually fired several of his guns. On this, the commodore poured a broadside into her, and compelled her commander to beg for mercy. This was the first check the British commanders had received from us on the ocean.

The conduct of Great Britain, which grew every day more insupportable, can only be accounted for, by her belief that we could not (to use the contemptuous expressions of the day) "*be kicked into a war.*" The experiment of war, on the part of the United States, was an awful one; any administration might be justly apprehensive of venturing upon an experiment, the consequences of which no one could foresee. This forbearance was construed into pusillanimity, and the name and character of the United States had sunk low, in consequence, with every nation of Europe. We had become the butt and jest of Napoleon and the English ministry, and who yet vainly essayed to draw us into a participation in their wars. A war with Napoleon could not have been more than nominal, unless we united in a close alliance with England; without this, we could inflict on him nothing more than a simple non-intercourse. But a war with England would be a very different matter; without forming any alliance with Napoleon, we might assail her commerce, her public ships, and her adjoining provinces.

But Great Britain was contending for her existence, she was fighting the battles of the civilized world; it was therefore cruel and ungenerous to press our demands at such a moment. This was by no means evident. If it had been true, why did she continue, at such a time, to insult and abuse us in every possible shape? Notwithstanding this appeal, there were many amongst us who could see only a contest between two great nations for the mastery of the world. We saw the stupendous schemes of British aggrandisement, in every part of the globe, which had little the appearance of fighting for her existence. We saw her already mistress of the seas; we regarded any actual invasion of her shores, as a thing too visionary, even for Napoleon; we saw, in the lawless and unbounded projects of this despot, at which England affected to be alarmed, her best security, as they kept alive the fears and jealousies of the surrounding nations, and silently undermined his throne. We have seen how inconsiderable were, in reality, all his conquests. The existence of England was never in danger; Napoleon could never have subdued Spain and Russia; two projects, which all now admit to have been the extreme of folly. England was not fighting the battles of the world, but of her ambition; she was not the bulwark of our religion, but the instigator of the savages; she was not the world's last hope—That last hope is America; not as the pretended champion in the cause

of other nations, but as a living argument that tyranny is not
necessary to the safety of man; that to be degraded and de-
based, is not the way to be great, prosperous and happy.

CHAPTER II.

Declaration of War—General Hull reaches Detroit—Crosses into Canada—Skirmishes on the River Aux Canards—Taking of Michilimackinac—Battle of Brownstown—Battle of Magagua—Taking of Chicago—Surrender of Hull.

An interesting period in the history of this youthful nation
was fast approaching. Our affairs with Great Britain had become every day more and more embarrassed. The storm
already lowered, and there was little hope that the gathering
clouds would pass harmless over us. In consequence of this
state of things, the first session of the twelfth congress had
been protracted to an unusual length, and the eyes of America
were turned towards it in anxious expectation. On the 5th of
June 1812, the President laid before congress the correspondence between our secretary of state and the British minister
near our government, which seemed to preclude all hope of
coming to an adjustment, in the two principal points in dispute,
—the orders in council, and the subject of impressment. But we
had so often been on the point of a rupture with Great Britain,
that even at this moment no certain conjecture could be formed
by the most intelligent, of the probable result. The public
voice called loudly for war, at least this was the sense of a
great majority of the nation. At length, on the 18th of June,
after sitting with closed doors, the solemn and important appeal
to arms was announced. The President had communicated
his message, in which all our complaints against Great Britain
were enumerated with great force, and an opinion expressed
that no remedy, no hope now remained, but in open war. The
committee of foreign relations, to whom the message was referred, concurred with the President, in recommending the
measure. An act of congress was accordingly passed, which
received the sanction of the President on the same day; and on
the day following, the 19th of June 1812, war was publicly
proclaimed.

Declaration of War

This highly important and eventful act of the national legislature was variously received. In some places it produced demonstrations of joy, similar to that which followed our declaration of independence. War as a calamity, although unavoidable in the present state of the world, where the strong disregard the rights of the weak, should be received without despondency, but not with gladness. Many, however, regarded the war with England, as a second struggle in support of national independence; and not in the course of ordinary wars, waged for the sake of mere interest, or in pursuit of the plans of state policy. On the sea board, and in the eastern states, the sensations which it produced were far from being joyful. The sudden gloom by which their commercial prosperity was overcast, caused an awful sadness, as from an eclipse of the sun. The commerce of the cities, although for some years greatly restricted by the depredations of the two great contending powers of Europe, still lingered in hopes of better times: it must now be totally at an end; their ships must be laid up, and business almost cease. In different parts of the United States, the war would necessarily be more severely felt; in an extensive country like this, it is impossible it should be otherwise. Moreover, there were those who regarded this measure as a most interesting and eventful experiment. An opinion was prevalent that the form of our government was not adapted to war, from the want of sufficient energy in the executive branch, and from unavoidable divisions in the national councils. But what was much more to be feared, the union of our states had scarcely yet been perfectly cemented; and if the interests of any extensive portion should be too deeply affected, a dissolution of our compact, "the noblest fabric of human invention," might ensue. A powerful party was opposed to the measure, on the grounds, that an accommodation with England might yet be made, that war could not be otherwise than in subserviency to the views of France, and that we were unprepared for so serious a contest. The opposition of a great portion of the population, of the talents and wealth of the country, was entitled to respect, and would certainly tend to throw embarrassments on its prosecution. Unanimity, in so important a measure, was not to be expected; yet the disadvantages of this opposition would be greatly felt. It was foreseen that our Atlantic cities would be much exposed; that the coasts of the southern states would be laid open to the incursions of marauding parties; and that the western frontier would feel all the horrors of a savage and murderous warfare. Many persons, on the other hand, entertained the belief, that the Canadas would

c*

fall, and that the Floridas, in case that Spain should be brought into the contest on the side of England, would be ours. Thus should we be freed from troublesome neighbours, and end forever, that dreadful species of hostility in which we had been so often engaged with the savages. These hopes were not ill founded; but we were not aware, at the time, of our deficiency in experience, and want of a full knowledge of our resources—the causes of many subsequent calamities.

For some years previous to the declaration of war, a military spirit was gradually diffusing itself amongst the people. Pains were taken in disciplining volunteer companies throughout the country; a degree of pride and emulation was every where felt, to excel in military exercises. The general preparations for war seemed to be prompted by instinct of the approaching event. But the military establishments were exceedingly defective. Acts of congress had already authorized the enlistment of twenty-five thousand men; but it was found impossible to fill the ranks of a regular army, from the small number of individuals who were not in easy circumstances, and therefore under no necessity of enlisting. The whole number already enlisted, scarcely amounted to five thousand men, and these scattered over an immense surface of country. The President was authorized to receive fifty thousand volunteers, and to call out one hundred thousand militia. This force could not be expected to be otherwise serviceable, than for the purpose of defending the sea coast, or the frontier. A difficulty of still greater importance existed; the best troops in the world are inefficient, unless they happen to be led by able and experienced officers. Our best revolutionary officers had paid the debt to nature, and those who remained, were either far advanced in life, or had not been tried in other than subordinate stations; and besides, from long repose, had laid aside their military habits. There prevailed, however, a disposition to place a degree of reliance on the skill of the revolutionary soldier, from the mere circumstance of having been such, which was not corrected until we had been severely taught by after experience. Such was the situation of things, at the commencement of hostilities.

Governor Hull, at the head of about two thousand men, was on his march to Detroit, with a view of putting an end to the Indian hostilities, when he received information of the declaration of war. His force consisted of about one thousand regulars, and twelve hundred volunteers from the state of Ohio, who had rendezvoused on the 29th of April. In the beginning of June they advanced to Urbanna, where they were join-

ed by the Fourth regiment of United States infantry, and immediately commenced their march through the wilderness, still in
possession of the Indians, and which separated the inhabited
part of the state of Ohio, from the Michigan territory. From
the town of Urbanna to the Rapids, a distance of one hundred
and twenty miles, they had to pass through a country without
roads, and abounding with marshes. From the Rapids to Detroit, along the Miami of the Lake, and along the Detroit river,
there were a few settlements chiefly of French Canadians, but
in general the territory was but thinly inhabited; the whole of
its scattered population scarcely exceeded five or six thousand
souls. It was near the last of June when this little army reached the Rapids, after having experienced considerable obstacles,
in passing through a gloomy, and almost trackless wilderness.
They now entered an open and romantic country, and proceeded
on their march, full of an ardent and adventurous spirit, which
sought only to encounter difficulties and dangers. The volunteers of Ohio consisted of some of the most enterprising and
active young men of the state; finer materials were never collected. After taking some refreshment here, they loaded a
schooner with a part of their baggage, in order to lighten their
march. By some misfortune, intelligence of the existing war
did not reach the army, until it was on this march, and was
followed by the news of the capture of the schooner, and a
lieutenant and thirty men who had been put on board. On the
5th of July, they encamped at Spring Wells, opposite Sandwich, and within a few miles of Detroit. For some days the
army had been under the necessity of proceeding with great
caution, to guard against surprises from the Indians and their
allies, and who, but for this timely arrival, would have possessed themselves of Detroit: they, however, had thrown up
breast-works on the opposite side of the river, and had made
an attempt to fortify a position about three miles below. From
both these holds, they were soon compelled to retreat, by a
well directed fire from the American artillery.

This was the favourable moment for commencing active operations against the neighbouring province of Upper Canada;
and as governor Hull had received discretionary power to act
offensively, an immediate invasion was determined on. Preparations for this purpose were directly made, and boats provided to effect the passage of the whole army at the same instant. The British, aware of this design, attempted to throw
up a battery, for the purpose of opposing the landing. This was
twice rendered abortive; on their attempting it a third time,
they were permitted to accomplish it unmolested, as our army

could either land above or below it, and thus keep out of the reach of their guns, which consisted of seven small cannon, and two mortars. On the 12th, every thing being made ready, the army embarked, and landed without molestation, some distance above the fort, and entered the village of Sandwich. The inhabitants made no show of resistance, and were therefore respected in their persons and property; the principal part, however, had been marched to Malden, for the purpose of aiding in its defence. A proclamation was immediately issued by Hull, in which he declared his intention of invading Canada, but gave every assurance of protection to the inhabitants, whom he advised to take no part in the contest. The proclamation was written in a spirited and energetic style, and had he been eventually successful, there is no doubt but that it would have been regarded as an eloquent production. It has been censured by the British, as intended to seduce her subjects from their allegiance, as if this were not justifiable in an invading army; and as violating the laws of civilized warfare, in the declaration that no quarter would be given to any white man, found fighting by the side of an Indian. When we consider, that Indians give no quarter, there may be as much justice in retaliating, upon those who are fighting by their sides, as upon the savages themselves, for it may be presumed that both are actuated by the same intentions. It is not to be supposed that Hull was seriously resolved on carrying this threat into execution; his object was to prevent, if possible, the employment of savages. It was altogether a suggestion of his own, unauthorized by the government, and never acted upon by himself.

In a few days, possession was taken of the whole country along the Trench, or Thames, a beautiful river, whose borders are well settled. This service was performed by colonel M'Arthur, of the Ohio militia, who returned to camp, after having collected a considerable quantity of blankets, ammunition, and other military stores. Colonel Cass was then despatched in an opposite direction, towards Fort Malden, with two hundred and eighty men, for the purpose of reconnoitering the British and Indians. This place is situated at the junction of Detroit river with Lake Erie, thirteen miles south of Hull's camp. Colonel Cass, following the course of the stream, reached the river Aux Canards, about four miles from Malden, where he found a British detachment in possession of the bridge. After reconnoitering the situation of the enemy, the colonel placed a rifle company under captain Robinson, near the place, with orders, to divert the attention of the guard, by keeping up a fire until the remainder of the party should appear on the opposite side. This part of the detachment, was to have forded the river about five miles below. The design was frustrated, by their want of a sufficient knowledge of the country; the detachment was unable to reach the designated spot, until late in the evening. In the meanwhile, the attempt to surprise the post had been discovered, and it was strengthened by considerable reinforcements; notwithstanding which, a smart skirmish ensued, and the enemy was compelled to abandon his position, after losing eleven killed and wounded, besides several deserters. Colonel Cass, having no orders to retain possession of it, although constituting the principal obstruction between the American camp and Malden, thought proper to retire.

These skirmishes, in which the Americans were generally successful, served to inspire confidence, and, together with the proclamation, had an effect upon the Canadians, many of whom joined our standard, and threw themselves on Hull for protection. These were, however, but preludes to the main object in view, the reduction of Fort Malden. Preparations for this purpose proceeded slowly; no artillery was provided for the occasion. It was not until the beginning of August, that two twenty-four pounders and three howitzers were mounted, and no attempt in the meanwhile had been made upon the fort. The capture of this place, which would have been necessary in the prosecution of any further design, had now become necessary to self-preservation. A most unexpected disaster had happened during the last month; an event, to which many of our subsequent misfortunes are to be attributed. This was the surrender of Michilimackinac.

On the 16th of July, a party of three hundred British troops, and upwards of six hundred Indians, embarked at St Joseph's, and reached the island next morning. A prisoner was despatched to inform the garrison, and the inhabitants of the village, that if any resistance were made they would all be indiscriminately put to death. Many of the inhabitants escaped to the British for protection. The garrison consisted of no more than fifty-six men, under the command of lieutenant Hanks, of the artillery. A flag was now sent by the enemy, to the fort, demanding a surrender. This was the first intimation of the declaration of war, which the garrison had received. Until this moment, the American commandant had considered this as one of the outrages on the part of the Indians, which of late had been frequent; he had therefore resolved to defend himself to the last extremity. He now considered it prudent to agree to a capitulation, as there was no hope of being able to defend himself successfully, against so great a disparity of force. The garrison was accordingly delivered up; security to the property and persons of individuals was stipulated, and the British put in possession of one of the strongest positions in the United States, on that account, sometimes called the American Gibraltar. The situation completely commands the northwest trade, which is compelled to pass immediately under the guns of the fort, and consequently affords the best means of intercepting the Indian supplies, and of checking the incursions of those restless warriors. The blame of this affair has been thrown by some upon the government, by others on Hull: the following facts will enable the reader to judge. Hull reached Detroit on the 5th of July, and the fall of Michilimackinac took place on the 17th. The distance is two hundred and forty miles. That the British at Malden should have had sooner intelligence of the declaration of war, than the American general, is less surprising when we consider the wonderful activity of those engaged in the Indian trade, as well as the circumstances of the regular establishments, all along the lakes. Notwithstanding this, it is not easy to account for the tardiness with which the news of war was transmitted from Detroit to Michilimackinac; nor was this satisfactorily explained by the American general.

Intelligence of this unfortunate occurrence, which so completely changed the face of affairs, reached Hull on the 23d of July, while engaged in making preparations for the attack on Malden. The British, by this time, were considerably reinforced, and aided by an additional number of Indians. The golden moment had been suffered to pass. It is generally conceded, that if an assault had been made on the fort in the first instance, it must have fallen. This was the opinion of the officers: the general, however, declined it under various pretexts. But having neglected this opportunity, there was no longer any hope of carrying the place without being provided with a train of artillery, and the necessary means for a regular assault. The necessity of possessing the post, became every day more apparent. With the fall of Michilimackinac, that of Chicago, and all the other western posts, might be expected to follow, and the Indian tribes would move down with all the force of the Northwest Company; rendering the situation of our army extremely critical. In anticipation of these events, the general had sent repeated expresses to procure reinforcements. His confident expectations of those reinforcements, may probably be one reason of the slowness of his movements against Malden, contenting himself with carrying on a vigilant partizan war, in itself of little consequence. Reinforcements were not hastened, from the belief that the force under his command, was more than sufficient for all the purposes that could be accomplished in this quarter.

The spirit which had animated the troops, in the first instance, was gradually giving way to the feelings of despondency; while their commander had by this time nearly lost their confidence. By the 1st of August, every thing being made ready for the attack on Malden, a council of war was convened, and the result was a determination to make it immediately. Desertions from the Canada militia still continued, and the whole force was animated with the prospect of undertaking an enterprise, which it was believed could not but be successful. The cannon was well mounted, and embarked on floating batteries. The general had approved the deliberations of the council, and the day was actually appointed for carrying them into execution.

Some time before this, a company of Ohio volunteers, under the command of captain Brush, had arrived at the river Raisin, with supplies for the army. As their march to Detroit, a distance of thirty-six miles, was attended with considerable dangers, from parties of the enemy, it was deemed prudent to remain here until an escort could be sent to guard them. This duty was confided to major Vanhorn, with a detachment of one hundred and fifty men. On his second day's march, near Brownstown, he was suddenly attacked on all sides by British regulars and Indians. His little force made a determined resistance, and being commanded by a brave and skilful officer, was at length brought off, with the loss of nineteen killed and missing, and nine wounded. Captains Gilcrease, M'Culloch, and Bostler were killed, and captain Ulry severely wounded.

Scarcely had this detachment left the camp at Sandwich, when a sudden and unlooked for change took place in the determination of the commander-in-chief. Without any apparent cause, or the occurrence of any new event, he announced his intention of abandoning not only the design upon Malden, but even the position which he then held. This operated very unfavourably upon the army; the volunteers murmured; they upbraided their commander with pusillanimity, and even treachery; and it was with difficulty they could be restrained by their own officers, in whom they confided. The disappointment and vexation which ensued, can better be imagined than described: all confidence in their leader was evidently at an end: if treacherous, he might deliver them up to be massacred; and it was evident he was deficient in the skill and ability necessary to command. It was with much reluctance this gallant little army was compelled to abandon, almost in disgrace, the flattering hopes which they thought themselves on the point of realizing. They reached the opposite shore on the 8th of August, where they received the intelligence of the affair of major Vanhorn, of the day before. Such was the termination of this expedition into Canada, of whose success, an account was every moment expected in the United States. Happy had it been if the misfortunes of our aims had terminated here! The enemy's territory was not, however, entirely evacuated; a detachment of about three hundred men was left to keep possession of Sandwich, principally with a view of affording some protection to the Canadians who had been induced by Hull's proclamation to join our standard.

One thing was now on all hands considered indispensable, the opening the communication with the river Raisin. In a few weeks, the army might stand in need of the supplies in the possession of captain Brush; and at all events, its situation was rendered extremely unpleasant, by being thus cut off from all communication with the state of Ohio. To effect this object, a respectable force was detached under lieutenant-colonel James Miller, of the United States army, consisting of three hundred regulars of the gallant Fourth regiment, which had distinguished itself under colonel Boyd, at the battle of Tippecanoe, and also about two hundred militia. The enemy, anticipating a renewal of the attempt, had sent reinforcements of regulars and Indians, so that their force was little short of seven hundred and fifty men: this force might, moreover, be increased during an engagement, from Malden, which is situated opposite Brownstown. They had also thrown up a temporary breast-work, of trees and logs, about four miles from this town, at a place called Magagua, behind which the greater part of the Indians, under Tecumseh, lay concealed, waiting the approach of the Americans; the whole commanded by major Muir, of the British army.

On the 9th, our detachment proceeded on its march, but with great caution, from the danger of surprise. They, however, drew near the ambuscade, before it was discovered; when suddenly the attack was commenced on captain Snelling, who commanded the advance, with the usual barbarous shouts of the enemy. This corps, undaunted by this sudden onset, kept its ground until the main body approached, when the Indians sprang up, and with the regulars furiously advanced to the front of the breast-work, where they formed a regular line, and commenced a heavy fire. Colonel Miller, with the utmost celerity and coolness, drew up his men, opened a brisk fire, and then charged. The British regulars gave way, but the Indians under Tecumseh, betaking themselves to the woods on each side, kept their ground with desperate obstinacy. The regulars being rallied, returned to the combat, which continued for some time, with equal resolution. The conduct of our countrymen, on this occasion, cannot be too much admired : the stoutest hearts might have failed when thus attacked on all sides by more than five hundred savages, painted in the most hideous manner, and yelling like demons; engaged at the same time with a body of regulars. Disregarding both the savage shrieks and the musketry of the British, the American leader repelled their attacks on every side, his troops gallantly maintaining their ground until the enemy was compelled to yield. They retired slowly to Brownstown, literally retreating at the point of the bayonet; here they hastily embarked in boats, provided for their reception. Had not this precaution been taken, it is probable the whole force would have fallen into the hands of the Americans. Their loss was, of the regulars, fifteen killed, and thirty or forty wounded, but of the Indians nearly one hundred were left on the field. In this battle, which lasted about two hours, we had fifteen killed, and about sixty wounded. The officers who chiefly distinguished themselves were captain Baker, lieutenants Larrabee and Peters, and ensign Whistler. The next day at noon, colonel Miller, who kept possession of Brownstown, received orders to return to Detroit. This was rendered necessary from the fatigue which his command had experienced in the engagement of the day before. It was thought more advisable to send a fresh detachment to accomplish the ultimate object.

An occurrence took place about this time in another quarter, which ought not to be passed in silence. Captain Heald, who commanded at fort Chicago, had received orders from Hull to abandon that post and make his way to Detroit. He accordingly consigned the public property to the care of some friendly Indians; and with his company, about fifty regulars, accompanied by several families, which had resided near this place, set out on his march. He had proceeded but a short distance along the beach of the lake, when he was attacked by a large body of Indians, who occupied the bank. Captain Heald ascended the bank, and fought them for some time, until they had gained his rear and taken possession of his horses and baggage. He then retired to an open piece of ground, where he was enabled to keep the Indians at bay. But finding that he would be compelled to yield at last, he accepted the offer of protection from an Indian chief. Twenty-six regulars were killed, and

D

all the militia; a number of women and children were inhumanly murdered. Captain Wells and ensign Warner were among the killed. Heald with his lady, who had received six wounds, himself severely wounded, after a variety of escapes, at length reached Michilimackinac.

The victory at Magagua, though brilliant and highly honourable to the American arms, was productive of no essential advantage. Two days afterwards, a despatch was sent to captain Brush, who was still in waiting for the escort at the river Raisin, informing him that in consequence of the fatigue of the victorious detachment, it had been rendered incapable of proceeding further, and that it was become impossible to send a sufficient force by the usual route; that he must therefore remain where he was until circumstances should be more favourable. In a postscript, the general advised him that an attempt would be made to open the communication in another quarter, by crossing the river Huron higher up the country. And accordingly, on the 14th, colonels Miller and Cass were despatched with three hundred and fifty men, for this purpose. Some time before this, an express had been received from general Hall, commanding at Niagara, bringing information that it was not in his power to send reinforcements.

On the 19th, the British took a position opposite Detroit, and immediately set themselves about erecting batteries. On their approach, major Denny, who commanded at Sandwich, abandoned his position, and crossed over to Detroit, it having been determined to act entirely on the defensive. The British continued their preparations for the attack. On the 15th, a flag of truce was sent by them to summon the place to surrender. A note to the following effect was directed to general Hull, by the British commander: "Sir—The forces at my disposal authorize me to require of you the surrender of Detroit. It is far from my inclination to join in a war of extermination, but you must be aware that the numerous body of Indians who have attached themselves to my troops will be beyond my control the moment the contest commences. You will find me disposed to enter into such conditions as will satisfy the most scrupulous sense of honour. Lieutenant-colonel M'Donald and major Glegg are fully authorized to enter into any arrangements that may tend to prevent the unnecessary effusion of blood." This was signed by major-general Brock.

To this summons an answer was returned, that the fort would be defended to the last extremity. The British immediately opened their batteries, and continued to throw shells during a great part of the night. The fire was returned, but

with little effect on either side. In the morning, it was discovered that the British were landing their troops at Spring
Wells, under cover of their ships. To prevent the landing
from the fort, at this moment, was a matter impossible; the
town lying between it and the river. But if Hull had not
neglected the advice of his officers, he might have effectually
prevented it, by erecting batteries on the bank, where they
would be compelled to debark. A strange fatality seemed to
attend this unfortunate man in every thing he did, or neglected
to do. The enemy having landed, about ten o'clock advanced
towards the fort in close column, and twelve deep. The fort
being separated from the town, by an open space of about two
hundred yards, they would be enabled to approach within this
distance, before its guns could be brought to bear upon them,
unless they could approach in the rear. The American force
was, however, judiciously disposed to prevent their advance.
The militia, and a great part of the volunteers, occupied the
town, or were posted behind pickets, whence they could annoy
the enemy's flanks; the regulars defended the fort, and two
twenty-four pounders charged with grape, were advantageously
posted on an eminence, and could sweep the whole of the
enemy's line, as he advanced. All was now silent expectation: the daring foe still slowly moved forward, apparently
regardless, or unconscious of their danger; for their destruction must have been certain, had they not been impressed with
contempt for a commander, who had so meanly abandoned
Sandwich a few days before. The hearts of our countrymen
beat high, at the near prospect of regaining their credit. But
who can describe the chagrin and mortification which took
possession of these troops, when orders were issued for them
to retire to the fort; and the artillery, at the very moment
when it was thought the British were deliberately advancing
to the most certain destruction, was ordered not to fire! The
whole force, together with a great number of women and children, was gathered into the fort, almost too narrow to contain
them. Here the troops were ordered to stack their arms, and
to the astonishment of every one, a white flag, in token of submission, was suspended from the walls. A British officer
rode up to ascertain the cause. A capitulation was agreed to,
without even stipulating the terms. Words are wanting to express the feelings of the Americans on this occasion; they
considered themselves basely betrayed, in thus surrendering to
an inferior force without firing a gun, when they were firmly
convinced that that force was in their power. They had provisions for at least fifteen days, and were provided with all the

requisite munitions of war. They were compelled, thus hu-
miliated, to march out, and to surrender themselves prisoners
at discretion. The British took immediate possession of the
fort, with all the public property it contained ; amongst which
there were forty barrels of powder, four hundred rounds of
fixed twenty-four pound shot, one hundred thousand ball cartridges, two thousand five hundred stand of arms, twenty-five
pieces of iron cannon, and eight of brass, the greater number of
which had been captured by the Americans during the revolutionary war.

The whole territory, and all the forts and garrisons of the
United States, within the district of the general, were also
formally surrendered, and the detachment under colonels
Cass and M'Arthur, as well as the party under captain Brush,
were included in the capitulation. Orders had been despatched
the evening before, for the detachment under Cass and M'Arthur to return, and they had approached almost sufficiently
near to discover the movements of the enemy, while their accidental situation might enable them to render the most
material service during the attack. They were surprised at
the silence which prevailed, when every moment was expected
to announce the conflict; and that surprise was soon changed
into rage, when they learned the capitulation. A British
officer was then despatched to the river Raisin, to convey the
intelligence to captain Brush, who at first gave no credit to so
improbable a tale, and actually put the officer in confinement.
The melancholy story was, however, soon confirmed by some
Americans who had escaped. Captain Brush indignantly refused to submit to the capitulation, declaring that Hull had no
right to include him, and determined to return to the state of
Ohio. He first deliberated, whether he should destroy the
public stores, which he had in his possession, and which he
could not carry away, but reflecting that this might be used as
a pretext for harsh treatment to his countrymen, he resolved
to abandon them. The greater part of the volunteers and
militia, were permitted to return home ; but the regulars, together with the general, were taken to Quebec.

In his official despatch, Hull took great pains to free his conduct from censure. In swelling the account of the dangers
with which he conceived himself beset, every idle rumour
which had operated on his fears, was placed under contribu-
tion, while his imagination conjured up a thousand frightful
phantoms. He magnified the reinforcements under colonel
Proctor, and gave implicit belief to the story that the whole
force of the Northwestern Fur Company, under major Cham-

bers, was approaching; nothing, in fact, was forgotten, which
could heighten the picture, or tend to take the blame from
him. While on the Canada side, it was impossible to effect
any thing against Malden, from the difficulty of transporting
his artillery. Every thing is difficult to a man who wants the
necessary talents. The British garrison had been wonderfully
strengthened, and at this critical moment, general Hall, of
Niagara, announced that it was not in his power to assist him.
What then could be done but to cross over to Detroit, that is,
to abandon the inhabitants of Canada, who had placed themselves under his protection; to fly, before the enemy had even
attempted to attack or molest him, and thus encourage them in
what they would never probably have thought it possible to
accomplish.

But what appears most to figure, in this attempted vindication, is the frightful display of Indian auxiliaries. The whole
" Northern hive," as he called it, was let loose: Winnebagos,
Wyandots, Hurons, Chippeways, Knistenoos and Algonquins,
Pottowatomies, Sacks and Kickapoos, were swarming in the
neighouring woods, and concealed behind every bush, ready
to rush to the indiscriminate slaughter of the Americans. He
represented his situation at the moment of surrender, as most
deplorable. In consequence of the absence of colonels Cass
and M'Arthur, he could not bring more than six hundred men
into the field, and he was, moreover, destitute of all necessary
supplies and munitions of war: yet, by the morning's report,
his force exceeded a thousand men fit for duty, besides the detachment which might be expected to arrive, about the time of
the engagement; and also three hundred Michigan militia who
who were out on duty, which would make his force upwards
of sixteen hundred. This force was much superior to that
of the British, which consisted of about seven hundred regulars, one half of which was nothing more than militia dressed
in uniform, for the purpose of deception, and about six hundred
Indians. Every other part of his statement was proved, by
the officers under his command, to have been incorrect or exaggerated. The most ordinary exertion would have sufficed,
to have completely destroyed the British force. He declared,
that he was actuated by a desire to spare the effusion of human blood! If he had designedly intended the destruction of
his fellow-citizens, he could not have fallen upon a more unfortunate measure; for by thus opening the frontier to the
tomahawk of the savage, and giving reasons to our enemy for
representing us as contemptible in arms, he invited those very
savages, which he so much dreaded, to throw off every re-

D*

straint, and declare themselves our foes.   He might have foreseen, that a considerable force would be sent by the British,
for the purpose of retaining this province, and that our country
would be compelled to suffer an immense expense of blood and
treasure, before our possessions here could be regained.   Although this afterwards became the theatre of war, where many
of our countrymen gained military renown, yet the effect of
this lamentable occurrence was visible in every subsequent
transaction on the borders of Canada.

The sensations produced by this occurrence, throughout the
United States, and particularly in the Western country, can
scarcely be described.   At first no one could believe an event
so extraordinary and unexpected ; the public mind was so entirely unprepared for it, that universal astonishment was occasioned.   Whatever doubts might have been entertained, of his
being able to subdue the country which he had invaded, there
were none of his being able to defend himself.   Never was any
people more deeply and universally chagrined.   This event,
in a country where every man has a personal feeling for the
honour and welfare of the nation, naturally awakened the strongest sympathy with the friends and families of the brave soldiers who had been thus wretchedly surrendered by their commander.

The general was afterwards exchanged for thirty British
prisoners.   Neither the government nor the people were satisfied with his defence.   The affair was solemnly investigated
by a court martial.   He was charged with treason, cowardice,
and unofficer-like conduct.   On the first charge, the court declined giving an opinion; on the two last he was sentenced to
death; but was recommended to mercy in consequence of his
revolutionary services, and his advanced age.   The sentence
was remitted by the President; but his name was ordered to
be struck from the rolls of the army.   The general afterwards
published an elaborate, but hopeless vindication.

CHAPTER III.

Naval Events—Cruise of Commodore Rodgers—The President captures the Belvidera—Cruise of Captain Hull—The Constitution captures the Guerriere—Commodore Porter captures the Alert—Cruise of the President and the Congress—of the Argus—The United States captures the Macedonian—The Wasp captures the Frolic—Exploits of American Privateers—Results of the Naval Warfare—Sensations excited in England

THE common observation, that evils do not come alone, but with others linked in their train, was happily not verified, at the period of the misfortunes of our arms in the west. The nation, overspread with gloom in consequence of this unexpected disaster, was suddenly consoled in the most pleasing manner. A new and glorious era burst upon our country. The historian will record the fact, that the same year which saw prostrated the despot of the land, also beheld the pride of the tyrant of the ocean completely humbled. A series of the most brilliant exploits, on that element, raised our naval renown, to a height which excited the surprise and admiration of Europe.

At the moment of the declaration of war, a squadron under commodore Rodgers, had rendezvoused under the orders of the government, off Sandy Hook. The squadron consisted of the frigates President, Congress, United States, and the brig Hornet. On the 21st of June they put to sea, in pursuit of a British squadron, which had sailed as the convoy of the West India fleet, the preceding month. While thus engaged, the British frigate Belvidera was discovered, to which they instantly gave chase. The chase was continued from early in the morning until past four in the afternoon, when the President, outsailing the other vessels, had come within gun shot. She opened a fire with her bow guns, intending to cripple the Belvidera, which returned it with her stern chasers. The firing was kept up for ten minutes, when one of the guns of the President burst, killed and wounded sixteen men, and fractured the leg of the commodore. By this accident, and the explosion of the passing-box, the decks were so much shattered, as to render the guns on that side useless. The ship was then put about, and a broadside fired, but without the desired effect, though considerable injury was done the Belvidera. This vessel, having thrown overboard every thing she could spare, now gained ground. The chase was continued until eleven o'clock at night, before it was deemed hopeless. The squadron then continued its pursuit of the convoy, which it did not give over until within sight of the British channel; then stood for the Island of Madeira; and thence, passing the Azores, stood for Newfoundland, and thence, by Cape Sable, arrived at Boston the 30th of August, having made prize of several British vessels; but, owing to the haziness of the weather, they were less successful than might have been expected.

The frigate Essex went to sea from New York, on the 3d of July; the Constitution sailed from the Chesapeake on the 12th, the brigs Nautilus, Viper, and Vixen, were at the same time cruising off the coast, the sloop of war Wasp was at sea on her return from France.

The Constitution, captain Hull, had sailed from Annapolis on the 5th of July. On the morning of the 17th, off Egg Harbour, she was chased by a ship of the line, the Africa, and the frigates Shannon, Guerriere, Belvidera, and Æolus. These vessels were approaching rapidly with a fine breeze, while it was nearly a calm about the Constitution. At sunrise the next morning, escape from the enemy was almost hopeless, as they were then within five miles. The Constitution was therefore cleared for action, determined to make a desperate resistance. The enemy still drawing near, captain Hull resolved to make another effort to escape. Boats were sent ahead, with anchors for the purpose of warping, there prevailing almost a calm. The others finding the Constitution gaining upon them, resorted to the same expedient. The chase continued in this manner for two days, partly sailing with light breezes, and partly warping, until the 20th, when the squadron was left entirely out of sight. This escape from so great a disparity of force, was considered as deserving a high rank in naval exploits, and was much admired at the time, as evincing superior nautical skill. The advantage to the British in this chase was considerable, when we reflect that their foremost vessel had the assistance of all the boats of the squadron, for the purpose of towing. The superiority of captain Hull, was that of seamanship alone. This superiority was sometimes afterwards proved in a most remarkable manner: while naval history lasts it will not be forgotten.

The Constitution again put to sea. on the 2d of September. On the 19th, a vessel hove in sight, and a chase instantly commenced. It was soon discovered to be the Guerriere, one of the best frigates in the British navy ; and which seemed not averse from the rencontre, as she backed her main topsail, waiting for the Constitution to come down. This was a most desirable occurrence to our brave tars, as this frigate had for some time been in search of an American frigate, having given a formal challenge to all our vessels of the same class. She had at one of her mast heads a flag, on which her name was inscribed in large characters, by way of gasconade, and on another, the words, " Not the Little Belt," in allusion to the broadsides which the President had given that vessel, before the war. The Guerriere had looked into several of our ports, and affected to be exceedingly anxious to earn the first laurel from the new enemy. The Constitution being made ready for action, now bore down, her crew giving three cheers. At first it was the intention of captain Hull, to bring her to close action immediately ; but on coming within gun-shot, she gave a broadside and filled away, then wore, giving a broadside on the other tack, but without effect. They now continued wearing, and manœuvring, on both sides, for three quarters of an hour, the Guerriere attempting to take a raking position ; but failing in this, she bore up, and ran with her topsail and jib on the quarter. The Constitution, perceiving this, made sail to come up with her. Captain Hull, with admirable coolness, received the enemy's fire, without returning it. The enemy, mistaking this conduct on the part of the American commander, continued to pour out his broadsides with a view to cripple his antagonist. From the Constitution, not a gun had been fired. Already had an officer twice come on deck, with information that several of the men had been killed at their guns. The gallant crew, though burning with impatience, silently awaited the orders of their commander. The moment so long looked for, at last arrived. Sailing-master Aylwin having seconded the views of the captain, with admirable skill, in bringing the vessel exactly to the station intended, orders were given at five minutes before five P. M. to fire broadside after broadside, in quick succession. The crew instantly discovered the whole plan, and entered into it with all the spirit the circumstance was calculated to inspire. Never was any firing so dreadful. For fifteen minutes the vivid lightning of the Constitution's guns continued one blaze, and their thunder roared with scarce an intermission. The enemy's mizen-mast had gone by the board, and he stood exposed to a raking fire, which swept his decks.

The Guerriere had now become unmanageable ; her hull, rigging and sails dreadfully torn ; when the Constitution attempted to lay her on board.   At this moment lieutenant Bush, in attempting to throw his marines on board, was killed by a musket ball, and the enemy shot ahead, but could not be brought before the wind.   A raking fire now continued for fifteen minutes longer, when his mainmast and foremast went, taking with them every spar, excepting the bowsprit.   On seeing this, the firing ceased, and at twenty-five minutes past five she surrendered.   "In thirty minutes," says captain Hull, "after we got fairly alongside of the enemy, she surrendered, and had not a spar standing, and her hull, above and below water, so shattered, that a few more broadsides must have carried her down."   The Guerriere was so much damaged, as to render it impossible to bring her in ; she was therefore set fire to the next day, and blown up.   The damage sustained by the Constitution was comparatively of so little consequence, that she actually made ready for action, when a vessel appeared in sight the next day.   The loss on board the Guerriere was fifteen killed, and sixty-three wounded : on the side of the Constitution, seven killed and seven wounded.   It is pleasing to observe, that even the British commander, on this occasion, bore testimony to the humanity and generosity with which he was treated by the victors.   The American frigate was somewhat superior in force, by a few guns ; but this difference bore no comparison to the disparity of the conflict.   The Guerriere was thought to be a match for any vessel of her class, and had been ranked amongst the largest in the British navy.   The Constitution arrived at Boston on the 28th of August, having captured several merchant vessels.

Never did any event spread such universal joy over the whole country.   The gallant Hull, and his equally gallant officers, were received with enthusiastic demonstrations of gratitude, wherever they appeared.   He was presented with the freedom of all the cities through which he passed on his way to the seat of government, and with many valuable donations.   Congress voted fifty thousand dollars to the crew, as a recompense for the loss of the prize, and the executive promoted several of the officers.   Sailing-master Aylwin, who had been severely wounded, was promoted to the rank of lieutenant, and lieutenant Morris, who had been also wounded, was promoted to the rank of post-captain.   This affair was not less mortifying to Great Britain, who for thirty years had in no instance lost a frigate in any thing like an equal conflict.

The public mind was now continually excited by some new

series of naval exploits. There was scarcely time for one victory to become familiar, before another was announced. On the 7th of September, commodore Porter of the Essex, entered the Delaware after a most active and successful cruise. He had sailed from New York on the 3d of July, and shortly after fell in with a fleet of merchantmen under convoy of a frigate. Having kept at a distance until night, she cut off a brig, with a hundred and fifty soldiers on board, which was ransomed for fourteen thousand dollars; the men were disarmed and released, on taking an oath not to serve against us during the war. The commodore regretted, in his letter to the secretary of the navy, that he had not had with him a sloop of war, as in this case he could have engaged the frigate, while the convoy were kept employed; and he could then have captured the whole fleet, consisting of several sail, and having two thousand men on board, including the crew and transports. On the 13th of August, the Essex fell in with the Alert sloop of war, and captured her, after an action of eight minutes: the Alert had mistaken this frigate for the Hornet, of which she was in pursuit, and actually commenced the engagement, by running down and pouring a broadside into the Essex. When she struck her colours but three men were wounded, but she had seven feet of water in her hold. The frigate did not suffer the slightest injury. Commodore Porter, being embarrassed with his prisoners, who exceeded five hundred in number, concluded to convert the Alert into a cartel, for the purpose of effecting an exchange. Her guns were thrown overboard, and she was ordered to proceed to St John's, under the command of a lieutenant of the Essex. The British commander at that place protested strongly against the practice of converting captured vessels into cartels; but in this instance was willing, in consequence of the attention which commodore Porter had uniformly shown to British prisoners, to consent to the proposed exchange. On the afternoon of the 30th of August, a British frigate was seen standing towards the Essex; preparation was immediately made for action, and she stood towards the enemy. Night intervening, the Essex hoisted lights to prevent a separation, which were answered; but at daylight, to the mortification of the crew, who were anxious to support the cause of "Free trade and sailor's rights," the enemy had disappeared. On the 4th of September, near St George's banks, two ships of war were been to the southward, and a brig to the northward, to which the Essex gave chase, but the winds being light, she made her escape. The Essex was afterwards chased by the two ship

seen to the southward, but escaped in the night by skilful manœuvring.

On the 8th of October, a squadron, consisting of the President, the United States, Congress and the Argus, sailed from
Boston on a cruise. On the 13th, the United States and
Argus parted from the rest in a gale of wind. A few days
afterwards, the President and Congress had the good fortune
to capture the British packet Swallow, with two hundred thousand dollars on board, and on the 30th of December arrived at
Boston, after a very successful cruise.

The Argus was not less fortunate; after parting from the
squadron, she cruised in every direction, between the continent
and the West Indies, and after being out ninety-six days, she
returned to New York, with prizes to the amount of two hundred thousand dollars. She made various hairbreadth escapes:
at one time she was chased by a British squadron for three
days, and several times almost surrounded; she was one moment within pistol shot of a seventy-four, and yet, in the midst
of all this peril, she actually captured and manned one of her
prizes.

The United States, commanded by that distinguished officer
commodore Decatur, soon after her separation from the squadron, had the good fortune to add another victory to our naval
chronicle, not less glorious than that of the Constitution. On
the 25th of October, off the Western Islands, she fell in with
the Macedonian, captain Carden, a frigate of the largest class,
carrying forty-nine guns and three hundred men. The Macedonian, being to windward, had it in her power to choose
her distance, and at no time were they nearer than musket
shot; from this circumstance, and the prevalence of a heavy
sea, the action lasted nearly two hours. The superiority of
the American gunnery, in this action, was very remarkable,
both for its greater rapidity and effect. From the continued
blaze of her guns, the United States was, at one moment,
thought by her antagonist to be on fire; a mistake of very short
duration. On board the Macedonian there were thirty-six
killed and sixty-eight wounded. She lost her mainmast, and
main topmast and mainyard, and was much cut up in her hull.
The United States suffered so little, that a return to port was
not necessary: she had only five killed, and seven wounded.
Among the killed were lieutenant Funk, of whom the commodore spoke in the highest terms. Lieutenant Allen was on
this occasion highly applauded. The commodore arrived at
New York on the 4th of December, with his prize. Decatur,
already a universal favourite, experienced the same demonstra-

HISTORY OF THE WAR.   49

The United States captures the Macedonian.....The Wasp captures the Frolic.

tions of gratitude, as were made to captain Hull: nor was there denied him that new species of praise, which the generous conduct of our heroic seamen has uniformly drawn forth, the praise of the enemy. All the private property belonging to the men and officers on board the Macedonian, was restored to the captured with the most rigid exactitude; and their treatment was the most polite and humane.

The feelings of the nation had scarcely time to subside, when the welcome news of another victory was received; a victory over an enemy most decidedly superior in force, and under circumstances the most favourable to him. This was the capture of the brig Frolic, of twenty-two guns, by the sloop of war Wasp. Captain Jones had returned from France, two weeks after the declaration of war, and on the 13th of October again put to sea. On the 16th he experienced a heavy gale, in which the Wasp lost her jib-boom and two men. On the evening of the following day, the Wasp found herself near five strange sail, and as two of them appeared to be ships of war, it was thought proper to keep at a distance. At daylight on Sunday morning, they were discovered to be six merchant ships, from Honduras to England, under a strong convoy of a brig and two ships, armed with sixteen guns each. The brig, which proved to be the Frolic, captain Whinyates, dropped behind, while the others made sail. The Wasp, being prepared for action, at thirty-two minutes past eleven o'clock, came down to windward in handsome style, when the action was begun by the enemy's cannon and musketry. This was returned, and approaching still nearer the enemy, brought her to close action. In five minutes the main topmast of the Wasp was shot away, and falling down with the main topsail yard, across the larboard fore and foretopsail, rendered her head yards unmanageable during the rest of the action. In two minutes more her gaft and mizen top-gallant mast were shot away. The sea being exceedingly rough, the muzzles of the Wasp's guns were sometimes under water. The English fired as their vessel rose, so that their shot was either thrown away, or touched the rigging of the Americans; the Wasp, on the contrary, fired as she sunk, and every time struck the hull of her antagonist. The Wasp now shot ahead, raked her, and then resumed her position. The Frolic's fire had evidently slackened, and the Wasp, gradually neared her, until in the last broadside, they touched her side with their rammers. It was now determined to lay her by the board. The jib-boom of the Frolic came in between the main and mizen mast of the Wasp, and after giving a raking fire, which swept the whole deck, they resolved to board.

E

Lieutenant Biddle sprang on the rigging of the enemy's bowsprit, where he was at first somewhat entangled, and midshipman Barker, in his impatience to be on board, caught hold of
Biddle's coat, and fell back on the deck, but in a moment
sprang up and leaped on the bowsprit, where he found one Lang
and another seaman. His surprise can scarcely be imagined,
when he found no person on deck, except three officers and
the seaman at the wheel. The deck was slippery with blood,
and presented a scene of havock and ruin, such as has been seldom witnessed. As he advanced, the officers threw down their
swords in submission. The colours were still flying, there
being no seamen left to pull them down. Lieutenant Biddle
leaped into the rigging, and hauled them down with his own
hands. Thus, in forty-three minutes, complete possession was
taken of the Frolic, after one of the most bloody conflicts any
where recorded in naval history. The condition of this unfortunate vessel was inexpressibly shocking. The birth deck
was crowded with the dead, the dying and the wounded; and
the masts, which soon after fell, covering the dead and every
thing on deck, left her a most melancholy wreck. Captain Jones sent on board his surgeon, and humanely exerted
himself in their relief, to the utmost of his power. The loss
on board the Frolic was thirty killed and fifty wounded; on
board the Wasp, five killed, and five slightly wounded. This
was certainly the most decisive action fought during the war.
The Wasp and Frolic were both captured that very day by a
British seventy-four, the Poictiers, captain Beresford.

Captain Jones spoke of all his officers and men in handsome
terms; but the noble part which he bore in this celebrated
combat, was touched upon with all that modesty for which our
naval heroes have been so justly admired. Lieutenant Booth,
Mr Rapp, and midshipmen Grant and Baker, were particularly
distinguished. Lieutenant Claxton, although too unwell to
render any assistance, crawled out of bed, and came on deck,
that he might witness the courage of his comrades. A seaman
of the name of Jack Lang, from Chester county, Pennsylvania,
a brave fellow, who had been twice impressed by the British,
behaved, on this occasion, with unusual bravery. Captain
Jones reached New York towards the latter end of November.
The legislatures of Massachusetts, New York, and Delaware,
of which latter state he was a native, presented him with their
thanks, and several elegant swords and pieces of plate; and the
congress of the United States voted him, his officers, and crew,
twenty-five thousand dollars, as a recompense for their loss, in not
being able to bring in the Frolic. He was soon after promoted to

the command of the Macedonian, captured by commodore Decatur.

Feats of naval prowess were not confined to national vessels: the exploits of private armed vessels daily filled the gazettes. Letters of marque were issued soon after the declaration of war, and privateers sailed from every port, to annoy and distress the enemy's commerce. They were generally constructed for swift sailing, an art in which the Americans excel every other people. In their contests they exhibited the same superiority over the vessels of the enemy, as was shown with respect to the ships of war. One of the first to sail, was the Atlas, commanded by captain Moffat. On the 3d of August he fell in with two armed ships, and after a severe action, captured them both, but was not able to bring more than one of them into port.

The Dolphin, captain Endicot, of Salem, in the course of a few weeks, captured fifteen of the enemy's vessels, and soon became noted for his activity and courage. He had the misfortune to be captured by a squadron, under commodore Broke, and in consequence of the prejudice entertained against privateers, and the irritation which his exploits had excited, he was treated somewhat roughly: this conduct, to the honour of the British officers, was soon changed, when they were informed, by the prisoners, of the humanity of his conduct. On one occasion, there happened to be on board one of the Dolphin's prizes, an old woman, who had her whole fortune on board, consisting of eight hundred dollars; she made a lamentable outcry at her misfortune: but the fact was no sooner known to the sailors, than they spontaneously agreed not to touch her pittance; and on arriving in the United States, she felt so much gratitude, that she could not refrain from giving publicity to it, in the newspapers. It soon became understood, that American privateers were under the same regulations as national vessels, a circumstance in which they differed from those of other nations; that, in fact, private cupidity was not the sole motive in arming them, but that they constituted a part of our mode of carrying on the war. by assailing the enemy in his most vulnerable part; and that the gallantry displayed on board of these vessels, conferred almost as high honour on the actors, as that which was won in the national ships: there were, therefore, the same inducements to correctness of deportment. Thus much may be said in mitigation of this species of warfare, which it is to be hoped will, at some future day, be suppressed by common consent.

Early in the war, one of our oldest and most distinguished naval heroes, but who had, for many years, led a private life, entered this service. Commodore Barney sailed from Baltimore in the Rossie, and, in the course of a few months, did more havock in the British commerce, than was experienced from the French cruisers for years. The fame of this gallant officer was already well known to the enemy, particularly as the captor of one of their vessels of war of superior force, the General Monk, during the revolution.

Such was the glorious beginning of our naval warfare against Great Britain. In the course of a few months, two of her finest frigates surrendered, each after a few minutes fighting; and a most decided victory was gained over an adversary confessedly superior. Before the meeting of congress, in November, nearly two hundred and fifty vessels were captured from the enemy, and more than three thousand prisoners taken. Upwards of fifty of them were armed vessels, and carrying five hundred and seventy-five guns. To counterbalance this immense loss, the enemy had but a small account. By the cruise of commodore Rodgers, our merchantmen had been much aided in getting into port, and the number captured was but trifling compared to theirs. The Frolic and Wasp, we have seen, were captured in a way to give no credit to the captors. Two other smaller vessels were also captured by squadrons: the first, on the 20th of July, the schooner Nautilus, of twelve guns, commanded by lieutenant Crane, captured by the frigate Shannon, the leading ship of the squadron. The Vixen was captured on the 22d of November, by the Northampton frigate, Sir James Yoe. Not long after the capture, both vessels ran ashore, and were wrecked. Through the exertions of captain Reed, of the Vixen, much of the property was saved from the wreck; and, in consequence of his services on the occasion, he was publicly thanked by Sir James, and permission given to him to return home on his parole. This he generously declined, as he could not think of receiving any benefits, in which his officers and crew did not partake. He accordingly accompanied them to Nova Scotia, where he fell a victim to the climate. He was interred by the British with the honours of war, accompanied by every demonstration of respect to the memory of a brave and gallant officer.

The navy now became the favourite of the nation; for thus far, contrasted with our armies, it was entitled to the most decided preference. There were not wanting occasions in which our arms by land had acquired reputation, but they had also brought upon us dishonour: on the contrary, the navy, in every instance, had added to our national renown. The modesty of our naval commanders, in the narratives of the most brilliant achievements, and which were read with delight in every cottage, and spread over the country by the means of our thousand newspapers, was peculiarly pleasing; whereas the proclamations of our generals were too often filled with idle fustian. The British had threatened to drive our "bits of striped bunting" from the ocean, and we had been seriously apprehensive that our little navy would be at once annihilated! We, however, sought consolation for this, in the prospect of possessing Canada, and freeing ourselves from troublesome neighbours. In both instances how greatly disappointed! The mortification of Great Britain was attended with no alleviation. She was wounded in the most vital part. In vain did she seek consolation in endeavouring to hide her misfortune from herself, by representing our vessels, in every instance, as greatly superior in size, and having every advantage in the various conflicts. This might do with respect to one engagement, but the same cause was insufficient to account for her defeats in every encounter. The American frigates were seventy-fours in disguise, and she turned her seventy-fours into frigates, that she might contend on equal terms! But she could not so easily account for the superiority in the management of the ships, and in gunnery. From the idle boast of being the sovereign of the seas (a claim as vain as that to the dominion of the air or the light), without whose permission not a sail could be spread, she was humbled by one of the youngest maritime states, actuated by no ambition of conquest, and merely contending for the privilege of navigating an element designed by the Almighty for the common possession of the human race.

CHAPTER IV.

Military Enthusiasm in the West—General Harrison takes command of the Northwestern Army—The Army advances under General Winchester—Expedition to the Rapids under General Tupper—Failure of the Expedition to the Rapids—Second Expedition to the Rapids under General Tupper—Foray under General Hopkins—Second Expedition under General Hopkins—Defence of Fort Harrison—Expedition under Colonel Russell—Expedition under Colonel Campbell—Security of the Frontier established.

THE public mind having recovered from the distress and chagrin occasioned by the surrender of Hull, was now carried to
E*

the contrary extreme. A spirit was roused, which produced effects not surpassed in the most enthusiastic periods of our revolution. To the westward and to the southward, volunteer corps were forming in every quarter, and tendering their services for any enterprise which might be undertaken. The western parts of Pennsylvania and Virginia exhibited great alacrity : but it was in the states of Kentucky, Ohio and Tennessee, that this generous zeal prevailed in the highest degree. Civil pursuits were almost forsaken, while this enthusiasm was shared by persons of both sexes and every age. The ladies set themselves to work in preparing military clothing and knapsacks for their relatives and friends, and cheerfully contributed from their household stock, such articles as their soldiers might require. Companies were equipped in a single day, and ready to march the next. There prevailed every where, the most animated scenes of preparation. The admiration which this excites, is not lessened by the reflection that they were but acting in self-defence ; for excepting in the remote settlements, and merely on the frontier, there was but little to apprehend from the Indians : the settlements having become so considerable in the western states, that it would be impossible for the enemy to penetrate far. They were actuated by an enthusiastic love of country, a generous spirit, which could not brook the thought of being worsted, or that a part of the territory of the United States, should fall by conquest into the hands of our enemy.

Louisville and Newport had been appointed as the places of rendezvous, for the troops destined to the aid of Hull. So numerous were the volunteers from Kentucky, who offered their services here, that it was soon found necessary to issue orders that no more would be received, and many companies, thus disappointed, were compelled to turn back. The command of the Kentucky militia, was assigned to general Payne. The same alacrity was manifested in the state of Ohio, which, in the course of a few days, embodied an equal force under general Tupper. The Pennsylvania volunteers, under general Crooks, were marched to Erie, and a brigade of Virginians under general Leftwich, was to join the troops of Ohio, at Urbanna. The Kentucky troops, together with the Seventeenth United States regiment under colonel Wells, the greater part of which had been enlisted in the Western country since the war, were destined for Fort Wayne, and thence for the Rapids, which was appointed as the general rendezvous. Thus in a few weeks, upwards of four thousand men were drawn out from their homes, completely equipped, embodied, and ready for the field. The command of this army was given to major-general Harrison, who was well known to the Western people, and whose recent conduct at Tippecanoe had raised him high in public estimation. In order to secure him this rank, a distinction of an unusual character, equally honourable to general Harrison, and to the person conferring it, who did not resolve upon it, however, without consultation and mature reflection, he received a brevet commission of major-general, from the governor of Kentucky; and some time after, the command of the Northwestern army was assigned him, by a special order from the department of war.

The first step taken by Harrison, was to relieve the frontier posts: principally Fort Harrison, on the Wabash; and Fort Wayne, situated on the Miami of the Lakes, and on the road to the Rapids. It might be expected that this fort, as well as Fort Defiance, situated lower down, would be attempted by the British, in order to obstruct the road to Detroit. Harrison arrived at Fort Deposit on the 12th of September, with about two thousand five hundred men.

The Indians who had laid siege to it, disappeared on his approach. It had been invested by a considerable body of them, who after repeated attacks, from the 6th to the 9th, in which they resorted to every stratagem, and several times attempted to take it by assault, were compelled to retire, after destroying every thing outside the fort. The garrison consisted of no more than seventy men.

After remaining here a few days, general Harrison, not thinking it advisable to proceed to the Rapids until sufficiently strengthened by the arrival of the other troops, resolved to occupy the intermediate time in laying waste the Indian country. Colonel Wells was despatched on the 14th, with his regiment, and that under the command of colonel Scott, together with two hundred mounted riflemen, against the Pottowatomy town on the river St Joseph, which discharges itself into Lake Michigan. Another detachment, under the command of general Payne, consisting of colonels Lewis and Allen's regiments, and captain Garrard's company, marched against the Miami villages. The detachments were in both instances successful, the bark and wooden huts of nine villages were destroyed, the inhabitants having abandoned them; their corn was also cut up, according to the mode of warfare practised on these people by all European nations. General Harrison returned to Fort Wayne about the 18th, where he found general Winchester, with considerable reinforcements from Ohio and Kentucky. This officer had been unexpectedly placed in command by the President; on which general Harrison resolved to retire, and set out on his return to Indiana, but was overtaken by a messenger, with information of the subsequent arrangements by the order of the President. On the 23d he accordingly resumed the command.

The day before his arrival, general Winchester had marched for Fort Defiance, on his way to the Rapids, the place of ultimate destination. His force consisted of a brigade of Kentucky militia, four hundred regulars, and a troop of horse, in all about two thousand men. The country which he was compelled to traverse, opposed great difficulties, particularly in the transportation of stores. Along the heads of the rivers which discharge themselves into the Ohio on the south, and those which discharge themselves into the lakes on the north, there is a great extent of flat land, full of marshes and ponds, in which the streams take their rise. In rainy seasons particularly, it is exceedingly difficult to pass, the horses at every step sinking to the knees in mud. The ground, besides, is covered with deep forests and close thickets. To facilitate the passage through this wilderness, each man was obliged to carry provisions for six days. General Harrison now proceeded in person to Fort St Mary's, for the purpose of organizing the ulterior movements of the army. A detachment under major Jennings was ordered to proceed with supplies by the Aux Glaize river.

General Winchester was obliged to advance slowly, on account of the precautions necessary to avoid surprise in a country highly favourable for Indian warfare. From the closeness of the thickets, the troops were under the necessity of cutting open a road each day, and were not able to make more than six or eight miles. They usually encamped at three o'clock, and threw up a breast-work to guard against a night attack. They had the precaution, on their march, to be preceded by a party of spies, under an active officer, captain Ballard, and an advanced guard of about three hundred men. On the 24th, they discovered an Indian trail for the first time, and pursued it some distance; but from the nature of the country, it was impossible to overtake the enemy. Ensign Leggett, having obtained permission to penetrate to Fort Defiance, still at the distance of twenty-four miles, set out accompanied by four volunteers. These gallant young men, not being sufficiently experienced in such enterprises, were killed the same evening, and found the next day by the spies, scalped and tomahawked in the most barbarous manner. On the 27th, captain Ballard, who had gone before for the purpose of burying the dead, discovered an Indian trail; but being aware of the stratagems of this wily people, instead of following it, he divided his com-

pany, and marched his men on each side. The stratagem of
the enemy being thus frustrated, they rose from their hiding
places, raised the war-whoop, and took possession of an elevated piece of ground; but were soon compelled, by the approach of the cavalry and the well directed fire of the spies, to
betake themselves to the swamps and thickets. The next day,
while the army was on its march, four Indians fired upon the
spies; the general instantly drew up his men, and sent forward
a detachment of horse, which returning with an account that
no enemy could be seen, the line of march was again resumed.
They had not proceeded far, when a trail was discovered,
which induced the general to cross the river, and shortly after
another trail was discovered, which was at first supposed to
have marked the march of colonel Jennings, who had been
ordered in advance with provisions, and was therefore hailed
with joy by the troops, who had begun to suffer for want of
them. The mistake was unpleasantly rectified by the arrival
of the scouts, who brought intelligence that about two miles
above Fort Defiance, they had seen the Indians encamped, with
their war poles erected, and bloody flag displayed.

On the evening of the 29th, a messenger arrived from colonel Jennings, with the information, that, on having discovered
the British and Indians in possession of Fort Defiance, he had
thought it prudent to land about forty miles above that place,
where he had erected a block-house, and awaited further orders.
Captain Garrard, with about thirty of his troopers, was despatched with orders to Jennings to forward the provisions; this was
promptly obeyed. Captain Garrard returned as the escort to a
brigade of pack-horses, on which they were loaded, after having been for thirty-six hours exposed to an incessant rain. This
occurrence gave new life and spirits to the starving army, which
had in the meantime taken possession of Fort Defiance. The
British and Indians had precipitately descended the river. On
the 4th of October, general Harrison left the fort, and returned
to the settlements, with a view of organizing and bringing up
the centre and right wing of the army; the left wing having
been placed under the command of general Winchester. Orders were given to general Tupper, by the commander-in-chief,
to proceed immediately to the Rapids, with about one thousand
men, for the purpose of driving the enemy from that place.

The intended expedition of general Tupper proved abortive.
The general, in consequence of the damaged state of the ammunition, and the length of time requisite to prepare the necessary provisions, was considerably delayed. In the meanwhile
the Indians had killed a man on the opposite side of the river,

and almost within gunshot of the camp. He beat to arms, and
ordered major Brush to cross over with about fifty men, and
explore the woods, while a strong detachment would be formed
for the purpose of supporting him, in case of attack. The
party had no sooner moved, than all in camp began to break
away, twenty or thirty together, in order to join in the chase,
and by no exertion of authority could they be kept back; so
totally insensible were they to any thing like regular military
subordination. Luckily these small bodies were not attacked,
or they must have been cut to pieces. Immediately after this,
orders were given by the commanding general, to go in pursuit
of the Indians, and if possible ascertain their number; general
Tupper represented his situation, and requested that the order
might be countermanded; but this was answered by a peremptory command, which he now attempted to obey. This unfortunately resulted in a misunderstanding between him and the
commanding general, in consequence of which colonel Allen
received private orders to supersede him in the command; on
this being made known to the corps of Ohio, they positively
refused to march, unanimously set off for Urbanna, and the
expedition was entirely broken up.

These are instances of insubordination much to be regretted;
but they spring from the want of that kind of habitual obedience,
and implicit confidence in their officers, incident to raw troops.
Such are the unavoidable evils attending a militia hastily called
together, and not kept in a body a sufficient length of time, to
learn the utility of perfect subordination.

It was now necessary to wait until the arrival of the other divisions of the army, before any thing further could be attempted
against the Rapids, and much less against Detroit. The army
was at this time accompanied by some friendly Indians, whom
general Harrison had received into his service at Fort Wayne,
the greater part under the command of Logan. No other course
would have prevented their becoming our enemies; it was in
vain to expect them to remain neutral, while surrounded by
war. However contrary to our maxims and policy to employ
such auxiliaries, we were compelled to do so in self defence;
and we afterwards sufficiently evinced, by the conduct of those
Indians, that it is not impossible to restrain them from the commission of acts of barbarity.

General Tupper, having returned to Urbanna with his
mounted men, was despatched with the division of the centre,
which consisted of a brigade of Ohio volunteers and militia,
and a regiment of regulars, to Fort M'Arthur, while the right
wing, consisting of a Pennsylvania and a Virginia brigade, was
ordered to Sandusky.

General Tupper, on his arrival at Fort M'Arthur, organized another expedition, for the purpose of proceeding to the Rapids. This force consisted of about six hundred men; and being provided with five days' provisions, marched on the 10th, and on the 13th approached within thirteen miles of the Rapids, which they found, by their scouts, to be still in the possession of the British and Indians. A number of boats and small vessels were seen lying below. On receiving this information, they advanced within a few miles of the Rapids, and then halted until sunset, with a view of crossing the river, and making an attack the next morning by daybreak. The rapidity of the current was such, that their attempts were ineffectual; many of the men, who endeavoured to cross, were swept down the stream, and it was thought advisable to order those, who had actually passed, to return. It was now resolved to resort to stratagem, and if possible, to decoy the enemy over. For this purpose, early in the morning, they showed the heads of their columns, by advancing some distance out of the woods, in an open space opposite the enemy's camp. A great confusion appeared to ensue; those in the vessels slipped their cables, and descended the river, while the Indian women were seen scampering off on the road to Detroit. A fire was then opened upon the Americans, with musketry and a four pounder. Tupper's stratagem did not perfectly succeed; but few Indians at first seemed disposed to cross, and then acted with great caution. A number, however, were observed in a little while crossing higher up the river; being now apprehensive that his camp might be attacked, the general thought proper to return. He had not proceeded far, when some of the men unfortunately, contrary to orders, fired on a drove of hogs, and pursued them some distance, and others, equally disobedient, entered a field to pull corn. At this moment, a body of mounted Indians rushed forward, killed four men, and attacked the rear of the right flank. The column, being thrown back, commenced a brisk fire, and caused the Indians to give ground. The Indians rallied, and passing along the van-guard, made a charge upon the rear of the left column: this column was also thrown briskly back; all attempts to break it were unsuccessful, and in twenty minutes, the Indians again retired. Conceiving this only preliminary to an attack of foot, general Tupper ordered the right column to move up in marching order, to prevent the attack from being made on the right flank. Information was now received, that the Indians were crossing in considerable numbers; on this, the general ordered the left column to take up the marching order, and proceed to the head of the right column, where a number of Indians had already crossed on horseback, while others were still in the river, and about two hundred on the opposite bank. These, a battalion was ordered to dislodge, which completely succeeded in the undertaking, many of them being shot from their horses in the river. The different charges of the Indians were led by the famous chief Split-Log, who rode a fine white horse, from which he sometimes fired, at other times alighted, and fired from behind a tree. The horses appeared to have been much superior to those which the Indians generally ride, and they were well supplied with holsters and pistols. The Americans were compelled to return in haste, as their provisions were by this time entirely exhausted, and they had to march forty miles before they could obtain a fresh supply.

While these things were taking place in the Northwestern army under general Harrison, other events, deserving attention, transpired further to the westward, under different leaders. We have seen that many of the companies equipped for the service of the United States, were dismissed, as exceeding the number required, or the number for which supplies had been provided. A spirit of volunteering prevailed, which reminds one of the enthusiasm of the crusades. Vincennes. on the Wabash, was appointed the place of rendezvous for an expedition against the Peoria towns, and others situated on the Illinois and Wabash rivers. Nearly four thousand men, chiefly mounted riflemen, under the command of general Hopkins, collected at this place, and early in October proceeded to Fort Harrison. This foray was sanctioned by the venerable governor Shelby, of Kentucky, and was, perhaps, the most formidable in appearance that had ever entered the Indian country.

The army reached Fort Harrison about the 10th, and on the 14th crossed the Wabash, and proceeded on its march against the Kickapoo and Peoria towns; the first about eighty miles distant, the others about one hundred and twenty. Its march lay through open plains covered with a luxuriant grass, which in autumn becomes very dry and combustible. Murmurs and discontents soon began to show themselves in this unwieldy and ill compacted body, which was kept together by no discipline or authority. Every one consulted his own will; in fact, but little could be expected from this "press of chivalry." They had scarcely been four days on their march, when they demanded to be led back; a major, whose name it is unnecessary to remember, rode up to the general, and peremptorily ordered him to return! An idea had begun to prevail, that the guides were ignorant of the country, and that their course was the opposite of that which they directed. An unlucky occurrence, towards evening, gave the finishing blow to this mighty expedition. A gust of wind had arisen, while they were encamped, which blew violently towards them; soon after, the grass was discovered to be on fire, and the flames approaching with great velocity. This was supposed to be an Indian attack; it would have been a formidable one, had they not set fire to the grass around their camp, and thus arrested the progress of the flames. The next morning a council of officers was called, and the general, seeing the state of the army, or more properly of the crowd, proposed to proceed against the Indian towns with five hundred men, if that number would volunteer their services, while the remainder might return to Fort Harrison. When the proposal was made to the men, not one would turn out; the general having entirely lost his popularity. He then requested to be permitted to direct the operations of that single day, this being agreed to, he placed himself at their head, and gave orders to march; but instead of following him, they turned round, and pursued a contrary direction, leaving him to bring up the rear. Finding it useless to attempt any thing further with such a body, he followed it to Fort Harrison.

The same officer, some time in November, led another party, with more success, against the towns at the head of the Wabash. On the 11th, he again set out from Fort Harrison, with about one thousand two hundred men; while at the same time, seven boats, under the command of lieutenant-colonel Butler, ascended the river with supplies and provisions. On the 19th, he reached the Prophet's Town, and immediately despatched three hundred men to surprise the Winnebago towns on Ponce Passu creek. The party under colonel Butler, came upon the place about daybreak, but found it evacuated. This village, together with the Prophet's Town, and a large Kickapoo village, containing one hundred and twenty cabins and huts, were destroyed, together with the winter's provision of corn. Until the 21st, no Indians were discovered; when they fired on a small party, and killed a man by the name of Dunn, a gallant soldier of Duvall's company. The next day, about sixty horsemen, under colonels Miller and Wilcox, being sent out to bury the dead, were suddenly attacked by a considerable party of Indians; and, in the skirmish which ensued, eighteen of our men were killed, wounded and missing. The principal camp of the Indians having been discovered, preparations were made to attack it, but on approaching it, the enemy were found to

F

have gone off. Their situation was remarkably strong, being on a high bank of the Ponce Passu, and no means of ascending but through some narrow ravines. The inclement season advancing rapidly, it was deemed prudent to think of returning, particularly as the ice in the river began to obstruct the passage. The success and good conduct of this detachment forms a favourable contrast with the first, and proves that militia may, in time, be trained to the discipline of the camp, so as to become efficient troops. This corps suffered exceedingly, and without a murmur; many of them were sick, and to use the words of the general, many were " shoeless and shirtless," during the cold weather of this season.

We have passed over, without noticing, but with the intention of recording in a more distinguished manner, the defence of Fort Harrison, which was timely relieved by general Hopkins, on his first expedition. This fort was invested about the same time with Fort Wayne, by a large body of Indians, some of whom had affected to be friendly, and had, the day before, intimated to captain Taylor, that an attack might soon be expected from the Prophet's party. On the evening of the 3d of September, two young men were killed near the fort, and the next day, a party of thirty or forty Indians, from the Prophet's Town, appeared with a white flag, under pretence of obtaining provisions. Captain Taylor, suspecting an attack that night, examined the arms of his men, and furnished them with cartridges. The garrison was composed of no more than eighteen effective men, the commander and the greater part of his company having suffered very much from sickness. For some time past, the fort had actually been considered incapable of resisting an attack. About eleven o'clock, the night being very dark, the Indians had set fire to one of the block-houses unperceived. Every effort was made to extinguish the flames, but without effect; a quantity of whiskey, amongst other stores belonging to the contractor deposited there, blazed up, and immediately enveloped the whole in a flame. The situation of the fort became desperate; the yells of the Indians, the shrieks of a number of women and children within, added to the horrors of the night, altogether produced a terrific scene. Two soldiers, giving themselves up for lost, leaped over the pickets, and one of them was instantly cut to pieces. The commander, with great presence of mind, ordered the roofs to be taken off the adjoining barracks; this attempt, with the assistance of Dr Clark, fortunately proved successful, although made under a shower of bullets. A breast-work was then formed, before morning, six or eight feet high, so as to cover the space which would be left by the burnt block-house. The firing continued until daylight, when the Indians retired, after suffering a severe loss ; that of the fort was only three killed, and a few wounded. The Indians, discouraged by the failure of this attack, thought proper to retire, and made no further attempts, until the place was happily relieved by the arrival of general Hopkins. In consequence of his conduct, captain Taylor was afterwards promoted to a majority.

Another expedition was undertaken by colonel Russell, with three companies of United States rangers, and a party of mounted riflemen, under governor Edwards, of Illinois. This party, consisting of three hundred and sixty men, was destined to meet general Hopkins at the Peoria towns, on the Illinois river. They were disappointed in this, in consequence of what has been already detailed ; but they, notwithstanding, persevered in their enterprize, and destroyed one of the towns known by the name of Pamitaris's town, and pursued the Indians into a swamp in its vicinity, where they had fled for shelter. The party waded into the swamp for several miles, in some places to the waist in water, and killed upwards of twenty of the enemy in this place, on the bank of the river. The village, which was populous and flourishing, was completely destroyed, together with their winter's provisions. The party returned to camp on the 21st of October, after an absence of only thirteen days.

Lieutenant colonel Campbell of the Nineteenth United States infantry, was, about the same time, detached against the towns on the Mississinewa river, a branch of the Wabash. A town, inhabited by Delawares and Miamis, was surprised on the 17th of November ; upwards of thirty persons were taken prisoners, and eight warriors killed. The next morning, at daylight, a furious attack was made on the American camp : major Ball, with his dragoons, sustained the onset for some time ; and a well directed fire from captain Butler's " Pittsburgh volunteers," compelled the enemy to give way. Captain Trotter, of the Lexington troop of horse, charged, and the Indians precipitately fled. Captain Pearce, of the Zanesville troop, was, unfortunately, killed in the pursuit. Lieutenant Waltz, of the Pennsylvania volunteers, was also killed. The officers particularly named on the occasion were lieutenant-colonel Simmeral, major M'Dowell, captains Markle, M'Clelland. Garrard and Hopkins. The loss in killed on the part of the assailants, amounted to forty ; and on our part to eight killed, and about thirty wounded. Several of their villages were afterwards destroyed.

Besides these affairs, there were others of less moment, in which the militia of Indiana, Illinois, and Missouri territories, greatly distinguished themselves. The Indians were now so much harassed, that they began seriously to repent of having taken up the war-club so hastily, and their sufferings, during the succeeding winter, were not likely to produce any change of feeling towards those who had thus urged them to encounter their own ruin. The security of the frontier from the murderous scalping knife of the savage, was thus, in a great measure, effected. The Indians would be compelled to remove to the distant British establishments for sustenance, during the winter, since their means of subsistence were cut off. As to the loss of their huts or wigwams, that was a matter of little consequence to them; a few days being sufficient to re-construct them. But by their being thus driven to a distance, with their wives and children, they were prevented from annoying the settlers, with their fiendlike warfare. Many a peaceful settler was saved from their midnight attacks; and "the slumbers of the cradle" were protected from the savage war-whoop.

CHAPTER V.

Troops on the Canada Frontier—Capture of the Caledonia—Battle of Queenstown, and Death of General Brock—Bombardment of Fort Niagara by the British—Abortive attempt of General Smyth—Northern Army—Incursion of Forsyth—of Colonel Pike—War on the Lakes—First Cruise of Commodore Chauncey.

It is now time to turn our attention to the Northern frontier, that we may take a view of the occurrences on that extensive line, from Niagara down the St Lawrence. Towards the close of the year, our forces had chiefly concentrated in two bodies: one near Lewistown, consisting of some regulars newly enlisted, and militia, amounting to four thousand men, under general Van Rensselaer, of New York; the other, in the neighbourhood of Plattsburg and Greenbush, under the commander-in-chief, general Dearborne. At Black Rock, at Ogdensburg, and Sackett's Harbour, some regulars and militia were also stationed. During the summer and autumn, a number of volunteer companies had marched to the borders, as also the new recruits, as fast as they could be enlisted. Bodies of

regulars were distributed in each of these places, with officers
of experience, for the purpose of drilling the raw troops as
they arrived. It was expected that before the month of October, every thing would be made ready for a formidable invasion of Canada. Considerable disappointment was, however,
experienced, in consequence of the refusal of the governors of
Massachusetts, New Hampshire, and Connecticut, to permit
the militia of those states to march under the requisition of the
president, on the ground of their being the proper judges,
under the constitution, of the exigency which might require
them ; and as they were not friendly to the war, and particularly so to rendering it offensive, they felt no disposition to
waive their privileges. Other constitutional objections were
also urged, which it is scarcely necessary to mention. As the
militia in those states were better disciplined, and more effective, than any in the union, their absence was severely felt.
It is highly probable, that had there been a full co-operation on
the part of these states with the views of the general government, Upper Canada, at least, would have fallen into our hands,
in the course of the first campaign. Military stores had been
collected at different points ; and general Dearborne, who had
been appointed in consequence of his experience in the revolutionary war, was actively engaged, with the assistance of
such officers as Pike, Boyd and Scott, in drilling, disciplining,
and organizing his army. General Smyth, who was considered an able tactician, was similarly engaged. Between eight
and ten thousand men were collected along this extensive line,
and it was hoped that something might still be done. Skilful
officers of the navy were also despatched, for the purpose of
arming vessels on lakes Erie, Ontario and Champlain, in order
if possible to gain the ascendency there, and to aid the operations of our forces. The army under the command of Van
Rensselaer was called the Army of the Centre, to distinguish
it from that under general Harrison. That under the immediate command of general Dearborne, the Army of the North.

On the morning of the 8th of October, the British brig
Detroit, formerly the Adams surrendered by Hull, and the
brig Caledonia, came down from Malden, and anchored under
the guns of Fort Erie, nearly opposite Black Rock ; lieutenant
Elliot, of the navy, conceived the idea of attacking them, and
sent an express to hasten the seamen, then on the way, and
who, about fifty in number, arrived in the evening, wearied
with a march of five hundred miles. Allowing them until
twelve at night for repose, he then embarked in boats with
about fifty volunteers, who joined him, and, crossing the

F*

river, slipped down to the brigs; suddenly boarded them, and took possession, and immediately got under weigh, but the wind not being sufficiently strong to bear them against the current, they were both run aground; the Caledonia, so as to be protected by the batteries of Black Rock; but the Detroit, after being defended, until a considerable part of the military stores on board were secured, was set on fire and destroyed. The Caledonia was laden with furs to the amount of one hundred and fifty thousand dollars. This was effected with the loss of only two killed, and four wounded.

This affair, having kindled the ardour of the Americans of the Army of the Centre, they demanded to be led to the invasion of Canada, and some of the volunteers threatened to return home, unless their wishes were complied with. But this was not the ardour of veterans, well acquainted with the dangers to be encountered, and despising them; it was the inconsiderate rashness of inexperienced men, ready to anticipate the proper moment, but not possessing the firmness to persevere when surrounded by unaccustomed terrors. After a conference with generals Smyth and Hall, general Van Rensselaer resolved to make an attack on the heights of Queenstown. From the information he could collect, the enemy's force had been chiefly drawn off for the defence of Malden, as it was supposed, under the command of general Brock, who had left the territory of Michigan under the government of general Proctor, until he could organize a force to return. Could this place be possessed by our troops, they would be sheltered from the approaching inclemency of the season, and the operations of the Western Army much facilitated. Accordingly, at four in the morning of the 11th, in the midst of a dreadful northeast storm and heavy rain, an attempt was made to pass the river; but, owing to the darkness of the night and various unforeseen accidents, the passage could not be effected.

This failure but served to increase the impatience of the troops, who became almost ungovernable. Orders were despatched to general Smyth, to advance with his corps, as another attempt would be made on Queenstown. Every arrangement was rapidly made; and early on the morning of the 13th, the troops embarked, under the cover of the American batteries. The force designated to storm the heights, was divided into two columns; one of three hundred militia, under colonel Van Rensselaer, the other of three hundred regulars, under colonel Christie. These were to be followed by colonel Fenwick's artillery, and then the other troops in order. The British, in the meanwhile, anticipating this attack, had obtained considerable reinforcements from Fort George, and if necessary, could be still further assisted by general Brock, who, it now appeared, commanded at that place. At daylight, as soon as the approach of the Americans could be discovered, a shower of musketry and grape opened from the whole line on the Canada shore and was returned by our batteries, with the addition of two sixes, which, after an extraordinary effort, lieutenant-colonel Scott had brought to their assistance from the Falls of Niagara. The fire of the enemy, and the eddies in the river, produced considerable embarrassment, in consequence of which, lieutenant-colonel Christie, who was wounded by a grape shot in the hand, and colonel Mulaney, fell below the intended point, and were obliged to return. Colonel Van Rensselaer, who commanded the whole, and who led the van, reached the shore, with only one hundred men, in the midst of a most galling fire. He had scarcely leaped on land, when he received four severe wounds, which retarded the onset. This gallant officer, being still able to stand, though suffering the most excruciating pain, ordered his men to move rapidly up the heights. Captain Ogilvie assumed the command, seconded by captain Wool, who was also wounded, and followed by lieutenants Kearney, Carr, Higginan, Sommers, and ensign Reeve of the Thirteenth. Lieutenants Gansevoort and Randolph ascended the rocks to the right of the fort, gave three cheers, and after several desperate charges, at the head of a handful of men, carried the heights, and drove the enemy down the hill in every direction. The enemy retreated behind a large stone house, and kept up their fire; but their batteries, with the exception of one gun, were silenced. The detachment under colonel Christie, on his second attempt, now landed. Considerable reinforcements soon after arrived, under captains Gibson, M'Chesney and Lawrence, and colonels Mead, Strahan, Allen, and other militia officers. About this time general Brock arrived in person, with the Forty-ninth regiment, six hundred strong. Perceiving him approaching to the rear of the battery, captain Wool, who commanded at this point, ordered a detachment of about one hundred and sixty men to charge. The detachment was driven back, but being reinforced, charged a second time. Encountering a great superiority of numbers, they were again repulsed, and on the point of being driven to the very verge of the precipice, when one of the officers, considering their situation hopeless, placed a white handkerchief on the point of a bayonet, in token of submission, which was instantly torn away by captain Wool, who ordered the men to stand their ground. At this instant, colonel Christie advanced with a reinforcement, which increased the number of the detachment to three hundred and twenty. This officer now led on a desperate charge, and completely succeeded in putting to flight a regiment twice his numbers, and bearing the name of Invincibles. General Brock, exasperated at this conduct, endeavoured to rally them, when he received three balls, which terminated his existence; his aid, captain M'Donald, at the same instant falling by his side, mortally wounded. At two o'clock, general Wadsworth of the militia, and colonels Scott and Mulaney crossed over. Captain Wool, having been ordered to retire to have his wounds dressed, again returned to the action. The Forty-ninth being repulsed, and the British commander having fallen, the victory was thought to be complete; and general Van Rensselaer crossed over, for the purpose of immediately fortifying a camp, to prepare against future attacks, should the enemy be reinforced. This duty he assigned to lieutenant Totten, an able engineer.

The fortune of the day was not yet decided. At three o'clock, the enemy having rallied, and being reinforced by several hundred Chippewa Indians, again advanced to the attack. At first, our men were disposed to falter, but being animated by such leaders as colonel Christie and colonel Scott, marched boldly to the charge, and at the point of the bayonet, once more compelled the British, who were now the assailants, to retire. This was the third victory gained since morning, and had the contest ended here, it would have been one of the most glorious for our country. General Van Rensselaer perceiving that the men on the opposite side embarked but slowly, and fearing another conflict, re-crossed for the purpose of expediting their departure. But what was his astonishment, on reaching the American side, when he found that they positively refused to embark! More than twelve hundred men under arms were drawn up on the bank, where they remained as idle spectators of the scene, and neither commands nor entreaties could prevail on them to move. They refused to do so on the ground of constitutional privilege; the same men, who a few days before had expressed so much impatience that their ardour was restrained. It seems that this boiling ardour had already been cooled, by what they had witnessed on the opposite shore.

At four o'clock, the British being reinforced by eight hundred men from Fort George, renewed the engagement with fresh vigour. General Van Rensselaer, perceiving that our men were now almost exhausted with fatigue, and their ammunition nearly spent, was compelled, under the most painful sensations, to address a note to general Wadsworth, communicating the unexpected circumstance, and giving him permission to consult his own judgment, and at the same time he despatched a number of boats, that in case it should be so resolved, he might return with his troops to the American side. A desperate contest soon followed, which was kept up for half an hour, by a continued discharge of musketry and artillery; when our troops were gradually overpowered by numbers, their strength rapidly declining, and their hopes being subdued by the information they had by this time received. The militia attempted to re-embark, but in this they were frustrated. It being impossible to hold out any longer, and more overcome by the apathy of their countrymen, who stood looking coldly on, than by the strength of their foes, they at length surrendered themselves prisoners of war. During the greater part of the engagement with the last reinforcement, the regulars, not more than two hundred and fifty in number, bore the brunt of the action entirely alone. The prisoners were generally treated well by the British, but they imposed no restraint on their allies, who proceeded immediately to the work of stripping and scalping the slain, and even many of the wounded. Amongst other indignities which these wretches were not restrained from committing, were those offered to the body of ensign Morris, brother to our naval hero. Contrasted with this, it is worthy of being mentioned, that the guns of the American fort were fired during the funeral ceremony of general Brock, a brave and generous enemy. Even savages, had they chosen to inquire the meaning of this, ought to have learned a lesson of humanity, which their civilized allies could not teach.

Every officer who crossed the river, it is said, distinguished himself. Colonel Scott, afterwards so highly distinguished, continued the greater part of the day in the hottest of the fight, and although dressed in uniform, and of a tall and elegant stature, did not receive the slightest wound. Several Indians afterwards declared that they had taken deliberate aim at him. A volunteer company of riflemen under lieutenant Smith, who took prisoner an Indian chief, when the enemy rallied a second time, was much distinguished. Lieutenant colonel Fenwick was severely wounded, but never left the ground during the action. Captains Gibson, Wool, and M'Chesney, were highly complimented by the general. The loss of the British and Indians is not exactly known; ours must have been at least one thousand in killed, wounded and prisoners. The greater part of the prisoners were taken to Montreal.

During the embarkation of the troops at Lewistown, a fire was opened from Fort George on the American Fort Niagara,

which was returned and kept up during the day on both sides.
The battery commanded by captain M'Keon, which was managed with ability, set fire to several houses near the British fort.
A twelve pounder happening to burst, and at the same time the
opposite garrison beginning to throw shells, captain Leonard
thought it prudent to leave the fort; but soon after, perceiving
the British about to cross, he returned with a guard of twenty
men, and kept possession during the night. The next evening
he was joined by the remainder of the garrison. Three days
afterwards the British batteries below Fort Erie, opened a fire
on the camp at Black Rock. One of the barracks was destroyed by a shell, which blew up the magazine, but no lives
were lost.

The garrison of Niagara, having been considerably reinforced,
was again attacked on the 21st, from the batteries of Fort
George. These places are situated nearly opposite each other,
and at the entrance of the Niagara. The cannonading continued
from sunrise until dark, the enemy throwing upwards of three
thousand red-hot shot, and upwards of two hundred shells; several
of the barracks and adjoining buildings were fired, but, through
the indefatigable exertions of major Armistead, of the United
States artillery, the fire was repeatedly extinguished. Colonel
M'Feeley, who commanded the fort, ordered the different batteries to open; and the enemy's fire was returned with interest.
Several houses in Newark, and about the fort, were burnt; a
schooner lying under its guns was sunk, and one of their batteries for a time completely silenced. Captain M'Keon commanded in the southeast block-house, and captain Jack, of the
militia artillery, in the northeast, the situation most exposed.
The different batteries were commanded by lieutenants Rees
and Hendal, both of which were very destructive. Lieutenant
Gansevoort commanded the Salt battery; Doctor Cooper, of
the militia, had the command of a six-pounder. Lieutenant
Rees having been wounded, his place was taken by captain
Leonard, during the remainder of the day. During this severe
bombardment, we had only four killed, and a small number
wounded, among whom was lieutenant Thomas. Colonel
M'Feeley spoke in high terms of colonel Gray, major Armistead, captain Mulligan, and all the other officers and men.
Such was their ardour, that having expended their wadding,
the officers tore off their shirts and the soldiers their pantaloons,
to be used for that purpose. An extraordinary instance of female bravery occurred on this occasion. The wife of a common soldier, of the name of Doyle, taken prisoner at Queenstown, and carried to Montreal, determined to revenge the

treatment of her husband, volunteered her services, and obtained permission to assist at one of the batteries, where she continued to serve hot shot until the last gun was fired, although the enemy's shells continually fell around her, and every moment threatened destruction.

Shortly after the unfortunate battle of Queenstown, General Van Rensselaer resigned the command, which devolved on brigadier-general Smyth, of the United States army. General Smyth announced his determination of retrieving the honour of the American arms, by another attempt on the British batteries and entrenchments on the opposite side. He conceived that the former attack had not been conducted with judgment, in the selection of the point of debarkation, directly in the face of their batteries, whereas it ought to have been between Fort Erie and Chippewa. This he had at first recommended to general Van Rensselaer, and to the neglect of his intimation he attributed the failure of the former attempt. Having now the sole command, and being at liberty to carry into execution his own plan, he set about preparing a force for the purpose ; that which he then had under his command being insufficient. As the most effectual mode to accomplish this, he issued a proclamation, appealing to the public feeling and patriotism of the American people, and inviting volunteers from every part of the country. Every topic which could influence the hearts and minds of the people, was strongly urged : they were reminded of the exploits of their ancestors of the revolution ; of the little honour which had thus far attended the prosecution of the war ; the recent failure, and the disgraceful surrender of Hull. They were told that even the Indians of the friendly Six Nations had offered their services, but that, through regard to the cause of humanity, he had refused to follow a disgraceful example, by letting loose these barbarous warriors upon the inhabitants of Canada. He then addressed himself particularly to the " Men of New-York," appealing to their patriotism, calling on them to retrieve the late disaster, and at the same time, by this step, secure their wives and children from the predatory and murderous incursions of the savage. This address was well calculated to reach the feelings of the moment, although eccentric in its style, and in some respects reprehensible, particularly in the reflections indulged at the expense of others. Moreover, it was not dictated by prudence as respected himself, for in the event of a failure, he would naturally be exposed to ridicule, for what would then be termed a pompous and inflated rhodomontade. It was, however, not without some effect ; particularly when seconded by an animated proclamation from general Porter, of

the New York militia. About the 27th of November, upwards
of four thousand five hundred men, consisting of regulars, and
the volunteers from Pennsylvania, New York and Baltimore,
were collected at Buffaloe ; and the officers were actively engaged in drilling, equipping and organizing them for the intended enterprise.

Seventy boats, and a number of scows, were prepared for
the reception of the army, that they might be at once transported to the Canadian shore. But, preparatory to the principal
attack, two detachments, one under colonel Boerstler, and another under captain King, received orders to pass over before
day : the first to destroy a bridge, about five miles below Fort
Erie, and capture the guard stationed there ; the other to storm
the British batteries. Before they reached the opposite shore,
the enemy opened a heavy fire ; the first detachment landed and
took some prisoners, but failed in destroying the bridge. The
other, under captain King, landed higher up at the Red House,
drove the enemy, and then advanced to their batteries, which
they stormed, and then spiked the cannon. Lieutenant Angus,
with a number of marines, accidentally separated from captain
King, and no reinforcements arriving from the opposite side,
they concluded that King and his party had been taken prisoners, and therefore returned. The party of King, now consisting of seventeen, besides captains Morgan and Sprowl, and
five other officers, was in full possession of the works, while
the enemy was completely dispersed. Finding, at length, that
they could not expect to be supported, they resolved to return.
But one boat could be found, to transport them all. Captains
Sprowl and Morgan passed over with the prisoners ; leaving
captain King, who was soon after, with his small party, surrounded and taken prisoner. On the return of captain Sprowl,
colonel Winder was ordered to pass over with about three hundred men. He instantly embarked, and led the van. His own
boat was the only one which touched the opposite shore, the
others having been swept down by the swiftness of the current.

From various causes the embarkation of the main body was
retarded much beyond the appointed time, so that it was twelve
o'clock in the day, when about two thousand men were ready
to move. General Tannehill's volunteers, and colonel M'Clure's
regiment, were drawn up ready for a second embarkation.
The enemy by this time had collected on the opposite shore,
and appeared ready to receive them. The departure of our
troops was, in the most unaccountable manner, delayed until
late in the afternoon, when orders were given to debark. Much
murmuring and discontent ensued ; which were in some mea-

ure silenced, by assurances that another attempt would be made. It was now resolved to land about five miles below the navy yard; and accordingly, on Monday evening, the 29th, all the boats were collected for the purpose. The whole body, with the exception of about two hundred men, were embarked at four o'clock; the men conducting themselves with great order and obedience, and affording every hope of success. Nothing was wanting but the word to move; when, after some delay, orders were suddenly given for the whole to land, accompanied with a declaration, that the invasion of Canada was given over for that season, while arrangements were made to go into winter quarters. One universal expression of indignation burst forth; the greater part of the militia threw down their arms, and returned to their homes, and those who remained continually threatened the life of the general. Severe recriminations passed between him and general Porter, who accused him of cowardice and of unofficer-like deportment. General Smyth, in vindication of his conduct, alleged that he had positive instructions not to risk an invasion with less than three thousand men, and that the number embarked did not exceed fifteen hundred. Be this as it may, great dissatisfaction was produced through the country, and his military reputation, from that time, declined in public estimation. Throughout the whole of this year, we were continually suffering the effects of our total want of experience in war. Every thing seemed to baffle our calculations, and to disappoint our hopes, particularly in our movements against Canada, although many acts of gallantry were performed both by regulars and militia.

It is now time to turn our attention to the Northern Army, collecting on the borders of the St Lawrence. But little was done in this quarter, until late in the autumn. At the declaration of war, but a small number of troops were stationed at any point along this frontier: and it would necessarily require a considerable length of time before the militia could be embodied and marched, or the regular troops, newly enlisted or already on foot, could be collected from over an immense surface of country such as ours. It was confidently expected that the upper provinces of Canada would fall an easy conquest to our troops of the Northwestern Army, and of the Army of the Centre, which might then move down, and join those on the St Lawrence, and, long before the winter, the war would be carried to Montreal. But the unlooked-for and lamentable surrender of Hull produced a total change in the situation of affairs. It was not until late in the autumn, that any thing worthy of note occurred in the Northern Army.

G

On the 15th of September, twenty-fiev barges of the British passed up the St Lawrence, and were attacked by a party of militia from Ogdensburg, and after a severe contest, the enemy were forced to abandon their boats, and fly for shelter to the woods; but soon after, receiving reinforcements, they compelled the militia to retire. Some time after this, captain Forsyth made an incursion into the enemy's country, with a party of his riflemen, and after twice defeating a body of regulars of superior numbers, burnt a block-house, containing the public stores, and returned with the loss of only one man. In revenge for that attack, the British, on the 2d of October, determined to attempt the destruction of Ogdensburg. A heavy fire was opened from the breast-works, at the village of Prescott, situated nearly opposite. On the 4th, they attempted to cross the St Lawrence, and storm the town, and embarked in forty boats, with about fifteen men in each; but they were warmly received by general Brown, of the New York militia, who commanded here in person. A sharp action continued for nearly two hours, when they were compelled to abandon their design, leaving one of the boats in our hands, and suffering a considerable loss.

Colonel Pike, to whose zeal and indefatigable exertions, the army was even at this time much indebted, on the 19th passed into the enemy's territory, surprised a block-house defended by a considerable body of English and Indians, put them to flight, and destroyed the public stores. Skirmishes like these were not unfrequent until the close of autumn, and even occurred during the winter; but nothing of moment transpired in this quarter, until the beginning of the year.

A new scene of warfare was about to open, upon those vast inland seas, which constitute so remarkable a feature of our continent. For the first time, their waves were to be lighted up with all the sublimity of naval combat: and they soon bore witness to achievements as glorious as those which immortalized our heroes on the ocean. In consequence of the failure of our arms at Detroit, it became necessary to form a navy on the lakes. We were now without a single armed vessel on Lake Erie, and our whole force on Lake Ontario was the brig Oneida, sixteen guns, commanded by lieutenant Woolsey. In October, commodore Chauncey, with a body of seamen, arrived at Sackett's Harbour, for the purpose of carrying this design into effect; he instantly purchased every trader capable of being fitted up as a vessel of war, and ordered lieutenant Elliot, as we have seen, to organize a naval force on Lake Erie. That his preparations proceeded with rapidity, cannot be doubted, when we

find, that on the 6th of November he considered himself able to
contend with the enemy's whole force.   Having received information that the enemy's fleet had sailed down the lake, for the
purpose of bringing up reinforcements to Fort George, he determined to intercept him at the False Ducks, on his way up.
The force of commodore Chauncey, created in this short space
of time, was composed of the Oneida, fourteen guns, in which
he sailed ; the Governor Tompkins, lieutenant Brown, six guns ;
the Growler, lieutenant Mix, of five guns ; the Conquest, lieutenant Elliot, of two guns ; the Pert, Arundel, of two guns ; and the
Julia, Trant, of one thirty pounder ; making in all thirty-two
guns.   The vessels of the enemy, which were supposed to
have passed up the lakes, constituted nearly the whole force of
the British, and consisted of the Royal George, twenty-six guns ;
ship Earl Moira, eighteen guns ; schooner Prince ,Regent,
eighteen guns ; Duke of Gloucester, fourteen guns , Torento,
fourteen guns ; Governor Simcoe, twelve guns.
    On the 8th, the squadron fell in with the Royal George, but
lost sight of her during the night, having chased her into the
bay of Quanti.   In the morning she was discovered in Kingston channel.   The commodore had made up his mind to board
her ; but the wind blowing directly in, and the enemy being
too well protected by the guns of the batteries, he changed his
intention.   The next morning he beat up in good order, and
commenced an attack on the Royal George, under a heavy fire
both from this ship and from the batteries.   The Conquest, the
Julia, the Pert, and the Growler pushed forward in succession ;
afterwards the brig General Hamilton, and the Governor Tompkins ; shortly after, the whole fire of the batteries was turned
upon the brig, and continued hot on both sides for an hour,
when the Royal George cut her cables, and ran higher up the
bay.   The squadron being now exposed to the cross fire of the
batteries, and not deeming it prudent to pursue the Royal
George, hauled off to the wind, and made sail out of the bay.
This was certainly a most daring exploit, and, to say the least
of it, merited success.   The Royal George suffered severely
in her hull ; the shot from the gun-vessels struck her frequently,
while the loss of commodore Chauncey was very inconsiderable.   The commander of the Pert, Arundel, was wounded by
the bursting of a gun, but refusing to quit the deck, was
knocked overboard and drowned.   The commodore captured
a schooner off the harbour, and sent the Growler as her convoy
past the entrance, for the purpose of decoying the Royal
George, but without success.   She then sailed with her prize
for Sackett's Harbour.   On her way she discovered the Prince

Regent and Earl Moira, convoying a sloop to Kingston; she immediately concealed herself behind a point, and when the armed vessels had passed, she ran out and captured the schooner and brought her into Sackett's Harbour. The prize had on board twelve thousand dollars in specie, and the baggage of general Brock, with captain Brock, the brother of that officer. Commodore Chauncey, soon after arriving, received the intelligence respecting the Earl Moira, and immediately set off in the midst of a severe storm, to intercept her at the False Ducks; but returned to the Harbour without being able to fall in with her.

He now occupied himself chiefly in superintending the new ship Madison, which was launched on the 26th of November. The winter set in soon after, and put an end to any further naval incidents for the season.

CHAPTER VI.

THE congress of the United States again assembled on the 4th of November, after a recess unusually short, on account of the new and interesting state of our affairs. Party spirit unfortunately raged amongst us, in a very high degree, and it was not difficult to foretell that no small portion would find its way into the national councils. Recriminations of French influence, and improper submission to the outrages of Great Britain, very much embittered this animosity. The existence of party spirit is necessary and healthful to our political system; it is like the current of the stream, which preserves it pure and untainted. In despotisms there is no party spirit; there all is conducted in the darkness and secrecy of intrigue. But party has its evils. In peace, it renovates the flagging energies of the nation, and keeps all things pure and sound; on the contrary, in a period of war, this animosity may clog the efforts of the party in power, and may be a useful ally to the enemy.

Unfortunately there prevailed a strong disposition to thwart the measures of the administration, and in this way compel it to sue for peace, without perhaps sufficiently reflecting, that the enemy might not be disposed to grant it, upon other terms than such as would be disgraceful to the nation. It is not becoming a true lover of his country, to desire that the government, with which the nation, as respects others, is identified, should be disgraced, in order that the power may be transferred to better hands. This would not be the maxim of Washington. But on this subject it is difficult, if not impossible, to draw the exact line between a manly and laudable opposition to what we conceive to be wrong, and such intemperance as may endanger the character and safety of the country. In the eastern states, the opposition to the war was the most violent.

The administration. soon after the war, had manifested a wish for the restoration of peace, could it be done consistently with prudence. About the time of the declaration of war in this country, the Prince Regent had repealed his orders in council, one of the principal causes of hostilities : an act, which was by no means dictated by a sense of what was due to justice and to us, but by the urgency of the particular interests of Great Britain. Having repealed them, he considered himself entitled to the same regard as if they had been expressly repealed on our account, and demanded that hostilities, on our part, should cease. To this the President replied, that being now at war, the United States would not put an end to hostilities, unless provision were made for a general settlement of differences, and a cessation of the practice of impressment, pending the negotiation. In the meantime, a law would be passed forbidding the employment of British seamen in our vessels, of whatsoever kind. A law to this effect was passed during the session.

Shortly after the commencement of the war, a proposition for an armistice had been made by the governor of Canada, but was rejected as a matter of course. The American minister in London was authorised to agree to a cessation of hostilities, even on the unofficial assurance that the practice of impressment would be discontinued, during the armistice. This was rejected. A proposition was afterwards made by admiral Warren ; which required as a preliminary to every other step, that our armies should be immediately withdrawn, and the orders to our cruisers recalled. This he alleged, was in consequence of our being the aggressors, and that as such it became us to take the first step, and unconditionally throw down

G*

our arms.　Here it might have been asked, whether this country had ever experienced so much good faith and forbearance from Great Britain, as to justify such confidence? But was she not the aggressor, by her own acknowledgement? for, by the repeal of the orders in council, if on our account, she acknowledged herself to have violated our neutral rights.　Moreover, it was well known that she had, at that moment, more than two thousand impressed American seamen, confined as prisoners of war, and persisted in refusing every arrangement which might remedy in future the odious practice.　So strangely inconsistent are the pretexts of injustice.　These attempts at reconciliation had failed, when the emperor of Russia interposed his mediation : which, on the part of our government, was instantly accepted; but, on being made known to England, was declined, as being incompatible with her naval interests. She professed a willingness, however, to enter into a direct negotiation; which, it will be seen, was merely thrown out as a pretext, to prolong the war at her pleasure.

A most important change had taken place in the affairs of Europe.　Napoleon had experienced a reverse, proportioned to the vastness of his designs.　This man, intoxicated with his former success, and with the vile flattery which is always paid to the despot who is the fountain of honour, and official emolument and power, had begun to think himself more than mortal.　It is thought that he had conceived the idea of universal empire; naturally enough the ultimate object of a conqueror—for what conqueror ever set bounds to his ambition?　The vanity of the scheme, if any such ever entered his head, of bringing all Europe to his feet, of mastering the fleet of England, and then extending his power over the globe, was now fully demonstrated.　The joy which many of our fellow citizens expressed on this occasion, was perhaps ill judged.　The fall of a despot and a tyrant, is certainly an agreeable theme to a republican; but the immediate connexion of this event with our welfare, was not easily traced. It was very evident that the enmity both of France and England towards this country, proceeded from the same cause; and, considering human nature, a very natural cause; to wit, the circumstance of our prospering and growing rich from their dissensions.　We had but little to fear that we should be molested by any European power, attempting to conquer our vast country; and as to universal dominion, England, in her claim to the sovereignty of the seas, already possessed it, as far as the thing, in its nature, was capable of being possessed. As to Europe, the mad attempt of Napoleon had been followed by an overthrow so complete; that so far from being dangerous to its repose in future, it became a matter of doubt with enlightened politicians of the day, whether he would be able to maintain his own ground, and whether, if France were reduced to a second rate power, Europe would not have to fear a more formidable enemy in Russia. Nothing but the pacific temper of its present sovereign, would be a guarantee to the safety of the neighbouring nations. The consequence of the rapid decline of the power of Napoleon, would be highly favourable to England, in the disposal of her forces against this country; and elated by her success against France, it was not probable that she would feel much disposition to treat with us on reasonable terms.

The first business, on the meeting of congress, with a view to the war, which now occupied its chief attention, was the providing an additional force. Enlistments had been extremely slow, and sufficient encouragement had not been held out for recruits. It was proposed to receive into the service of the United States, twenty thousand volunteers, for a year, to be clothed and paid in the same manner as regular troops. The inefficacy of mere militia, under no discipline, and under no control, had been sufficiently seen, both during the present and the revolutionary war. But there was no mode of remedying the evil; for regular soldiers could not be raised, or at least, in sufficient numbers.

The navy attracted much attention. On this subject there prevailed the most perfect unanimity; and it was resolved, that it should be fostered, as the best and safest reliance of our country. Such as had once been inimical to it, became its warmest friends. The national legislature now engaged with great assiduity, in devising such measures as were necessary, for a vigorous prosecution of the war, and as would tend to remedy the evils already experienced.

The seaboard, although sometimes threatened by the enemy, had not yet experienced any serious molestation. In the month of December, the whole coast was proclaimed in a state of blockade, but with no force actually applied. This paper blockade had no pretence of retaliation, like that declared against the coast of France; and the United States did not choose to follow an example so contrary to the laws of nations, and in turn declare the coast of England in a state of blockade, and under that pretence interrupt the commerce of neutrals going to her ports. The British vessels were chiefly employed in the protection of her commerce against our cruisers; and her attention was so much taken up with the mighty affairs which were then passing on the continent, that we fortunately remained, during this season, unmolested; at least our homes and our firesides were not disturbed.

A war, however, threatened us in another quarter, to which we now looked with no small anxiety. The southern Indians, equally ferocious in their modes of warfare, and perhaps more daring than the northern, began to exhibit signs of hostility. No people had ever less cause to complain. The Creeks within the territorial limits of the United States, had been uniformly protected by the Americans; intruders upon their lands were turned off at the point of the bayonet; immense sums were expended in teaching them the arts of civilized life; persons were employed to reside among them, for that purpose, and implements of agriculture were furnished at the public expense. This humane system, commenced by Washington, was strictly pursued by subsequent administrations; and the effects were visible in the course of a few years. Their country and climate, probably the best in the United States, were capable of affording every thing essential to their happiness. The domestic arts had taken root amongst them ; that strong stimulant to industry, separate property on the soil, was beginning to be understood; they possessed numerous herds, and all the domestic animals; their situation was, in every respect, equal to that of the peasants in many parts of Europe. They had thrown off their clothing of skins, and wore cottons of their own manufacture; and their population was rapidly increasing. They had always lived on terms of friendship with the United States; their lands had never been encroached upon; and they had become considerably intermingled, by marriages, with the whites. According to one of their laws, no white man, except the Indian agent, was permitted to reside in their territory, unless married to a native.

The benevolent societies of the United States, had opened schools through the country, for the purpose of giving the finish to this state of manners; for in every other respect they had entirely thrown off their savage habits. Nearly the same state of improvement existed amongst the other tribes, the Choctaws, Chickasaws, and Cherokees. The same regular industry was visible in the villages of these people, in their daily occupations, in their cultivation of the soil, in their attention to their lands, and even in the construction of their dwellings, which, in many cases, were built by white carpenters employed for the purpose, and were little inferior to those of the generality of white settlers.

To seduce these people into a war, would be an act of cruelty to them ; and hostilities on their part would be the extreme

of folly. For although, if united, their number would be thrice
that of the northern Indians, yet being completely surrounded
by white settlements, their destruction must be inevitable. The
United States agent, colonel Hawkins, an enlightened man,
had devoted his life to the civilization of these unfortunate people, and had acquired a considerable ascendency over them.
But, among them, there was a large proportion of the idle and
the worthless, who had not acquired any property, and who
were inclined to return to the old state of savage manners, as
more favourable to their loose, unrestrained propensities, than
the habits newly introduced, which they pretended to despise.
During the summer, while war raged on the northern frontier,
the disorderly Creeks began to show much uneasiness; they
collected in small bands, roamed about the country, committed
depredations on the property of the well-ordered class, and
often upon the whites. Shortly after the surrender of Hull,
this disposition broke out into open violence. A party of these
vagabond Muscogees fell upon some people, who were descending the Mississippi, and murdered them near the mouth of the
Ohio. The affair was represented to the nation, who caused
the perpetrators to be seized and put to death. A civil war,
soon after, was the consequence, in which the savage part, as
might be expected, prevailed ; and the greater number of those
who had been friendly to the United States, were either obliged
to fly, or to join their standard.

Other causes contributed to bring about this ruinous state of
things. The celebrated chief, Tecumseh, had, the year before,
visited all the southern tribes, for the purpose of kindling a
spirit unfriendly to the United States. This savage Demosthenes, wherever he went, called councils of their tribes, and
with that bold and commanding eloquence, which he possessed
in a degree infinitely superior to what had ever been witnessed
amongst these people, exhausted every topic calculated to operate on their minds, and alienate their affections from their
benefactors. Among all these nations his speeches had great
effect, but with the Creeks particularly, although the more
considerate rejected his interference. Amid the usual topics
of his discourses, he was in the habit of reproaching them with
their civilization ; and in the keenest and most sarcastic manner
contrasted their degenerate effeminacy, with every thing that
was great and noble in the opinion of Indians. Demosthenes,
in his reproaches of his countrymen, was not more terribly vehe-
ment and audacious. Against the United States, he pronounced
the most furious invectives, which might be compared to the

Philippics of the Grecian orator; and he unquestionably left a strong impression on the minds of the southern Indians.

There existed, however, another and more immediate cause of their enmity towards us. The Seminoles, and the tribes of the Creeks who resided within the territory of Spain, were frequently supplied with arms and presents from the British government, with a view of engaging them to make war upon the United States, and also to prevail upon the other Creeks to join them. The town of Pensacola, which was then, to every purpose, under the control of Great Britain, was the usual place at which these presents were distributed, and where the vagabond Indians could be supplied with arms; and they resorted to it, from all the different tribes, for the purpose of receiving them. It was no difficult matter, thus to excite hostilities; and the attempt, unfortunately, proved but too successful. Such was the disposition of the southern Indians, during the first year of the war.

The Choctaws, Chickasaws and Cherokees, the latter particularly, being further removed from British influence, and within reach of our power, were disposed to be friendly; but many of their restless young men, in spite of the nation, strayed off and joined our enemies. Hostilities did not commence on the part of any of these Indians, within our territory, during the first year of the war. The government, however, fearing the worst, called on the governors of Georgia and Tennessee, to hold their militia in readiness; and general Jackson, at the head of two thousand men, early in the spring, marched through the Choctaw and Chickasaw country to Natchez, a distance of five hundred miles; but every thing appearing peaceful in this quarter, he shortly after returned. This expedition had the effect of fixing the tribes through which it passed, and of retarding the Creek war. The tribes within the limits of the Spanish part of Florida, on the contrary, declared themselves at once, and brandished the scalping knife against the frontier of Georgia.

The Seminoles, very soon after the declaration of war, began to make incursions into Georgia, accompanied by a number of negro runaways, who had taken refuge amongst them. They proceeded to the usual work of murdering the inhabitants, and plundering their property. Early in September, a party of marines, and about twenty volunteers under captain Williams, were attacked near Davis's Creek by about fifty Indians and negroes. After a desperate resistance, in which captains Williams and Fort were both severely wounded, the party retreated, leaving the savages in possession of their wagons and teams.

On the 24th of the same month, colonel Newman, of the Georgia volunteers, with about one hundred and seventeen men, marched to the attack of the Lochway towns. When within a few miles of the first of these, he met a party of one hundred and fifty Indians on horseback, who instantly dismounted and prepared for battle. Colonel Newman ordered a charge, and the Indians were driven into one of the swamps which abound in this part of the country. As they fled, the fire of the musketry did considerable execution, and, amongst others of the slain, they left their king in the hands of the whites. The Indians discovering this, with a spirit which deserves to be admired, made several desperate charges, in order to recover the body of their chief, and were each time driven back. But in another attempt, still more desperately furious, they succeeded in carrying off the dead body; when they retired from the field, after a severe conflict of two hours. This, however, did not free the Georgians from their unpleasant situation. Before night, the Indians returned with considerable reinforcements of negroes; and after a loss more severe than the first, they again fled. The volunteers now found their situation becoming every moment more critical; the number of their wounded, would neither permit them to retreat nor to advance, and the enemy was hourly increasing on all sides. A messenger was despatched for reinforcements; and in the meanwhile, they threw up a small breast-work. Here they remained until the 4th of October, waiting for assistance; having in the meantime repelled numerous assaults from the Indians, who continued to harass them day and night. The Indians, observing that a perfect silence prevailed within the breast-works, suspected that they had been deserted in the night; and approached under this assurance, until within thirty or forty paces, when the Georgians suddenly showed themselves above the breast-work, fired their pieces, and sent them yelling to the swamps. The volunteers then decamped, and reached unmolested the village of Peccolatta, whence they had set out. Intelligence of this affair reached the government about the commencement of the session of congress, and it was found necessary to make suitable preparations to meet a war in this quarter. The defence of this important frontier was assigned to general Pinckney, of South Carolina, a gentleman of great distinction and ability, who was appointed a brigadier in the service of the United States.

Congress had not been long in session, when the public feelings were once more excited by news of the most flattering kind. Another naval victory was announced, not less splendid

Third Naval Victory over a British Frigate (the Java)

than that of the United States, and the first of the Constitution : the flag of another British frigate was transmitted to our capitol, and was placed amongst the other trophies of our naval prowess.

In October, the Constitution, commodore Bainbridge, and the Hornet, captain Lawrence, sailed from New York, and were to effect a junction with the Essex, captain Porter, which sailed about the same time from the Delaware ; the object of which was to cruise in the South Seas, and destroy the British fisheries and commerce in that quarter. The junction not happening at the time and place appointed, commodore Porter passed round Cape Horn alone. In the meanwhile, on the 29th of December, a few leagues west of St Salvador, the Constitution, which had a few days before parted company with the Hornet, descried a British frigate. Commodore Bainbridge tacked, and stood for her. At two P. M. the enemy was within half a mile of the Constitution, and to windward, having hauled down his colours except the union jack, which was at the mizen-mast head. A gun was then fired ahead to make him show his colours, which was returned by a broadside. The enemy's colours being now hoisted, the action commenced with round and grape ; but he kept at so great a distance that this had little effect; and in this position, if he were brought nearer, the Constitution would be exposed to raking. At thirty minutes past two, both ships were within good canister distance, when the Constitution's wheel was shot away. At forty minutes past two, the fore and main sail were set; and commodore Bainbridge, being now determined to close with her, luffed up for that purpose : in ten minutes afterward the enemy's jib-boom got foul of the Constitution's mizen rigging, and in another ten minutes his bowsprit and jib-boom were shot away. At five minutes past three, his maintopmast was shot away just above the cap. This was followed by the loss of his gaff and spanker-boom, and soon after his mainmast went nearly by the board. At fifteen minutes past three, the enemy was completely silenced, and his colours at the mainmast being down, it was thought he had surrendered: under this idea the Constitution shot ahead to repair damages ; after which, discovering the enemy's flag still flying, she wore, stood for him in handsome style, and got close athwart his bows in an effectual position for raking, when his mainmast went entirely by the board, and he lay an unmanageable wreck. He now struck his colours ; and being taken possession of by lieutenant Parker was found to be the British frigate Java, of thirty-eight guns, but carrying forty-nine, commanded by a distinguished officer, captain Lambert, who was mortally wounded. She had on board four hundred men, besides one hundred seamen whom she was carrying out to the East Indies for the service there. The Constitution had nine men killed, and twenty-five wounded; the Java sixty killed, and one hundred and twenty wounded. She had on board despatches for St Helena, the Cape of Good Hope, and the different establishments in the East Indies and China, with copper for a seventy-four, building at Bombay. There were also on board a number of passengers, among whom were lieutenant-general Hislop, governor of Bombay; major Walker; and one staff-major; captain Marshall, master and commander, of the royal navy; and several officers appointed to ships in the East Indies.

The conduct of all the American officers on this occasion, was as conspicuous for gallantry during the engagement, as for humanity to the vanquished. It is this true chivalric courtesy which gives estimation to valour. Lieutenant Aylwin, so favourably known to the reader, received a severe wound, of which he soon after died. He was in the act of firing his pistols at the enemy from the quarterdeck hammock, when he received a ball in his shoulder blade, which threw him on the deck. Midshipman Dulany, who had fought by his side in both actions of this ship, ordered two men of his division to carry him below; to this he would not consent until he saw the issue of the battle, at the same time declaring that no man should quit his post on his account. Lieutenant Parker, James Dulany of Pennsylvania, and James Packett, of Virginia, were much distinguished; the latter was afterwards presented with a sword by his native state, and was promoted to a lieutenancy. Many extraordinary instances of bravery were manifested by the seamen, one of whom, after being mortally wounded, lay upon deck during a great part of the action, apparently expiring; but no sooner was it announced that the enemy had struck, than he raised himself up, gave three cheers, fell back and expired.

On the 1st of January, the commodore, finding the prize in such a state as to render it impossible to bring her in, and leaving every thing on board except the prisoners' baggage, blew her up. On arriving at St Salvador, the commodore received the public acknowledgements of governor Hislop, who presented him with an elegant sword in consideration of the polite treatment which he had shown. He dismissed the private passengers without considering them as prisoners; the public passengers, officers and crew were released on their parol. At this place the Constitution met with the Hornet; and leaving this vessel to blockade the Bonne Citoyenne, the commodore

H

sailed for the United States, changing the original destination for the South Seas.

On the arrival of commodore Bainbridge in the United States, he was universally hailed by the applauses of his countrymen, he received the freedom of the city of New York in a gold box; a piece of plate from the citizens of Philadelphia, and the thanks of many of the state legislatures. Congress also presented him a medal. and voted fifty thousand dollars to himself, officers and crew.

In the midst of these affairs, news of fresh disasters to the westward, and accompanied by circumstances such as rarely occur in the annals of history, tended much to temper the public joy for the second victory of the Constitution.

CHAPTER VII.

Harrison returns to Ohio—General Winchester sends a Detachment to the relief of Frenchtown—Defeat of the British and Indians—Winchester arrives with Reinforcements—Surrender at the River Raisin—Cruelty of the British and Indians at the River Raisin—Humane Conduct of the People of Detroit—March of General Harrison—Siege of Fort Meigs—Defeat of Colonel Dudley—Sortie under Colonel Miller—Siege of Fort Meigs raised—Exploit of Major Ball.

We have seen with what indefatigable industry general Harrison was engaged, in placing the western frontier in a posture of defence, and in attempting to regain what we had lost. The Indian tribes had been made to feel the war in their own country, and were driven to such a distance by the destruction of their villages, as to prevent them from annoying our settlements; they were compelled to remove their wives and children to the distant British establishments, in order to obtain the means of subsistence. The close of the season was now chiefly occupied in strengthening the frontier posts, and in establishing others. Great exertions were made by governor Meigs, of Ohio, to keep up the necessary supply of men, and to provide the means of subsistence. General Harrison established his head quarters at Franklinton, whence he could with greater facility organize and distribute to the different forts the reinforcements and supplies which must arrive. His object was to concentrate a considerable force at the Rapids, and thence, unless a change of circumstances forbade, proceed to Detroit. The government was compelled, in consequence of the taking of that place, to transport artillery and public stores at an enormous expense across the mountains, and down the Ohio; and afterwards to the different forts. This necessarily consumed much time, and delayed the operations of the army.

In the meanwhile, general Winchester continued at Fort Defiance, with about eight hundred men; many of the volunteers having returned home on the expiration of their term of service. Those who remained were chiefly from Kentucky, and the greater part ranked amongst its most respectable citizens. Early in the month of January, General Winchester received intimations from the inhabitants of the village of Frenchtown, which is situated on the river Raisin, between the Rapids and Detroit, that a large body of British and Indians were about to concentrate at this point, for the purpose of preventing the further progress of the Americans. The inhabitants, becoming alarmed at their situation, besought the Americans to march to their protection, as they would probably be exposed to the horrors of Indian massacre, in the midst of ferocious savages, whom the British were obliged to indulge, that they might be kept in good humour. Threats against them had, besides, been thrown out by one of the Indian chiefs. The sensibility of the young American volunteers, officers and privates, was strongly excited; and they earnestly besought the general to lead them to the defence of the distressed inhabitants. With some reluctance, he yielded to their wishes, and, contrary to the general plan of the commander-in-chief, resolved to send a force to their relief. Accordingly, on the 17th of January, he detached a body of men under colonels Lewis and Allen, with orders to wait at Presque Isle, until joined by the main body.

On their arrival, information was received that an advance party of British and Indians had already taken possession of Frenchtown. It was determined to march instantly and attack them. As they drew near, the enemy became apprised of their approach, and prepared for their reception. Colonel Allen commanded the right wing, major Graves the left, and major Madison the centre. On coming to the river, which was bridged with ice, they displayed, and moved forward under a fire from a howitzer and musketry. Majors Graves and Madison, with their battalions, were ordered to dislodge the enemy from the houses and picketing, which they in a moment effected, under a shower of bullets, and drove the British and Indians to the woods. Colonel Allen made a simultaneous movement upon

their left, and after several spirited charges compelled these to
take to the wood also.   Here, availing themselves of the fences
and fallen timber, they attempted to make a stand ; but were
attacked a second time, and after a conflict more obstinate than
the first, again fled.   They now attempted to draw their pur-
suers into a wood; and partly succeeding, they charged in turn
furiously, but were unable to break the American line.   A
severe conflict now ensued, but the enemy were finally beaten,
pursued with a continual charge for several miles, and entirely
dispersed.   The American loss was twelve killed, and fifty-five
wounded : that of the enemy could not well be ascertained, but
fifteen of the Indians were left on the field.   The volunteers,
having thus gallantly effected their object, encamped on the
spot, where they remained until the 20th, when they were
joined by General Winchester.   With this addition, their whole
force exceeded seven hundred and fifty men.

Six hundred men were placed within a line of pickets, and the
remainder, to the number of one hundred and fifty, encamped
in the open field.   On the morning of the 22d, a combined force
of about fifteen hundred men, under Proctor and the Indian chiefs
Round-Head and Split-Log, suddenly attacked our little army.
They were in an instant ready for the reception of the enemy,
who planted six pieces of artillery, and opened a heavy fire,
accompanied with musketry, against the slight breast-work of
pickets.   The body of men belonging to the encampment, and
composing the right wing, was soon overpowered by numbers,
and endeavoured to retreat across the river.   Two companies
of fifty men each, seeing the situation of their comrades, sallied
out of the breast-work to their relief, but were obliged to retreat
with them.   Nearly all these unfortunate men were either cut
off, or surrendered themselves prisoners to the British, under promise of protection.   The left wing within the pickets, still continued a cool and steady resistance.   Three successive assaults
were made by the British Forty-first, but they were driven
back, with the loss of thirty killed and one hundred wounded.
When the right wing broke at the commencement of the action,
great efforts had been made by general Winchester and colonel
Lewis, to rally and bring them within the pickets; but in the
attempt these officers were taken prisoners.   Notwithstanding
these misfortunes, and the overwhelming force which assailed
them on every side, they still continued, with firmness and determination seldom surpassed, to repulse every assault of the
enemy, until eleven o'clock in the day ; making prodigious
slaughter in his ranks.

Finding at length that it would be vain to contend openly

with such men, resolved to defend themselves to the last, and that even if they had now been successful, their victory would have been dearly bought, the enemy attempted to prevail on them to surrender. The general was told by colonel Proctor, that unless his men surrendered, they would be delivered over to the fury of the savages, or what amounts to the same thing, no responsibility would be taken for their conduct, and that the houses of the village would be burnt. The general sent a flag communicating these particulars, and stating that in order to preserve the remainder of his brave troops, he had agreed to surrender them as prisoners of war, on condition of their being protected from the savages, of their being allowed to retain their private property, and of having their side arms returned them. The flag passed three times; the Americans being unwilling to surrender with arms in their hands, until they received a positive engagement from a British colonel that they should not be murdered, and that they should have the privilege of burying their dead. Thirty-five officers, and four hundred and fifty non-commissioned officers and men, still remained, after fighting six hours against artillery, surrounded by the yells of a thousand savages, waiting like wolves for their prey. At this time the killed, wounded and missing, of the little army, including those that had been outside the pickets, amounted to more than three hundred. The loss of the British could not have been less. The little band, thus solicited by their general, and giving way to that ray of hope which the bravest in desperate situations will seize, at last consented to a surrender.

The office of the historian sometimes imposes a melancholy duty. The mind may be allowed to indulge a generous satisfaction, in recording those actions where a high, but mistaken ambition calls forth our energies at the expense of humanity. Who can read without admiring, the retreat of the ten thousand Greeks, and what heart can be insensible to the recital of the fate of Leonidas and his immortal band! The virtues of such men, their fortitude, their love of country, their unconquerable minds, give a sanctity to their fate; and while we grieve for them, we rejoice that we also are men. Far otherwise, when we trace, in characters of blood, the cold, deliberate, fiendlike depravity, which assimilates men to the most odious and ferocious of the brute creation.

The task I must now fulfil is painful; I must speak of such things as I almost shudder to name; neither can it be done without tearing open the yet bleeding wounds of my country. But faithful history forbids that they should be passed over in silence; they must stand forth in all the awfulness of truth:

H*

and that impartial judgment must be passed upon them, which
will doom them to the detestation of all posterity.   The vengeance of heaven does not sleep.   There is a measure of retri-
butive justice even in this world, which soon or late overtakes
the swiftest guilt.   Not the most infuriated passions of the worst
times, ever caused the perpetration of more shocking cruelties than were now practised towards this band of brave men.
Impelled by feelings of humanity, they had marched to protect
the feeble and the helpless from savage violence : and assailed by
overwhelming numbers, they might have contended to the last
man ; but yielding to the solicitations of their captured general,
and to the threats of the conflagration of the village and the murder
of its inhabitants, they surrendered in an evil hour to a faithless
and treacherous foe, that they might be consigned to cruel suffering, to butchery, to murder, to unrelenting torture, to every
species of savage death.   Well might those disposed to wage
such a war, wish to destroy the pen of history.   Would, for the
honour of Britain ; would, for the sake of humanity ; would, for
the sake of our common relationship to a nation which pos-
sesses so many virtues, that the odious tale of the river Raisin
and Frenchtown, might be consigned to eternal oblivion !   But
it cannot be.   The sacred call of truth must be obeyed.   The
savage and wanton massacre of our heroic countrymen, in the
presence of a British officer, has not been denied, or palliated.
Other atrocities the perpetrators have attempted to cover, by
some flimsy veil of unsubstantial excuse ; but this charge has
always been met with silence.   They have not dared directly
to deny ; and, gracious Heaven, where could they find an excuse !
    Scarcely had the Americans surrendered, under the stipu-
lation of protection from the British officer, than our brave
citizens discovered, too late, that they were reserved to be
butchered in cold blood.   Of the right wing, but a small number had escaped ; the work of scalping and stripping the dead,
and murdering those who could no longer resist, was suffered
to go on without restraint.   The infernal work was now to
begin with those who had so bravely defended themselves.
The infamous Proctor and the British officers turned a deaf ear
to the just remonstrances of these unhappy men.   Contrary to
express stipulation, the swords were taken from the sides of the
officers ; and many of them stripped almost naked, and robbed.
The brave dead were stripped and scalped, and their bodies
shockingly mutilated.   The tomahawk put an end at once to
the sufferings of many of the wounded, who could not rise ; in
allusion to which, some days afterwards, a British officer ob-

served, " The Indians are excellent doctors." The prisoners, who now remained, with but a few exceptions, instead of being guarded by British soldiers, were delivered to the charge of the Indians, to be marched in the rear of the army to Malden. This was, in other words, a full permission to indulge their savage thirst for blood; and in this they were not disappointed; for the greater part of these ill fated men were murdered on the way, through mere wantonness. All such as became too weak for want of nourishment, from excessive fatigue, from their wounds, in this most inclement season of the year, were at once despatched. But small was the remnant of this little army, that ever reached the British garrison ; the greater part of the prisoners had been carried off by the Indians, that they might satiate their fiendlike hatred by roasting them at the stake; or if reserved, it was to gratify their cupidity, by rendering them the objects of traffic. Alas! what heart does not shrink with horror, from the recapitulation !

About sixty of the wounded, many of them officers of distinction, or individuals of much respectability, had been suffered to take shelter in the houses of the inhabitants, and two of their own surgeons permitted by Proctor to attend them, from whom they also obtained a promise that a guard should be placed to protect them, and that they should be carried to Malden the next morning in sleds. But this affected humanity, was but an aggravation of his cruelty, by awakening a hope which he intended to disappoint. No guard of soldiers was left, and on the next day, instead of sleds to convey them to a place of safety, a party of Indians returned to the field of battle, fell upon these poor wounded men, plundered them of their clothing, and every article of any value which remained, tomahawked the greater part of them, and, to finish the scene, fired the houses, and consumed the dying and the dead!

The terrible tale is not yet told. Those rites, which in every civilized country are held sacred, which are not withheld from the vilest malefactor, which are paid alike to enemies and to friends, and for which there existed an express stipulation with the monster who commanded (a stipulation unnecessary amongst civilized men)—the rites of sepulture, were not only denied, but the humane inhabitants of the village dared not perform them under pain of death. And why was this refused? Because, said Proctor, his majesty's allies would not permit! Was there any attempt made to bury them? None. Notwithstanding this, some of the inhabitants, although it " was as much as their lives were worth," did venture to perform this last and pious office to captain Hart, to captain

Woolfolk, and a few others ; but the remainder, nearly two hundred in number, never had this office performed for them, until their friends and relatives triumphed in turn, the autumn following, and then gathered up their bleaching bones and laid them in one common grave. Their mangled bodies had been suffered to lie on the ground exposed to the ferocious beasts of prey, or to the more horrible pollution of domestic animals.

The tragedy was diversified by the most afflicting scenes of individual suffering. The fate of the brave and accomplished captain Hart, a near relative of two of our most distinguished statesmen (Henry Clay and James Brown), a young gentleman of finished education and polished manners, cannot be related without a tear. He had in a particular manner distinguished himself during the engagement, and had received a severe wound in the knee. On being surrendered with the other prisoners, he was recognized by colonel Elliot, a native of the United States, with whom he had been a classmate at Princeton, but who had become a British officer and an ally to the savages. Base indeed must be that man, whose soul, under such circumstances, would not be touched! Elliot voluntarily offered his services to the friend of his youth, his countryman, and promised to take him under his special protection and to transport him to Malden ; but whether he changed his mind, or was forbidden by Proctor, certain it is, that he gave himself no further concern on the subject. The next day a party of Indians came into the room where he lay, and tore him from his bed ; he was then carried to another apartment by one of his brother officers, where he soon experienced the same treatment. He then, by the offer of a large sum of money, induced some Indians to take him to Malden ; they had proceeded but a short distance, when they dragged him from his horse, shot him and scalped him. The same species of suffering was undergone by colonel Allen, by captains Hickman, Woolfolk, and M'Cracken. This ill-fated band was composed of the flower of Kentucky ; we may name Mr Simpson, a member of congress, captains Bledsoe, Matson, Hamilton, Williams and Kelly, and majors Madison and Ballard With the exception of three companies of United States infantry under captains Hightower, Collier and Sebree, they were, all, the volunteers of that patriotic state. On the evening succeeding the engagement, rum was distributed to the Indians, for a frolic in which they were disposed to indulge, and we may easily suppose what was the nature of their infernal orgies.

Proctor now beginning to fear the infamy attached to his conduct, offered a price for those whom the Indians still preserved—those prisoners who had surrendered on the faith of a capitulation with him, and whom he ought never to have abandoned. The humane inhabitants of Detroit had already exhibited a degree of tenderness and solicitude for their unfortunate countrymen which will ever entitle them to our gratitude and esteem. Many of them parted with every thing they possessed of value, for the purchase of the prisoners ; for, to the disgrace of the British arms must it be recorded, persons of the first respectability, who composed this Spartan band, were suffered, under the eyes of colonel Proctor, to be hawked about the streets from door to door, and offered for sale like beasts ! The only restraint on the cruelty of the savage wretches, arose from permitting them to consult their avarice. Even such prisoners as were more fortunate, no matter what their rank or character, were treated with every species of contumely and contempt.

The conduct of the people of Detroit was such as might have been expected from humane Americans. The female sex, ever the foremost in acts of benevolence to the distressed, were particularly distinguished; they gladly gave their shawls, and even the blankets from their beds, when nothing else remained for them to give. Mr Woodward, the former judge of the supreme court, and appointed by the President of the United States, a man of enlightened mind, now openly and boldly remonstrated with Proctor, and in the manly tone of his injured country depicted the infamy of the British conduct "The truth," said he, "must undoubtedly eventually appear, and that unfortunate day must meet the steady and impartial eye of history." Those facts have been established by a cloud of witnesses, and the appeal of judge Woodward will reach posterity. Let the reader of this history now remember, that this was but the commencement of a series of barbarities, both upon the Atlantic bord and upon the frontier, which was afterwards systematically pursued : that so far from this having been covered by the base excuse of retaliation, it is a charge which has never otherwise been met than with the silence of conscious guilt.

Never did any calamity so deeply affect the sensibilities of a people. All Kentucky *was literally in mourning ;* for the soldiers thus massacred, tortured, burnt, or denied the common rites of sepulture, were of the most respectable families of the state ; many of them young men of fortune and distinction, with numerous friends and relatives.

It would be unjust, in this common anathema, to include all the British officers : the names of some deserve to be rescued from this indelible reproach ; major Muir, captains Aikins, Curtis, Dr Bowen, and the reverend Mr Parrow. Elliot was also spoken of in favourable terms by the American officers, as having on some occasions interested himself for the sufferers. Enough has certainly been said on this distressing subject; one part, however, cannot be omitted. Proctor, perceiving the eagerness of the people of Detroit in purchasing the unhappy captives, actually issued an order prohibiting any further purchases, on the ground that they gave more than the government. This officer was afterwards promoted to the rank of a brigadier, in consequence of his good conduct, particularly in *saving the prisoners from the fury of the Indians* If any thing can move indignation, it is this climax of insult. The facts were afterwards proved to the satisfaction of every one, but the British government was silent, instead of making a signal example of the man who had brought such disgrace upon her name.

A few days after the affair, a Dr M'Keehan was despatched by general Harrison for the purpose of attending the sick, and provided with gold to purchase such things as they might want. The doctor, notwithstanding his flag, his sacred errand, and an open letter directed to any British officer, stating the object of his mission, was actually wounded and robbed, then dragged to Malden, whence he was taken to Quebec. After the sufferings of several months, having been dragged from place to place, from dungeon to dungeon, he at length reached home, with a constitution totally impaired. Such are the distressing occurrences which it becomes the painful duty of the historian to record.

The news of this melancholy affair soon after reached general Harrison, who was on his march with reinforcements to general Winchester. He had heard with chagrin the movements of that officer, and apprehensive of the consequence, had ordered a detachment of three hundred men, under major Cotgreves, from general Perkins's brigade of Ohio militia, to march to his relief. Hearing of the disaster, they fell back upon the Rapids, where general Harrison was then stationed, who retreated to Carrying river, for the purpose of forming a junction with the troops in the rear, and favouring the convoy of artillery and stores then coming from Upper Sandusky. He first, however, despatched a chosen body of one hundred and seventy men for the purpose of picking up such of the unfortunate fugitives as might have escaped. The number of these was very small, on account of the depth of the snow, which rendered it almost im-

possible for them to make their way. Governor Meigs having
promptly despatched two regiments to the assistance of Harrison, the latter again advanced to the Rapids, and immediately
set about constructing a fort, which, in honour of the governor
of Ohio, he named Fort Meigs. Fortifications were at the
same time constructed at Upper Sandusky by general Crooks,
who commanded the Pennsylvania militia. Excepting some
partizan excursions, nothing additional transpired during the
severe winter months. The movement of general Winchester
had entirely deranged the plans of Harrison; and it was necessary to organize a new system. He returned to Ohio, for the
purpose of obtaining an additional force from that state, and
Kentucky. Towards the beginning of April, he received information which hastened his return to Fort Meigs.

The enemy for some time past had been collecting in considerable numbers, for the purpose of laying siege to this place :
and as the new levies had not yet arrived, the Pennsylvania
brigade, although its term of service had expired, generously
volunteered for the defence of the fort. Immediately on his
arrival, general Harrison set about making preparations for the
approaching siege. The fort was situated upon a rising ground,
at the distance of a few hundred yards from the river, the
country on each side of which is chiefly natural meadows. The
garrison was well supplied with the means of defence, and
Harrison, with unremitted exertions, laboured, night and day,
to improve its capacity for resisting the siege. The assistance
of captains Wood and Grauot, his principal engineers, enabled
him to put in practice whatever was necessary to improve his
fortifications. The troops in the fort, to the number of twelve
hundred, the greater part volunteers, were in high spirits, and
determined to defend themselves to the utmost. On the 28th,
one of the parties constantly kept out for the purpose of noting
the advance of the enemy, reported that he was in great force
about three miles below. A few British and Indians showed
themselves on the opposite side ; but a few shot from an eighteen pounder, compelled them to retire. A despatch was now
sent to hasten the march of general Clay, who was approaching with twelve hundred militia from Kentucky. These brave
people, so much sufferers during the war, were ever the foremost to meet danger, and the first to fly to the relief of their
friends. On the three following days, the enemy was occupied in selecting the best positions on either side of the river,
around the fort, whence it might be annoyed, and in erecting
batteries on the opposite side : in the latter, they were considerably impeded by the fire from Fort Meigs ; but they usually

availed themselves of the night, to proceed in the work. A
fire of small arms had been kept up by them, which was returned by the American artillery, but without any loss of importance on either side.

The garrison suffered somewhat from want of water, their
well not being completed; and it was attended with great risk
to obtain their supply during the night from the river. The
perpetual vigilance necessary to be observed in guarding against
a surprise, required them to lie constantly on their arms, and
was calculated to wear them down. On the 1st of May, the
enemy had mounted his batteries, and opened a fire with one
twenty-four pounder, one twelve, one six, and one howitzer.
No material injury was done on either side : the commander-
in-chief made a narrow escape, a ball having struck a bench on
which he was sitting; and some days before, a man was mortally wounded by his side.   On the 3d, an additional battery
was opened, at the distance of two hundred and fifty yards
from the fort, mounted with a mortar; and a number of bombs
were thrown : but this was several times silenced.   In this
part of the siege, major Chambers approached the fort with a
flag, and, for the first time, summoned the place to surrender.
He stated, that the British commander *was desirous of sparing
the effusion of human blood;* that his force was so immense
that it would be impossible to withstand it; and that, unless the
Americans threw themselves at once upon the tender mercy of
Proctor, they might expect to be massacred in cold blood.
This summons was received by Harrison, with the contempt
and indignation it merited.   To look for mercy from the hands
of Proctor, yet reeking from the murder of the Kentuckians
at the river Raisin, would have been imbecility indeed; and if
he had not been able to restrain the Indians then, how could he
now, when, according to his own account, the number of
these collected, was greater than had ever been known?   The
commander expressed his surprise, that the garrison had not
been summoned before; this at least implied they thought him
resolved to do his duty and that as to the number of his force,
which he represented as of such unusual magnitude, it was a
trick which he perfectly understood.   He then requested major Chambers to return for answer to general Proctor, that
while he had the honour to command an American fort, it
should never surrender to a combined force of British and Indians.

The siege was renewed with great vigour, and the firing was
hotly kept up on both sides. The Indians mounted on trees at
some distance from the fort, fired into it, and killed and wounded

several. On the 5th, a small party from the advancing corps
under general Clay, reached the fort, with the information that
he was in his boats not many miles above. Orders were instantly despatched by the commander-in-chief to the general,
requiring him to detach eight hundred men for the purpose of
landing on the opposite side and destroying the enemy's batteries ; and in the meanwhile he projected a sortie against those
on the side of the fort, under the command of lieutenant-colonel Miller of the Nineteenth United States infantry. This
simultaneous attack was well planned : should it succeed, the
enemy would be compelled to raise the siege instantly. Colonel Dudley, who was charged with the execution of the order
by general Clay, landed his men in good order, and then advanced on the enemy's cannon. The four batteries were carried in an instant, and the British regulars and Indians compelled to take to flight. A large body of Indians, under the
celebrated Tecumseh, were on their march to the British camp,
when they met the fugitives : this body was instantly ordered
to form an ambush, and wait the approach of the Americans ;
and, to decoy them, a few Indians showed themselves out of
the woods, as if to renew the action. Colonel Dudley having
executed his orders, commanded a retreat ; but his men, flushed
with victory, and roused with the desire of avenging their
slaughtered countrymen, pushed forward with irresistible impetuosity. Their commander in vain attempted to check their
career ; he even turned his spontoon against them ; but nothing
could restrain them. In a few moments, they found themselves
surrounded by three times their number. A desperate fight
now ensued, which was followed by a slaughter of the Kentuckians, almost as terrible as that at the river Raisin, though
not to the same extent after the battle. The chief who now
commanded, was of a much more generous character than
Round-Head, or Proctor; and even on the field of battle per-
sonally interposed to save those who yielded. But one hundred and fifty made their escape ; the rest were either killed
or missing. Colonel Dudley attempted to cut his way through
to the river ; but was killed, having himself slain an Indian after he was mortally wounded. The other party, under general Clay, landed upon the side of the fort, and was near being
drawn in like manner into an ambush, when general Harrison
ordered a troop of horse to sally out and cover their retreat.

The impetuosity of colonel Dudley's party, in some measure,
disconcerted the plan of the sortie under colonel Miller. Notwithstanding this, he sallied forth at the head of three hundred
men, assaulted the whole line of their works, manned by three

I

hundred and fifty regulars and five hundred Indians, and after
several brilliant charges, drove the enemy from their principal
batteries, spiked the cannon, and returned to the fort with forty-two prisoners.   The first charge was made on the Canadians
and Indians by major Alexander's battalion; the second by
colonel Miller, against the regulars : the officers of these were
Croghan, Langham, Bradford, a gallant officer, Nearing, and
lieutenants Gwynne and Campbell. A company of Kentuckians, commanded by captain Sebree, who had distinguished
himself in the battle of Frenchtown, was particularly remarked :
it maintained its ground with unshaken firmness, at one time
against four times its numbers ; and being entirely surrounded,
would have been cut to pieces, had not lieutenant Gwynne, of
the Nineteenth, gallantly charged through the enemy, and
released it.
   A cessation of hostilities took place during the three following days ; flags frequently passed between the besiegers and
the besieged, and arrangements were entered into for the
exchange of prisoners. Tecumseh agreed to release his claim
to the persons taken by the Indians, provided some Wyandots,
to the number of forty, were delivered up : and Proctor promised to furnish a list of the killed, wounded and prisoners ;
with this, however, he never complied. On the 9th, the enemy appeared to be engaged in making preparations for raising
the siege : a schooner, and some gun-boats had been brought
up during the night, for the purpose of embarking their artillery ; a few shot from the fort compelled them to relinquish
this design, and at ten o'clock, they raised the siege, and moved
off with their whole force.
   Thus terminated a siege of thirteen days, in which our enemies were taught, that in future they must expect to meet with
resistance different from that which they had experienced from
Hull , and that, if they should succeed in taking an American
garrison, it must be after severe fighting. The loss of the
Americans in the fort, was eighty-one killed, and one hundred
and eighty-nine wounded. The loss of the Kentuckians, as
usual, was much the most severe, amounting to upwards of
seventy killed and wounded, besides the loss under colonel Dudley. This officer was much regretted, few men in Kentucky
were more generally esteemed: his body, after much search, was
found unburied, and horribly mangled. He was interred, together with some of his companions, with the honours of war.
   The force under general Proctor was reported at five hundred and fifty regulars, eight hundred militia, and fifteen hundred
Indians ; the latter of whom fought with great courage, and, on

several occasions, rescued their allies in the sorties from the garrison. On the day of the last affair, Tecumseh arrived in person, with the largest body of Indians that had ever been collected on the northern frontier; and had not the sortie taken place, it is probable the situation of the army would have been extremely critical. The Indians, after the battle, according to the custom which prevails amongst them, had returned to their villages, in spite of the exertions of Tecumseh and his subordinate chiefs. Thus weakened, Proctor was obliged precipitately to retreat, leaving behind many valuable articles, which in his haste he was unable to carry away. Besides the American officers already named, there were many others who distinguished themselves: major Ball, an active officer, who was frequently complimented in general orders, rendered great service during the siege; captain Croghan on one occasion made a brilliant sortie on the British regulars; majors Todd, Johnson, Sodwick, Ritzen, and Stoddard, were also mentioned in the most honourable terms. The latter, a man of distinguished literary attainments, received a severe wound, of which he afterwards died. Captain Butler's Pittsburgh Blues, which behaved so handsomely at the battle of Mississiniwa, composed chiefly of young gentlemen of Pittsburgh, suffered severely; the accomplished young officer who commanded them, was a son of the lamented general Butler, who fell in St Clair's defeat. It would be in vain, on this occasion, to enumerate all who deserved the applauses of their country.

After the siege of Fort Meigs, offensive operations were for a considerable time suspended on both sides. Until the completion of the naval preparations on Lake Erie, which were then in considerable forwardness, the troops were to remain at Fort Meigs, and Upper Sandusky. Without the command of the lake, little of consequence could be effected; the troops would, therefore, continue a great part of the summer in a state of inactivity, awaiting this event. In the meantime general Harrison returned to Franklinton, for the purpose of organizing the forces expected to concentrate at that place. A deputation from all the Indian tribes residing in the state of Ohio, and some in the territories of Indiana and Illinois, made a tender of their services to follow general Harrison into Canada. Hitherto, with the exception of a small band commanded by Logan, a distinguished chief and nephew of Tecumseh, none of the friendly Indians had been employed by the United States. The advice to remain neutral, could not be understood by them: they considered it in some measure a reproach upon their courage; more particularly, as several hostile incursions had been made of late into their settlements by the hostile Indians. General Harrison consented to receive them into the service; but, expressly on condition, that they should spare their prisoners and not assail defenceless women and children. Logan was killed not long afterwards.

Although the settled parts of the country were shielded from the depredations of the Indians; they still continued to attack the settlements along the borders of the lake, from Frenchtown to Erie. These inroads received a temporary check, from a squadron of horse under major Ball. This officer was descending the Sandusky with twenty-two men, when he was fired upon by about the same number of Indians in ambuscade. He charged upon them; drove them from their hiding places; and, after an obstinate contest on a plain, favourable to the operations of cavalry, killed their chiefs. The savages, seeing no hope of escape, contended with dreadful fury until their whole band was destroyed. During the heat of the fight, the major was dismounted, and had a personal conflict with a chief of prodigious strength. They fought with desperation, until an officer shot the Indian.

We now return to the operations of our armies on the northern frontiers; where, since the winter, by which hostilities had been suspended, events of a very important character had transpired.

CHAPTER VIII.

DURING the winter, Great Britain had sent a number of troops to Halifax, for the purpose of being employed, in the spring, in the defence of Canada. The recent success of the allies on the continent, had taken away any disposition she might have had for a peace, as was clearly proved by the rejection of the Russian mediation. The militia of Canada was disciplined with great care, and from the greater energy of the British government, it was enabled to bring them more promptly into service, and to retain them for a longer term ; while on our side, during the past year, from the unpopularity of the war, it was difficult to prevail on the states to call out the militia; and volunteers, by which the war to the westward was so spiritedly carried on, came forward, in the northern sections of the union, in but small numbers. It was still hoped that such preparations would be made, during the winter, as would lead to something of more importance than had been done the year before ; although the golden moment for the conquest of Canada had passed, the British having so strengthened themselves, as to render the execution of such a project a matter of extreme difficulty. It was thought, however, that by one vigorous effort more, particularly if the spirit of the northern states could be roused, and the nation be made to come forth in its strength, something might yet be effected. If the complete command of the lakes could be obtained, the whole of Upper Canada, at least, must fall before winter.

A mutual exchange of prisoners had taken place, and arrangements were entered into, to effect this in future ; by which means some valuable officers, taken in the first campaign, were restored. The troops, enlisted in the midland and northern states, were marched to the frontier, and all the necessary supplies and munitions of war were assiduously collected at the different posts along the line. Excepting some partizan affairs, nothing of consequence transpired during the winter.

In the month of February, a party of the enemy, who crossed in search of some of their deserters, committed many wanton depredations on the houses and property of the inhabitants. Major Forsyth, who commanded at Ogdensburgh, resolved to return the visit. Taking a part of his riflemen, and such volunteers as offered, some of whom were private gentlemen of the neighbourhood, he crossed the St Lawrence, surprised the guard at Elizabethtown, took fifty-two prisoners, among whom were one major, three captains, and two lieutenants ; and captured one hundred and twenty muskets, twenty rifles, two casks of fixed ammunition, and other public property. He then returned, without the loss of a single man.

Soon after, it was discovered that the British meditated an attack on Ogdensburgh. Colonel Benedict called out his regiment of militia, to aid in the defence of the place. They appeared on the 21st of February, with twelve hundred men ; and with this force, so much superior to that of Forsyth, succeeded in expel-

ling him from the town, after a sharp conflict. The British
attacked in two columns, of six hundred men each, at eight
o'clock in the morning, and were commanded by captain
M'Donnel, of the Glengary light infantry, a corps trained with
peculiar care, and colonel Frazier, of the Canada militia. The
Americans kept up the contest for an hour, with the loss of
twenty men killed and wounded ; and from the cool and deliberate aim of the riflemen, the enemy must have lost twice
that number, among whom were five officers of distinction.
A flourish was made by the British of this affair ; and a message
was sent with the news to colonel M'Feelcy, commanding the
American garrison of Niagara, informing him that a salute
would be fired from Fort George. The American officer expressed his satisfaction at being able to return the compliment,
as he had just received intelligence of the capture of his majesty's frigate Java, by an American frigate of equal force ; and
intended to fire a salute from Niagara, at the same time, in
honour of this brilliant victory.

Bodies of new levies were daily arriving at Sackett's Harbour, and the vicinity of that place. To convert new recruits,
in the course of a few months, into efficient troops, was an
operation not easily performed. Indefatigable industry was
displayed in this essential duty by Pike, lately promoted to the
rank of a brigadier, in consequence of his meritorious services,
and increasing reputation. Pike was cradled in the camp ; his
father, a revolutionary officer, was still in the army, but too far
advanced in life for active service. He was acquainted with
all the details of the military profession, having served in
every grade from a soldier to the general. He possessed an
ardent mind, and was animated by a desire of martial glory and
renown ; but such glory and renown as were compatible with
the welfare of his country. The models which he had placed
before him, were somewhat of a romantic cast ; he desired to
combine the courage of the soldier, and the ability of the commander, with those ornaments of character which become the
man. Pike was already a favourite in the United States, and
distinguished as the adventurous explorer of the immense Western desert, traversed in another direction by Lewis and Clarke.
He had here given proofs of much fortitude of mind, vigour of
body, and great prudence and intelligence. His zeal and activity
were afterwards conspicuous, in the success with which he formed the regiment placed under his command. He was beloved
by his troops, whose affections he knew how to engage, and into
whom he could infuse a portion of his own generous spirit. It
is not surprising, therefore, that the progress made by the
troops, at Sackett's Harbour, under the unceasing attention of

this accomplished officer, should be unusually rapid.   Nothing
was wanting but an opportunity, on opening of the campaign,
to lead them to the achievement of some glorious exploit.

This opportunity was not long in presenting itself.   The
lake was no sooner clear of ice, than a descent on the Canada
shore was projected.   York, the capital of Upper Canada, was
the depot of all the British military stores, whence the western posts were supplied.   It was known that a large vessel
was on the stocks, and nearly completed.   The importance of
the place to either party was immense.   Should an attack on
it prove successful, it might be followed up by an immediate
attempt upon Fort George ; and the forces then, concentrating,
and aided by the fleet, might, with every prospect of success,
move against Kingston.

About the middle of April, the commander-in-chief, after conference with Pike and other officers, determined on attacking
York.   Major Forsyth, who had returned to Ogdensburg on
the retreat of the British, was ordered with his riflemen to repair to Sackett's Harbour ; and commodore Chauncey received
orders from the navy department, to co-operate with general
Dearborne, in any plan of operations which he might wish to
carry into execution.   On the 25th of April, the fleet moved
down the lake, every arrangement having been made for the
projected attack.   The plan, which had been principally suggested by Pike, was highly judicious ; and, at his particular request, he was entrusted with its execution.   On the 27th, at
seven o'clock in the morning, the fleet safely reached the place
of destination.   The spot fixed on for this purpose was an
open space at the ruins of Toronto, the former site of the fort,
about two miles above the present town of York.   The debarkation commenced at eight o'clock, and was completed at ten.
The British, on discovering the fleet, hastily made the necessary
dispositions to oppose the landing of the American forces.
General Sheaffe advanced from the garrison, which was situated above York, with his whole force, consisting of about seven
hundred and fifty regulars and militia, and five hundred Indians, besides a body of grenadiers, and a corps of Glengary
fencibles.   The Indians were placed in the thickets at the
water's edge, near the expected points of debarkation, while
the regulars were drawn up on the bank, and partly concealed
in a wood.   In pursuance of the plan of attack, the batteaux
carrying Forsyth and his riflemen, first moved to the shore,
at the point where the principal force of the enemy was stationed.   A galling fire of musketry and rifles was instantly
opened on him.   To have gone higher up would have deranged

the general plan; he determined therefore to dash at once into the thickest of the enemy; but first ordered the oars to cease a moment, that he might give his riflemen an opportunity of returning their fire.

Pike, who was attentively watching this movement, observed the pause, and not knowing its reason, instantly leaped into the boat provided for himself and his staff, at the same time ordering major King to follow, with a part of his regiment. Before he reached the shore, however, Forsyth had landed, and was closely engaged with the whole British force. The detachment under King, consisting of the light artillery under major Eustice, a volunteer corps commanded by colonel M'Clure, and about thirty riflemen under lieutenant Riddle, now landed; and Pike, placing himself at the head of those first formed, ordered the rest to follow rapidly; then gallantly ascended the bank with this handful of men, under a shower of bullets from the grenadiers. He charged impetuously upon them; they were thrown into disorder and fled. This had scarcely been achieved, when the bugles of Forsyth announced that he had also been victorious; the Glengary fencibles still kept up an irregular fire, but the Indians had fled. A fresh body of grenadiers now suddenly issued from the wood, and made a desperate charge on major King's regiment, which by this time was drawn up on the bank: at first it faltered; but in a moment was rallied, returned to the charge, and drove the enemy from the field. The British were again seen forming at a distance; but considerable reinforcements having by this time landed from the fleet, and formed in column, the British retreated to the garrison below.

The whole of the troops having now landed, they were formed in the order contemplated in the plan of attack. The different bodies of troops under majors Lewis and Eustis, and colonels M'Clure and Ripley, were disposed in the most judicious manner, while Forsyth and his riflemen were to act on the flanks. The column then moved forward with the utmost precision, and with as much regularity as the nature of the ground would permit, until they emerged from the wood, when a twenty-four pounder opened upon them from one of the enemy's batteries. The battery was soon cleared, and the column moved on to the second, which was abandoned on the approach of the Americans, the enemy retreating to the garrison. General Pike here ordered the column to halt, for the purpose of learning the strength of the garrison, and obtaining further information: as the barracks appeared to have been evacuated, he suspected a stratagem, to draw him within the reach of some secret force. Lieutenant Riddle was sent forward to learn the situation of the enemy. In the meanwhile, Pike, as humane as he was brave, occupied himself in removing a wounded British soldier from a dangerous situation, and having performed this act of humanity, which speaks volumes in his favour, had seated himself on the stump of a tree, and entered into conversation with a serjeant, who had been taken prisoner: when suddenly the air was convulsed by a tremendous explosion. The magazine, at the distance of two hundred yards, near the barracks, had blown up. The air was instantly filled with huge stones and fragments of wood, rent asunder and whirled aloft by the exploding of five hundred barrels of powder. This was the treacherous attack which the British had prepared, but which Pike could not have suspected. Immense quantities of these inflamed and blackened masses fell in the midst of the victorious column, causing a havock which the arms of the enemy could not have effected, killing and wounding upwards of two hundred, and amongst them their beloved commander, the heroic Pike. The brave troops, though for a moment confounded by the shock, were soon called to their recollection by the national music, Yankee Doodle: the column was instantly closed up; and they rent the air, in their turn, with three loud huzzas!

The wound of Pike, a severe contusion, was soon found to be mortal; he still, however, preserved his undaunted spirit : " Move on my brave fellows, and revenge your general,'' he cried, addressing them for the last time. This they instantly obeyed. He was then taken up by some of his men, to be conveyed on board the ship; scarcely had he reached the shore of the lake, when a loud and victorious shout from his brigade brightened, for a moment, the expiring lamp of life; a faint sigh was all his strength would permit him to express. Shortly after being carried on board the Pert, the British flag was brought to him; at the sight of it, his eye again resumed its lustre for a moment, and making signs for it to be placed under his head, he gloriously expired. Thus fell a warrior who will live with honour in the page of history. Brave, prudent and chivalrous, he was adorned with that moral excellence which is essential to the accomplished soldier and the real hero. As he terminated his career in the very day-spring of life, we can but imperfectly estimate what the ripened age of so much promise would have brought forth. No officer entertained a more refined sense of honourable warfare; a proof of it is to be found in the orders which he gave on this memorable day, that any of his soldiers who should molest the possessions or persons of the inhabitants, or wantonly destroy the public property, should suffer instant death.

On the fall of general Pike, the command devolved on colonel Pearce, who advanced to the barracks, which he found already in the possession of Forsyth ; the enemy having retreated to the fort. No one now being acquainted with the further execution of the plan of attack, the enemy was not immediately pursued ; otherwise the whole of the regulars and public stores must have fallen into our hands. The Americans, after halting a short time, moved on towards the town ; and on drawing near it were met by officers of the Canada militia, with offers of capitulation. This produced some delay ; but it being suspected that it was only intended to facilitate the escape of general Sheaffe and the principal part of his regulars, and to gain time while they could destroy the military stores, and burn the vessel on the stocks, Forsyth and Ripley pushed forward, and were soon after followed by Pearce. The strictest observance of Pike's order, with respect to the treatment of the inhabitants and their property, was enjoined. At four o'clock the Americans were masters of the town. Although with justice they might be enraged at the conduct of the British, for their barbarous and unmanly attempt to destroy them by a mine, the troops conducted themselves with the most perfect order and forbearance ; perhaps considering this the best testimonial of respect for their brave leader. The stipulations of surrender were entered into with colonel Pearce, at the very moment the British were engaged in the destruction of the public property. By the terms of the stipulation, the troops, regulars and militia, naval officers and seamen, were surrendered prisoners of war ; all the public stores were given up, and all private property was to be guarantied to the citizens of York ; every thing relating to the civil departments was to be respected ; and the surgeons, attending on the wounded, were not to be considered as prisoners of war.

It is gratifying to reflect that the deportment of the victors, on this occasion, was such as to extort praise even from the vanquished. So far from inflicting any injury on the inhabitants, a considerable portion of the public stores, which could not easily be transported, were distributed among them, and they expressed themselves highly satisfied with the conduct of the Americans. The principal civil officers of the place addressed a letter of thanks to general Dearborne, for the strict regard which was manifested by the troops under his command, for the safety of the persons and property of the inhabitants.

The commander-in-chief landed soon after the fall of Pike, but did not assume the immediate command until after the surrender of the town.

Great assistance was rendered during the engagement by the co-operation of commodore Chauncey, after landing the troops. The vessels, in consequence of a contrary wind, were compelled to beat up to their several positions with great difficulty, and under a heavy fire from the batteries. When this was effected, they opened a galling and destructive fire, which contributed much to the success of the attack. In the squadron, three were killed and eleven wounded; among the first, midshipmen Thompson and Hatfield, both much regretted.

The loss on the American side was inconsiderable until the explosion of the " infernal machine," which caused it to amount to three hundred in killed and wounded. Several officers of merit were killed or wounded by the explosion. The aids of the general, captains Nicholson and Frazier, were wounded; the first mortally: also, captain Lyon, captain Hoppock, lieutenant Bloomfield, and many other valuable officers. Much praise was bestowed on lieutenant-colonel Mitchell, of the third regiment of artillery: he formed the column after the explosion, and throughout the whole of the affair behaved with the greatest gallantry. Major Eustis; captains Scott, Young, Walworth, M'Glassin, and Stephen H. Moore of the Baltimore volunteers, who lost a leg by the explosion; and Lieutenants Irvine, Fanning and Riddle, were named among the most distinguished of the day.

There were taken from the British, one lieutenant-colonel, one major, thirteen captains, nine lieutenants, eleven ensigns, one deputy adjutant-general, four naval officers, and two hundred and fifty-one non-commissioned officers and privates; and it was contended, that according to the capitulation, the commanding general, his staff, and all his regulars, ought to have been surrendered. There was certainly an unfair procedure on the part of the British general, as well in this business, as in the destruction of the public property after it had been fairly surrendered. With respect to the explosion, it was attributed by general Sheaffe to accident; and as a proof, he mentioned the circumstance of forty of his own men having been killed and wounded in the retreat. But the American officers, who witnessed the affair, were perfectly satisfied that it was designed. After the conflict had ceased for some time, and the magazine and barracks had been entirely abandoned by the enemy, the occurrence of such an *accident* was almost impossible; and leads to the conviction, that a match had been purposely laid, intended to explode on the approach of the American troops; which, but for the fortunate precaution of their commander, would have involved them in one general destruction. It is unjust, on light grounds, to impute to the British general, conduct so dishonourable ; and but for the circumstances we have mentioned, it might be regarded as the unauthorized act of some base individual. The fact of a part of his own column having been overtaken by stones propelled to an immense distance, has no weight in his exculpation : this may have proceeded from his not having calculated with sufficient accuracy for their own safety, although nothing could have been better timed for the complete destruction of our gallant countrymen. Had the explosion taken place in the midst of the fight, there might then be room for supposition that it was the result of accident; but, under the circumstances, that this should have been the case, appears next to impossible. The loss of the British, amounted to seven hundred and fifty men in killed, wounded and prisoners . of these, the killed and wounded were not less than two hundred; the prisoners amounted to fifty regulars, and five hundred militia. Property to an immense amount was destroyed, and there still remained to the value of at least half a million of dollars : in his hasty retreat, general Sheaffe abandoned his baggage, containing all his books and papers, which proved a valuable acquisition. Upon the whole, the capture of York was a brilliant achievement, and worthy of Pike, its projector. It was the first dawn of that military distinction, to which we afterwards so rapidly attained under the gallant officers, whom the school of experience had fashioned.

The object of this expedition being now fully attained, the American forces evacuated York on the 1st of May, and re-embarked. The fleet, however, did not leave the harbour until the 8th. A schooner had in the meantime been despatched to Niagara, to inform general Lewis of the success of the expedition, and of the intended movements of the troops.

The next thing to be undertaken, was the attack of Fort George and Fort Erie, which had been unsuccessfully attempted the year before. Commodore Chauncey having the command of the lake, forces could be transported to any part with facility. On the evening of the 8th, the troops were landed at Four Mile creek, so called, from being four miles distant from Niagara. The next day, two schooners, under the command of lieutenant Pettigrew, sailed with a detachment of one hundred men, commanded by captain Morgan of the Twelfth, for the purpose of destroying some of the enemy's stores at the head of the lake. On their approach, the guard, about eighty men, retired; the public buildings were burnt, and the party returned with the greater portion of the property. On the 10th, commodore Chauncey sailed to Sackett's Harbour, for the purpose of leaving the wounded men and officers, and of bringing such additional force as could be spared from that place. He again sailed on the 22d, leaving the Pert and the Fair American to watch the movements of the enemy. Two days afterwards he arrived safely at Niagara, with three hundred and fifty men of colonel Macomb's regiment of artillery, and an additional number of guns.

Arrangements were now made for carrying the contemplated enterprise into immediate execution. Commodore Chauncey having, on the 26th, reconnoitered the opposite shore, and ascertained the best places for landing, and the stations for the smaller vessels to occupy; the next morning was fixed upon for the attack. A number of boats were made ready, and others, which had been building for the occasion, were launched in the afternoon; this being observed by the enemy, a fire was opened upon the workmen, from a battery, erected for the purpose, nearly opposite. This brought on a severe cannonade from the forts and batteries, which continued for some hours, and in which the Americans had the decided advantage. Fort George appeared to suffer considerable injury. The guns of the American battery were directed with so much precision, that the halliards of the flag-staff were shot away; and the buildings of every description around the fort were much damaged: while the loss on the American side was very inconsiderable. All the boats in the meanwhile passed safely to the encampment at Four Mile creek: and as soon as it grew dark, the artillery was put on board the Madison, the Oneida, and the Lady of the Lake: the troops were to embark in the boats and follow the fleet. At three o'clock in the morning, signal was made to weigh; but in consequence of the calm which prevailed, the schooners were obliged to resort to sweeps to gain their stations. These consisted of the Julia, Growler, Ontario, Governor Tompkins, Conquest, Hamilton, Asp, and Scourge; each within musket shot of the shore, and skilfully disposed to attack the different batteries, and cover the landing of our forces. The troops had now all embarked, and amounted to about four thousand men, and at daybreak, generals Dearborne and Lewis, and suits, went on board the Madison. The enemy's batteries immediately opened, as the troops advanced in three brigades. The advance was led by that accomplished officer colonel Scott, who had so much signalized himself in this place the year before; and was composed of Forsyth's riflemen, and detachments from various infantry regiments: it

K

landed near the fort, which had been silenced by the Governor
Tompkins. General Boyd, to whom the brigade lately commanded by general Pike had been assigned, formed the first
line, which was flanked by the Baltimore and Albany volunteers under colonel M'Clure. He reached the shore immediately after the advance had landed. General Winder followed,
at the head of the second brigade ; and was closely succeeded
by the third, under general Chandler. The wind suddenly
springing up from the east, and producing a considerable
swell, the troops from the Madison and Oneida could not
reach shore until the second and third brigades had advanced ;
Macomb's regiment, and the marines under captain Smith,
therefore, did not land until the debarkation had been completed

The advance under Scott, consisting of five hundred men,
had been exposed, on its approach to the shore, to an incessant
volley of musketry, from at least twelve hundred regulars, stationed in a ravine. This spirited corps, composed of the flower
of the army, moved on without faltering, and briskly returned
the fire from the boats. As they drew near the shore, a surprising degree of emulation manifested itself both amongst
officers and soldiers ; many of them leaping into the lake, and
wading to land. Captain Hindman, an accomplished young
officer of the second artillery, was the first on the enemy's territory. No sooner were the troops formed on the beach, than
they were led to the charge, and instantly dispersed the enemy
in every direction ; some flying to the woods for shelter, and
others seeking refuge in the fort. The first were briskly assailed by Forsyth ; while the advanced corps and the first brigade, under general Boyd, vigorously attacked the latter. The
prevailing panic had seized the garrison, which made but a
feeble resistance. Fort Niagara, and the batteries on the American side, opened at the same time; and Fort George having
become untenable, the British laid trains to their magazines,
abandoned all their works, and retreated with the utmost precipitation by different routes. Colonel Scott and his light
troops followed closely in their rear, when he was recalled by
general Boyd. Lieutenant Riddle, with his party, not receiving the order, pursued the enemy almost to Queenstown, and
picked up a number of stragglers. The light troops took possession of Fort George ; captains Hindman and Stockton entering first, and extinguishing the fire intended to explode the
magazine. The former withdrew a match at the imminent hazard of his life. General Boyd and colonel Scott mounted the
parapet for the purpose of cutting away the staff; but Hind-

man succeeded in taking the flag, which he forwarded to general Dearborne. The American ensign was then immediately
hoisted; and the troops ordered in and quartered. At twelve
o'clock the whole of the British fortifications on this shore,
from Fort George to Fort Erie inclusive, were in the quiet
possession of the Americans. The enemy had moved off with
such rapidity, that in a short time nothing more of them was
to be seen; and our troops, having been eleven hours under
arms, were too much fatigued to pursue them far. The loss
of the British in this affair, considering the time during which
the contest lasted, was very considerable. There were one
hundred and eight killed, and one hundred and sixty wounded,
who fell into our hands : besides which, one hundred and
fifteen regulars, and five hundred militia, were taken prisoners.
The loss of the Americans was thirty-nine killed, and one
hundred and eight wounded : among the former, lieutenant
Hobart of the light artillery ; and of the latter, major King of
the Thirteenth, captains Arrowsmith of the Sixth, Steel of the
Sixteenth, Roach of the Twenty-third (who had been wounded
the year before at the heights of Queenstown, and promoted
to the rank of captain for his good conduct on that occasion),
and lieutenant Swearingen of the rifle corps. The Forty-ninth
British regiment, the Invincibles, was in this affair, and its commander, colonel Myers, wounded and taken prisoner. The action, notwithstanding, was fought on the American side with
inferior numbers; the advance, and part of Boyd's brigade only
having been actually engaged. Shortly after the surrender of
the fort, the lake became so rough as to render the situation of
the fleet somewhat dangerous. Commodore Chauncey, therefore, made signal to weigh ; and proceeding up the river, chose
a place of safety between the two forts, where he anchored.

High praise was given, both by the commodore and general
Dearborne, to the forces under their respective commands.
Scott and Boyd were particularly mentioned. The commander-
in-chief also acknowledged himself much indebted to colonel
Porter, of the light artillery, to major Armistead, of the Third
regiment of artillery, and to captain Totten of the engineers,
for their skill in demolishing the enemy's forts and batteries.
We here find the first mention of the hero of Lake Erie, lieutenant-commandant Oliver H. Perry, who had volunteered his
assistance on the night of the 26th, and had rendered good
service in the arrangement and debarkation of the troops.
Much of the success of this gallant enterprise was attributable
to the judicious plan of commodore Chauncey, in attacking the
different batteries of the enemy with his vessels, and rendering

them untenable. General Dearborne had been much indisposed; but he refused to yield the command of the expedition, and issued his orders from his bed.

Lieutenant Perry was despatched, the day after the battle, to Black Rock, with fifty men, for the purpose of taking five vessels to Erie as soon as possible, and also of preparing the squadron at that place, to commence operations, in conjunction with general Harrison, by the 15th of June.

A few days afterwards, it was ascertained that the enemy, under general Vincent, had retired to the Beaver Dams, and formed a junction with the command of lieutenant-colonel Bishop from Fort Erie and Chippewa. The day after this was effected, the British general retreated hastily to the upper end of Lake Ontario, and took a position on the heights at the head of Burlington Bay. His force, it was supposed, did not exceed a thousand men. General Winder, at his request, was detached, by the commander-in-chief, in pursuit, with his brigade. Having reached Twenty Mile creek, on the second day's march, the general received information, that the enemy had been reinforced by several hundred men from Kingston; that his force, besides Indians, and a few militia, might amount to fifteen hundred men: he, in consequence, thought it prudent to despatch an officer to general Dearborne for an additional force; that under his command not exceeding twelve hundred infantry, exclusive of the dragoons under colonel Burns, and Towson's artillery. He nevertheless continued his march to Forty Mile creek, where, selecting a good position, he proposed to wait for the expected reinforcement. This, consisting of Chandler's brigade, in a short time arrived, after a rapid march; when general Chandler, being the senior officer, assumed the command.

On the same day, the united force proceeded to a rivulet called Stony Creek, where they encamped, having in the course of the afternoon skirmished with, and driven back the advance parties of the enemy In order to secure the baggage of the army, which had been conveyed in batteaux along the lake shore, colonels Christie and Boerstler, with their respective regiments, the Thirteenth and Fourteenth, were detached, to take a position at the distance of two miles from the main body, on the neck of land which divides the lake from Burlington Bay, and on the road from Fort George to York and Kingston. The distance of the main body of the British was about eight miles.

The ground occupied by general Chandler was a high bank on Stony Creek: on the opposite side of the stream there was a small meadow, and the bank was much lower.   He halted immediately on the road, as the centre of his encampment.   The Fifth, a small detachment of the Twenty-third, and one company of the Sixteenth infantry, occupied a height, a short distance to the left.   The object of this was to prevent, in case of a night attack, the occupation of ground which commanded the road ; while, at the same time, the troops stationed there could with facility be wheeled into line with the Twenty-fifth, along the high bank of the creek.   The light artillery of captains Towson and Leonard, were posted immediately to the right of the last mentioned regiment, so as to command the road in the direction of the enemy.   The cavalry, under colonel Burns, were placed in the rear, to be ready at a moment's warning. A guard of eighty or a hundred men was posted a quarter of a mile in advance, at a wooden chapel on the road side.   In other respects the usual precautions were taken.

The situation of the British army was almost hopeless.   To contend openly with the superior force of the Americans, was out of the question.   No possibility of escape remained but by marching through the thinly inhabited country towards Detroit, and joining general Proctor ; or attempting the fortune of a night attack.   The first, in their present deficiency of supplies, was considered almost impracticable : the latter was, therefore, resolved upon.   The existence of this alternative could not have escaped the penetration of the American generals ; and therefore the necessity of the utmost precaution.   To the ultimate character of the campaign, the capture of the British would be of the greatest importance : as the necessary consequence, the contest to the westward would terminate, for it would no longer be possible for Proctor to hold out, after his communication with the lower provinces had been cut off.

Until late in the evening, the soldiers of the Twenty-fifth had occupied the meadow ground on the opposite side of the creek, where they had kindled fires for the purpose of cooking ; but towards midnight they were withdrawn to the position assigned them on the brow of the high bank.   This precaution had well nigh proved fruitless, from the negligence and misconduct of the main guard.   Several of the sentinels in advance were silently bayoneted by the enemy, who unmolested pushed a column of seven or eight hundred men past the chapel : our guard must have been buried in sleep, since not a shot was fired. On approaching the fires made by the Twenty-fifth, and which had not yet been extinguished, the enemy raised a tremendous Indian yell, expecting no doubt to bayonet the Americans, whom they supposed to be asleep a few paces from them.

K *

This yell was most fortunate for the Americans, who were instantly roused on the opposite bank. The Twenty-fifth had lain on their arms, and instantly commenced a heavy fire on the British, who were revealed by the fires which had deluded them. General Winder, who commanded the troops on the left of the road, succeeded in a few moments in stationing the greater part of them on the edge of the creek, to the left of the artillery, and joined his fire with that of the Twenty-fifth, which was by this time returned by the enemy, though with little effect. In twenty minutes the firing on the part of the British ceased; and as they had become invisible after passing the fires, the night being excessively dark, it was uncertain whether they had retired, or meant under cover of the darkness, to charge with the bayonet. The firing on the part of the Americans was ordered to cease; and arrangements were rapidly made to repel an attack. At this moment some shots in the rear of the army induced the general, who was apprehensive that an attempt might also be made in that quarter, to order one of the regiments to face about, and take such a position, as would enable him to meet it, whether made on flank or rear. Whilst general Chandler was directing these movements on the right, his horse fell under him. After recovering somewhat from the fall, which had stunned him, he attempted to walk towards the centre, near the artillery, where he and general Winder had met from time to time, to receive and communicate information and orders. In the meantime, favoured by the excessive darkness, which had been increased by the smoke, the enemy stole along the road unperceived; and mingling with the American artillerists, drove them from their pieces. At the same moment general Chandler, being surrounded by them, was taken prisoner.

General Winder, in returning from maintaining the dispositions on the left, met with a part of the Sixteenth, which had either never reached its position, or had fallen back; and was posting it to protect the artillery: when, discovering some confusion there, he rushed forward to ascertain the cause, and was made prisoner in attempting to turn back what he supposed to be the American artillerists. The British finding two pieces limbered, drove them off, overturned one or two more, and then retreated with precipitation and disorder. Before clear daylight they had covered themselves from the view of the Americans by a wood. General Vincent, the British commander, was thrown from his horse, and did not rejoin his troops until evening, almost exhausted with fatigue. Several gallant efforts were made by the American troops, to recover the artillery.

Lieutenant W. M'Donough prevented the capture of one piece, and lieutenant M'Chesney another; these officers, as well as colonel Burn and colonel Milton, and captains Hindman, Archer, Steel and Leonard, were highly complimented in general orders.

The American loss was sixteen killed, and thirty-eight wounded; and two brigadiers, one major, three captains, and ninety-four men missing. The loss of the enemy was much more severe, particularly in officers; one hundred prisoners were taken. Blame was attached to general Chandler, who commanded, and also to general Winder: to the former with very little reason; and to the latter with still less justice, as he only met with such misfortune as the bravest and most prudent are subject to. Had the enemy been immediately pursued, there is little doubt they would have fallen into our hands; but colonel Burn, who now commanded, after consultation with the officers, judged it most prudent to fall back on Forty Mile creek. Here he was joined by colonel Miller's regiment, which had been sent to guard the boats; and generals Lewis and Boyd: the former of whom now assumed the command.

The British claimed in this affair a splendid victory. The accidental capture of the American generals would seem to give it the appearance of one; but in the action they were certainly beaten with great loss. Their object, however, was effected by the attack, though not to the extent which they had expected.

A flag having been sent into our camp under pretence of obtaining information of the killed and wounded, and permission to bury the dead, but in reality to procure information; general Vincent immediately despatched a messenger to sir James Yeo, advising him of the position of the Americans. On the 8th, sir James, with his squadron, appeared abreast of the encampment, and within a mile of the shore. He attempted to destroy the boats, and warped in a large schooner for the purpose; but capains Archer and Towson, hastily constructing a furnace, opened a fire with hot shot, which compelled him to haul off. A party of Indians now appeared upon the brow of the mountain, but were soon dislodged by lieutenant Eldridge, who gained the summit with a few volunteers, in advance of the detachment which was ordered for the purpose. Sir James demanded a surrender, with the usual story of Indians in the rear, a fleet in front, and regulars on the flanks; but this artifice had grown stale, and could be played off no longer. Orders having been received from general Dearborne, for the army to return to Fort George; the greater part of the camp equipage and baggage were put in boats. These were intercepted by an armed schooner of the enemy, and twelve of them taken. The army broke up its encampment about ten o'clock, and took up its march for Fort George, harassed nearly the whole way by Indians, who hung upon its flank.

The movements of general Dearborne against the British fortifications on the Niagara, had well nigh cost him dear. The British, having obtained information of it, resolved to seize the opportunity of the absence of our troops and fleet, to attack Sackett's Harbour. They well knew the importance to us of this place. It was the depository of all our naval and military stores ; both those captured at York, and those which had been collecting for a year with a view to the operations against Canada. Its convenient locality had caused it to be selected as the place at which to fit out our navies of the lake ; and great quantities of timber and other materials were here collected for the construction of vessels. The new ship, the General Pike, was on the stocks, nearly ready to be launched, and the prize, the Gloucester, lay in the harbour. No time was lost in carrying into effect this important enterprise. Sir George Prevost selected a thousand of his best men, and embarked them on board the fleet under commodore James Yeo. Scarcely had commodore Chauncey arrived at Niagara, when sir James showed himself off the harbour, with the Wolf, the Royal George, the Prince Regent, the Earl Moira, and some smaller vessels. The small vessels under lieutenant Chauncey, placed to give notice of the enemy's approach, espied the squadron, on the 27th, and hastened to the harbour, firing guns of alarm. This was immediately followed by the alarm guns on the shore, to bring in the militia, and to give notice to such regulars as might be near enough to hear them. Lieutenant-colonel Backus, of the dragoons, had been left in command of the place ; but in case of attack, general Brown, then at his residence eight miles off, was requested to take the command, although his brigade of militia had retired to their homes, their term of service having expired. The whole of our regular force consisted of a few seamen, lieutenant Fanning's artillery, and about two hundred invalids, not exceeding in the whole five hundred men ; and colonel Mills's Albany volunteers and some militia, amounting to about five hundred more. On the 28th, the enemy was seen at the distance of about five miles, and seemed to be standing for the harbour, when a fleet of American barges was discovered coming round North Point, with troops from Oswego. Their attention was now occupied by these, and they succeeded in cutting off twelve of them; and taking it for granted that there were many more, they stood off all the day, with a view of intercepting them. In the meanwhile general Brown was diligently occupied in arrangements for the defence of the place, in making which he discovered much judgment. But a small part of the ground adjacent to the village was cleared, the rest being surrounded by woods. At the only point of landing, a battery and breast-work were hastily constructed, and the militia placed behind them ready to receive the enemy as they landed, and to open a fire upon them in conjunction with the artillery. The regular troops, and the light artillery, were stationed in a second line, nearer the barracks and public buildings. On the approach of the enemy's boats, which were commanded by sir George Prevost in person, a well directed fire, which had been reserved until then, compelled them to pause; and several officers and men were seen to fall. Encouraged by this fire, our militia were engaged in loading a second time; with the artillery to sustain them: when suddenly they were seized by some unaccountable panic; a panic to which corps composed of the bravest men individually are liable on being engaged for the first time; and fled in confusion. Their officers in vain attempted to rally them; and their brave commander, colonel Mills, in attempting to effect it, was shot dead from his horse. The enemy now landed with little opposition, and having formed, advanced to the barracks; but were for a moment checked by a vigorous attack from a party of infantry under major Aspinwall, and the dismounted dragoons under major Laval. These were compelled, by numbers, to retreat. A sharp conflict now commenced with the regulars and artillery under colonel Backus; which retired gradually, taking possession of the houses and barracks, and thence continuing to annoy the enemy. The colonel, about this time, fell, severely wounded. Shortly after the flight of the militia, general Brown succeeded in rallying the company of captain M'Nitt, about ninety in number: with this he assailed the rear of the British, and in his own words, "did some execution." Finding that there was now little hope of repelling an enemy so superior in force, and every moment gaining ground; he resorted to a ruse de guerre: a considerable part of the militia, now ashamed of their panic, having collected near the scene of action; he instantly formed them, and marched them silently through the woods, so as to be discovered by the enemy. On which, sir George Prevost, believing that his rear was about to be cut off, ordered a retreat, which became a precipitate flight, to the boats, and left all his wounded and a number of prisoners.

The resistance at the barracks had been exceedingly obstinate: a destructive fire was poured from the buildings, while lieutenant Fanning, though severely wounded, still directed one not less so from his piece of artillery. Captain Gray, a valuable British officer, and an accomplished gentleman, was shot by a small boy, a drummer, who snatched up a musket and fired at him, as he was advancing at the head of a column, to storm one of the barracks. This boy, who was an American, had served him in his kitchen, and on the war breaking out, had returned home; he now approached his former master while in his last agonies, and owned that he had shot him. Captain Gray generously forgave him, and with a nobleness of soul of which there are but too few examples, took out his watch and presented it to him, with these words, "My brave little fellow, you have done well." It is delightful to read such traits even in an enemy: whether the boy deserved this encomium is a matter to be settled by casuists.

During the battle, information having been communicated to lieutenant Chauncey, that our troops had been defeated; he immediately, according to orders previously received, set fire to the public store houses: and the fire was not extinguished until considerable damage had been done. The loss of the Americans in this affair was, one colonel of volunteers, twenty regulars, and one volunteer, killed; one lieutenant-colonel, three lieutenants and one ensign, and seventy-nine men, non-commissioned officers and privates, of the regulars, wounded; and twenty-six missing. The loss of the enemy amounted to three field officers, two captains, and twenty rank and file, found dead upon the ground; two captains, and twenty rank and file, wounded; besides those killed and wounded in the boats, and carried away previous to the retreat. On the same evening lieutenant-colonel Tuttle arrived, after a forced march of forty miles, with about six hundred men; and other reinforcements were rapidly coming in from every quarter.

Notwithstanding this, a modest demand to surrender was made by Sir George Prevost, which he soon after as modestly changed into a request that the killed and wounded in our hands should be respectfully attended to; in answer to which he received satisfactory assurances. On his return to Kingston, he issued a vaunting proclamation, in which he announced a splendid victory, which no one believed. The injury inflicted on us was certainly considerable, but fell far short of the object of this expedition; and that the enemy was compelled precipitately to retreat, he could not pretend to deny. General Brown received and deserved applause for his conduct on this occasion: he here laid the groundwork of his military celebrity.

Shortly after this affair, commodore Chauncey returned with his squadron; and General Lewis, taking command of the place, set about repairing the buildings and public store houses : while general Dearborne, whose increasing indisposition disqualified him for active command, retired from service, leaving colonel Boyd in command of Fort George.

On the 16th of June, lieutenant Chauncey, who had been ordered to cruise off Presque Isle with the Lady of the Lake, captured the Lady Murray, with some officers and privates, besides a quantity of military stores.

About the same time, a devastating and plundering party of the British made an attack on the village of Sodus, where some public stores were deposited. On their approach, these were concealed in the woods, until the militia could be assembled to defend them. The British, exasperated at their disappointment, set fire to all the valuable buildings in the town ; destroyed the private property of individuals ; and were only induced to desist from the entire destruction of the place, on the stipulation of the inhabitants to deliver the public stores at the wharf. The militia soon after appearing, the British were compelled to decamp with the booty they had already collected. They made a second attempt a few days afterwards, but were prevented from landing by the appearance of the militia. This marauding expedition had no pretext of retaliation to cover it.

Shortly after, an affair of some moment took place at Beaver Dams, in which our arms again experienced a severe reverse. A detachment of our troops had been ordered out for the purpose of dislodging the enemy at La Coose's house, about seventeen miles from Fort George, where they had been stationed for some time, in the neighbourhood of two other parties of them still more formidable, but which were both nearer to Fort George. Lieutenant-colonel Boerstler was selected to command it.   The expedition had no rational object, was dangerous, and ill-judged. The Americans had not proceeded more than half way, when Indians were seen skulking across the wood in their rear : a camp of several hundred of these lay between them and the point to which they were going. The Indians now made an attack from the adjoining woods ; and although at last compelled to fly, they kept up the fight long enough for the British parties to come up to their assistance on all sides. Colonel Boerstler made a brave resistance ; which he continued until his ammunition was nearly expended, and a third of his detachment placed *hors de combat*. His rear was assailed by a large body of British and Indians ; and no way of retreat remaining but by cutting his way through the enemy, he proposed a charge upon them. He had been twice summoned to surrender ; and on consultation with his officers, it was agreed to capitulate under stipulations similar to those made by general Winchester, and which were but little better respected.

A few days after this, the British, having been greatly reinforced by general De Rottenburgh, invested the American camp: general Vincent was stationed at Burlington heights, and De Rottenburgh at Ten Mile creek.

The New York volunteers were detained at the head of the lake, contrary to their parol, and on the 12th were ordered to Kingston; but on the way a number effected their escape.

During the remainder of this and the succeeding months, a war of posts was kept up between the two armies. On the 8th of July, a severe skirmish was brought on, in which nearly the whole force on each side was engaged, without any thing of moment resulting from it. An incident, however, occurred, which exasperated the Americans to a greater degree than any thing which had transpired during the war in this quarter. Lieutenant Eldridge, a gallant and accomplished youth, with about forty men, was drawn by his impetuosity too far, and was surrounded by British and Indians. The greater part resisted until they were killed; but lieutenant Eldridge, and ten others, were taken prisoners, and never afterwards heard of. The bodies of the slain were treated in the most shocking manner by the Indians; their heads were split open, and their hearts torn out, by those monsters, the allies of a Christian king! General Boyd, considering the forbearance hitherto practised in declining the aid of Indian allies as no longer justifiable, and by way of preventing a recurrence of these barbarities of the British Indians, accepted the services of four hundred warriors of the Seneca nation, under Young Cornplanter, or Henry O'Beal, an Indian, educated at one of our colleges, but who on his return had resumed the blanket. It was, however, positively stipulated, that the unresisting and defenceless should not be hurt, and that no scalps should be taken; a stipulation which was abided by during the whole war.

On the 11th of July, a force of two hundred of the enemy crossed the Niagara, and attacked Black Rock; the militia stationed there at first fled, but soon returning, with a reinforcement of regulars and Indians, compelled them to fly to their boats, with the loss of nine of their men killed, and their commander, colonel Bishop, mortally wounded.

On the 28th of July, a second expedition was undertaken against York, which had been re-captured by the enemy after the battle of Stony Point. Three hundred men, under colonel Scott, embarked in commodore Chauncey's fleet, and suddenly landing at that place, destroyed the public stores and property, released a number of colonel Boerstler's men, and returned to Sackett's Harbour, with a trifling loss.

The British, who were at this time pursuing a system of devastation along our seabord, which will be recounted in the next chapter, were at the same time engaged in laying waste the country on the borders of Lake Champlain. A small navy had been set on foot by both sides, on this lake, in the beginning of the year; but that of the United States was thus far less prosperous than that of the enemy. The whole American force, on this lake, consisted of a few armed barges, some gun boats, and two schooners, the Growler and Eagle, under lieutenant Sydney Smith. In the beginning of July, the schooners were attacked near the entrance of this lake into the St Lawrence, and after a severe resistance of three hours, against a very superior force, were compelled to surrender. The British, being now masters of the lake, cruised along its borders, landing in various places, and committing many depredations on the property of the inhabitants. On the 31st of July, twelve hundred men landed at Plattsburgh, where no resistance was made, a sufficient body of militia not being collected in time : they first destroyed all the public buildings, and then wantonly burnt the store houses of several of the inhabitants, and carried off great quantities of private property. The same outrages were committed afterwards at Swanton, in the state of Vermont. These acts served only to provoke the inhabitants, and render them better disposed to give the enemy a warm reception at some other period.

On Lake Ontario, a naval armament which might be termed formidable for this inland sea, was arrayed on either side; and an interesting contest ensued, between two skilful officers, for the superiority. The General Pike, of twenty-two guns, having been launched, and proving to be an excellent sailer; commodore Chauncey was now fully equal. in point of strength, to his antagonist. Sir James Yeo, though somewhat inferior in force, had the advantage in an important particular: his ships sailed better in squadron, and he could therefore avoid or come to an engagement as he thought proper. It being a matter all important to the British, to prevent the Americans from becoming masters of the lake; sir James prudently avoided a general action: while, on the other hand, to bring him to action, was the great object of commodore Chauncey. On the 7th of August, the two fleets came in sight of each other. Commodore Chauncey manœuvred to gain the wind. Having passed to the leeward of the enemy's line, and being abreast of his van ship, the Wolf, he fired a few guns to ascertain whether

L

he could reach the hostile fleet. The shot falling short, he wore, and hauled upon a wind to the starboard tack; the rear of his schooners being six miles astern. Sir James wore also, and hauled upon a wind on the same tack; but observing that the American fleet would be able to weather him in the next tack, he tacked again and made all sail to the northward. Commodore Chauncey pursued him. He continued the chase until night; but the schooners not being able to keep up, a signal was made to relinquish the pursuit, and to form in close order. The wind now blew heavily; and at midnight, two of the schooners, the Scourge and the Hamilton, were found to have overset in the squall. Lieutenants Winter and Osgood, two valuable officers, were lost, and only sixteen men of the crews saved. The next morning the enemy, discovering this misfortune, and having now the superiority, manifested a disposition to engage the Americans, and bore up for the purpose. Two schooners were ordered to engage him; but when they were within a mile and a half of him, he attempted to cut them off. Failing in this, he hauled his wind, and hove to. A squall coming on, commodore Chauncey was fearful of being separated from his dull sailing schooners, and ran in towards Niagara and anchored. Here he received on board, from Fort George, one hundred and fifty men to act as marines, and distributed them through his fleet. On the morning of the 9th, he again sailed. At eleven o'clock, after much manoeuvring on both sides, the rear of the enemy's line opened its fire; and in fifteen minutes the action became general on both sides. At half past eleven, the American weather line bore up, and passed to the leeward, the Growler and Julia excepted, which soon after tacking to the southward, brought the British between them and the remainder of the American fleet. Sir James, after exchanging a few shot with the American commodore's ship, pursued the Growler and Julia. A firing commenced between them, which continued until one o'clock in the morning of the 10th; when, after a desperate resistance, the two schooners were compelled to yield. The fleets had lost sight of each other in the night; but as Sir James on the next day, when they were again visible, showed no disposition to renew the action, commodore Chauncey returned to Sackett's Harbour. A victory for this affair was claimed by the British commander.

CHAPTER IX.

War on the Coast—British Attack Lewistown—Gun Boats attack some British Vessels of War—Exploits of Cockburn—Attack on Frenchtown—Plundering and Burning of Havre de Grace—of Georgetown and Fredericktown—Arrival of Admiral Warren and Sir Sydney Beckwith—Southern Cities threatened—Attack on Craney Island—gallantly repulsed—Hampton assaulted and plundered—Enormities committed there—Correspondence between General Taylor and Sir Sydney Beckwith—Cockburn plunders the Coast of North Carolina—Blockade of the American Squadron at New London by Commodore Hardy—Torpedo System.

DURING the first year of the war, Great Britain, being deeply engaged in the important transactions then going on in Europe, had little time to attend to the war with this country. The forces which she could spare, had been sent to Canada; and not one of our ports could be said to have been in a state of actual blockade. The change in the face of things in Europe, however, gave her a greater disposable force, and more leisure; while our victories on the ocean awakened her attention, and kindled a desire for revenge. Long before spring, it was known that a British squadron had arrived at Bermuda, with a body of troops on board, and well supplied with bombs and rockets, for the purpose of attacking some of our southern cities and towns. A distinction was made between the north and south, from the belief, that the northern states were not merely unfriendly to the war, but were strongly inclined to secede from the union, and return to their former allegiance to the king of England.

We are now about to enter upon a species of hostilities, entirely new among civilized people. The scenes which we must pass in review, can scarcely be spoken of with moderation: and the chief actors of them can never be otherwise regarded, than as the perpetrators of enormities from which the honourable warrior would shrink with instinctive horror.

It was soon understood that the war to be carried on against the Atlantic coast in the spring, was to be a war of havock and destruction; but to what extent was not exactly known. The

enemy "talked of chastising us into submission." It was therefore expected that our large commercial towns, now somewhat
fortified against the approach of their shipping, would be vigorously attacked; and it was probable that they would be much
injured, and not impossible that they might be reduced to ashes.
Preparations for resistance were made, by stationing small
bodies of regular troops at different points along the seabord;
which were to form rallying points for the militia, when their
aid should be required. A number of marines and seamen,
belonging to public vessels which did not put to sea, were
directed to co-operate in this service.   .
   On the 4th of February, a squadron consisting of two ships
of the line, three frigates and other vessels, made its appearance
in Chesapeake Bay, apparently standing for Hampton Roads.
The alarm was immediately caught at Norfolk, and the militia
were called in from the upper part of Virginia. No attempt, however, was made upon the town ; the enemy contenting himself
with destroying the smaller vessels employed in the navigation
of the bay, and effectively blockading its waters. About the
same time, another squadron, under the command of commodore
Beresford, consisting of the Poictiers, the Belvidera and some
other vessels, entered the Delaware, which in the same
manner destroyed a number of small trading vessels, and attempted several times to land some men, who were as often
repulsed by the militia, hastily collected.   On the 10th of April,
sir John Beresford made a demand on the people of the village
of Lewistown, for a supply of provisions, which was spiritedly
refused by colonel Davis, commanding at that place.   Captain
Byron, of the Belvidera, was ordered to move near the village,
and bombard it until the demand should be complied with.
This was obeyed, but without effect: after a cannonade of
twenty hours, the enemy were unable to make any impression on
the place.   Their fire had been returned from some batteries
rapidly thrown up on the bank, with considerable effect.   On
the 10th of May, the same squadron sent out their barges in
the neighbourhood of Lewistown, to procure water.   Major
George Hunter was detached by colonel Davis, with one hundred and fifty men, to oppose their landing, which the major
did with so much gallantry, that they were compelled to hasten
to their shipping.   The squadron soon after returned to Bermuda, where sir John Borlace Warren, who commanded on this
station, was engaged in fitting out a more considerable armament, for the attack of our sea coast during the summer.
   Soon after the departure of this squadron, the Spartan and

some other vessels entered the Delaware. One of them, the sloop of war Martin, was discovered on the 29th of July, slightly grounded on the outer edge of Crew's shoals. A detachment of the gun boat flotilla, at that time near the place, immediately moved, and anchoring about three quarters of a mile from the sloop, opened a destructive fire upon her. The Junon frigate soon after came to her relief. A cannonade was kept up during an hour between the gun boats and these two vessels, in which the latter suffered great injury. Finding it impossible to drive off this musquitto fleet, the enemy manned their launches, tenders and cutters, to cut off the gun boats at the extremity of the line. Gun boat No. 121, commanded by sailing-master Head, was unfortunately taken, after a desperate resistance against eight times her number. The British soon after retired, having extricated the Martin from her situation.

Scenes of a different kind were, in the meanwhile, acting in the Chesapeake. The blockading squadron, which had returned in February, was engaged in carrying on a predatory war along the shores and inlets. It was here that Cockburn, a rear admiral in the British service, commenced those exploits, for which he afterwards became so notorious ; and of which he may justly claim to be the originator. At first they were directed against detached farmhouses, and the seats of private gentlemen unprepared for and incapable of defence. These were robbed, and the owners treated in the rudest manner. The cattle which could not be carried away, were doomed to wanton destruction; and the slaves, armed against their owners. were persuaded, in imitation of the example of their new friends, to attack and plunder the defenceless families and property of their masters. It was impossible to station a force at each farmhouse, to meet these miserable and disgraceful incursions. Yet, in several instances, they were bravely repelled by militia, who collected without authority and under the guidance of no leader. Cockburn took possession of several islands in the bay, particularly Sharp's, Tilghman's and Poplar islands; whence he seized the opportunity of making descents upon the neighbouring shores, at such times as the inhabitants happened to be off their guard: but the spirited citizens of Maryland, by stationing bodies of infantry and cavalry at intervals along the shore, ready to be drawn out at a moment's warning, prevented the success of many of them.

Encouraged by the results of his attacks on the farmers and their hen roosts, and rendered more rapacious by the booty already obtained, Cockburn now resolved to undertake something of a bolder and more adventurous character, in which his

L *

thirst for plunder, and his love of mischief, might be gratified
in a higher degree.   He therefore directed his attention to the
unprotected villages and hamlets along the bay ; carefully avoiding the larger towns, the plundering of which might be attended
with some danger.   The first of his exploits was against the
village of Frenchtown, containing six dwellinghouses, two large
store houses, and several stables.   This place was important, as
a point of intermediate deposit for the lines of transportation
between the cities of Philadelphia and Baltimore ; and Cockburn rightly conjectured that here there might be private property to a considerable amount.   He accordingly set out on this
expedition, from his ship the Marlborough, in barges, with five
hundred marines ; a number sufficient to have carried the town on
their backs.   Some show of resistance was made by a small
party of militia collected from Elkton, which retired as the admiral approached.   The store houses were destroyed ; together
with such goods as could not be carried off, to an immense amount.
Amongst other objects of wanton destruction, was an elegant
drop-curtain, belonging to the theatres of the cities before mentioned.   The brand was applied to some of the private dwellinghouses, and to several vessels lying at the wharf ; after
which, the British, fearing the approach of the militia, hastily
returned to their shipping.

The next exploit of the admiral was of still greater importance.   The town of Havre de Grace is situated on the Sus-
quehanna, about two miles from the head of the bay, and is a
neat village, containing twenty or thirty houses.   An attack
on this place was the next object in the plan of his operations.
Accordingly, on the 3d of May, before daylight, his approach
was announced by the firing of cannon and the discharge of
numerous rockets.   The inhabitants, thus awakened from their
sleep, leaped up in the greatest consternation ; and the more
courageous repaired to the beach, where a few small pieces
of artillery had been planted on a kind of battery, for the
purpose of defence against the smaller watering or plundering parties of the enemy.   After firing a few shots on the
approaching barges, they all, with the exception of an old citizen of the place of the name of O'Neill, fled, abandoning the
village to the mercy of Cockburn.   O'Neill alone continued
the fight, loading a piece of artillery, and firing it himself, until,
in recoiling, it ran over his thigh and wounded him severely.
He then armed himself with a musket, and keeping up a fire
on the advancing column of the British, which had by this time
landed and formed, limped away to join his comrades, whom
he attempted in vain to rally.

No sooner had the enemy taken possession of the village by this sudden and bold assault, than they set themselves about destroying the private dwellings, and plundering their contents. Having glutted their avarice, they then amused themselves with every species of barbarous and wanton mischief. The houses being now on fire, they cut open the beds of the inhabitants, and threw in the feathers to increase the flame. Women and children fled shrieking in every direction, to avoid the brutal insolence of the British seamen and marines, and no where did they find a protector amongst these savages. Their clothes were torn from their backs, and they felt themselves at every moment in danger of being massacred. Not on women and children alone were these outrages committed; the horses belonging to the public stages were cruelly maimed, and the stages themselves broken to pieces. Determined that their character should not be equivocal, these worse than Vandals, selected as the next object of their barbarous vengeance, a neat and beautiful building, dedicated to the worship of the Almighty, and took unusual pains to deface its doors and windows. One building yet remained undemolished, an elegant dwelling belonging to commodore Rodgers. Here the most respectable females of the town had taken refuge with their children; believing that a naval officer would not wantonly insult the unprotected wife of a brave and gallant seaman, who was then absent in the service of his country. The officer to whom the task of conflagration had been assigned, already held the torch, when by much solicitation he was induced to wait a few moments, until an appeal to the admiral could be made. It proved successful; and it is mentioned to his praise, that he refrained on one occasion only from that the doing of which would have been the climax of brutality. No further mischief remaining to be perpetrated in the village, the enemy divided their force into three bodies; and while one remained to keep watch, the others proceeded to lay waste the adjacent country. One party pursued the route towards Baltimore for several miles, plundering the farm-houses, and robbing the travellers on the road of their clothes and money; the other marched up the river, committing similar outrages. It were endless to enumerate the acts of cruel and wanton injury, inflicted by this party, during the short time which they remained. On the 6th, to the great satisfaction of the inhabitants, these savages. than whom those of the west were not worse, returned to their fleet. O'Neill, who had been taken prisoner, was carried with them and detained several days; at the end of which time they thought proper to release

him. The inhabitants of the village, many of whom were almost ruined, threw themselves on the humanity of their fellow
citizens of Baltimore, who contributed generously to their relief; and they were soon after enabled to commence the rebuild-
ing of their houses.

Elated with the profitable issue of this descent, in which
a rich booty was obtained with so little danger, the enemy was
eager for some other enterprise equally honourable to the British arms.   On the river Sassafras, which empties itself into the
bay, stood Georgetown and Fredericktown, two beautiful villages situated nearly opposite to each other, one in Kent, the other
in Cecil county.   These had attracted the attention of the admiral.   His hired agents, for miscreants may be found in every
country for such purposes, had informed him, that here he might
glut his crew with plunder.   On the 6th, placing himself at the
head of six hundred men, in eighteen barges, he ascended the
river, and proceeded towards Fredericktown.   Colonel Veazy
had collected here about fifty militia ; and, on the approach of the
barges, he immediately commenced a heavy fire with langrel
shot and musketry   The greater part of the militia soon fled,
leaving the colonel to oppose the enemy as he could; he, notwithstanding, kept up a steady fire, until they approached so near
that he was compelled to retreat.   The admiral boldly advanced
to the town, plundered the houses, and in spite of the entreaties
of the women and children, again acted the incendiary.   Leaving Fredericktown in flames, he passed to the opposite side of
the river, whence, after treating the village of Georgetown in
the same manner, he returned, glutted with spoil and satiated
with wanton havock.

Not long after this, admiral Warren entered the bay with a
considerable reinforcement to the fleet, and a number of land
troops and marines under the command of sir Sydney Beckwith. He had seized some of the vessels employed in the navigation of the bay, with the view of using them in penetrating
those inlets which were impervious to the larger tenders.   To
oppose the small parties which he sent out, the government hired
a number of barges and light vessels, which, by moving from
place to place with great rapidity, tended to keep him in check.

By the arrival of admiral Warren, the hostile force in the
Chesapeake was increased to seven ships of the line, and twelve
frigates, with a proportionate number of smaller vessels.   The
appearance of this formidable armament created much alarm in
the more considerable towns along the neighbouring coast.
Baltimore, Annapolis and Norfolk were threatened; and it

soon became evident that the latter of these places was selected
to receive the first blow.

On the 18th, commodore Cassin, having received intelligence
that a squadron of the enemy had arrived in Hampton Roads,
commenced the necessary dispositions for repelling the invader.
The frigate Constellation was anchored between the two forts,
commanding Elizabeth river, on which the city of Norfolk is
situated. At this place nearly ten thousand of the Virginia militia had collected. A detachment of the gun boat flotilla was
ordered in the meanwhile to descend the river, and engage the
foremost of the enemy's frigates. Captain Tarbell, by whom
it was commanded, proceeded in two divisions: the first commanded by lieutenant Gardner, and the other by lieutenant
Henly. On the 20th, having brought his gun boats into a favourable position, he opened a rapid fire upon the Junon frigate, at the distance of half a mile. This was returned; and
the cannonade continued for half an hour; the frigate receiving
much injury, while the gun boats suffered but little. Another
vessel, which proved to be a *razee*, was now seen coming to her
assistance; and the fire of the Junon, which for a short time had
been silenced, on the arrival of her consort and additional
frigates again opening, Captain Tarbell thought proper to retire.
By this affair, the Junon was much shattered; and her loss,
considering the great disparity of force, was considerable.

A formidable attack on Norfolk having been resolved upon
by the British; it was necessary, preparatory to this, to subdue
the forts by which it was protected. The nearest obstruction
to the enemy's advances, was Craney island; and in the course
of the day, the fleet in the bay dropped to the mouth of James
River. Captain Tarbell gave orders to lieutenants Neale, Shubrick and Saunders, of the frigate Constellation, to land a hundred
seamen on the island, for the purpose of manning a battery on
the northwest side; while he stationed the gun boats in such a
manner as enabled him to annoy the enemy from the opposite
side. On the 22d, at daylight, they were discovered approaching in barges, round the point of Nansemond river, to the number of four thousand men; most of whom, it was afterwards
ascertained, were wretched French troops, which had been taken
prisoners in Spain, and induced to enter the British service by
the promise of being permitted to pillage and abuse the citizens of the United States. They selected a place of landing
out of the reach of the gun boats; but, unfortunately for them,
not out of the reach of danger. When they had approached
within two hundred yards of the shore, lieutenant Neale, assisted by lieutenants Shubrick and Saunders, opened a galling fire

from his battery, and compelled them to pause. The battery was manned by one hundred and fifty men, including lieutenant Breckenridge's marines. An eighteen pounder which had been mounted on it was directed with so much precision, that several of the enemy's boats were cut in two, and the men with difficulty escaped. The Centipede, the admiral's barge, was sunk, and the whole force compelled to make a precipitate retreat. No sooner was this discovered, than lieutenant Neale ordered his men to haul up the boats which had been sunk, and to afford the unfortunate sufferers every assistance in their power. A large party of the enemy which had landed on the main shore, and were crossing a narrow inlet to the west side, were not less warmly received by the Virginia volunteers. A short time before the approach of the barges, this body of men, about eight hundred in number, attempted to cross to the island by the inlet of which we have spoken. Colonel Beatty, who had been posted, with about four hundred men, on the island, planted two twenty-four pounders, and four sixes, to oppose the passage, under the direction of major Faulkner, aided by captain Emerson, and lieutenants Howel and Godwin. The conflict commenced at the same moment that the attack was made on the party approaching by water; and the enemy was compelled to relinquish his attempt in this quarter also. His total loss was upwards of two hundred in killed and wounded. besides a number of his men, who seized the opportunity to desert.

The safety of the city of Norfolk, and of Gosport, Portsmouth and other surrounding towns, is to be attributed to the resolute defence of Craney island. The conduct of lieutenant Neale, and his brave companions Shubrick, Saunders and Breckenridge, received the grateful acknowledgements of the inhabitants. Colonel Beatty and his officers, and two noncommissioned volunteers, sergeant Young and corporal Moffit, were no less entitled to praise for the parts which they took in this interesting affair.

This unexpected repulse enraged the enemy beyond measure; but at the same time that their desire of revenge was excited, they were taught greater prudence in the selection of the object of attack. A consultation took place between admiral Warren, sir Sydney Beckwith and Cockburn, which resulted in a determination to attack the town of Hampton, about eighteen miles distant from Norfolk. There was a garrison here, consisting of about four hundred men, artillerists and infantry. The fortifications of the place were very inconsiderable; and the town itself was of little more importance than the villages which had been pillaged by Cockburn. It was thought, that by the possession of this place, the communication between Norfolk and the upper part of Virginia would be entirely cut off. On the 25th, the plan of attack having been adjusted, admiral Cockburn advanced towards the town, with a number of barges, tenders and smaller vessels, throwing rockets, and keeping up a constant cannonade ; while sir Sydney landed below, at the head of two thousand men, intending to march up and gain the rear of the Americans. Admiral Cockburn was so warmly received by major Crutchfield, the officer commanding at Hampton, who opened upon him a few pieces of artillery, that he was compelled instantly to draw back, and conceal himself behind a point. In the meanwhile, sir Sydney made his appearance, and was severely handled by a rifle company under captain Servant, which had been posted in a wood, near which he had to pass. Major Crutchfield soon after drew up his infantry in support of the riflemen ; but finding himself unable to contend with numbers so superior, he made good his retreat, not however without great difficulty. Captain Pryor had been left to command the battery which opposed the enemy's approach from sea. The royal marines, having landed, had advanced within sixty yards of him ; and his corps, considering their situation hopeless, already regarded themselves as prisoners of war; when, ordering the guns to be spiked, and charging upon the enemy, he threw them into such confusion, that he actually effected his escape without the loss of a single man. The loss of the Americans in this affair, amounted to seven killed and twelve wounded: that of the British, according to their statement, was five killed and thirty-three wounded ; but it was probably much more considerble.

Scarcely was this village in the possession of the invaders, when full permission was given to the troops to gratify their worst passions and propensities. After enacting the usual scenes of shameless plunder and devastation, they proceeded to offer violence to the persons of those of the unfortunate inhabitants, whose age, sex or infirmities had prevented them from escaping. Was there no British officer who, on this occasion, felt for the honour of his country, and endeavoured, at the risk of his life, to rescue it from indelible reproach ? It seems there was not one. An old man of the name of Kirby, unable to rise from his bed, was set upon and murdered in the arms of his aged wife, who, on daring to remonstrate, received the contents of a pistol in her breast! To complete this barbarous act, they wantonly put to death his faithful dog! Two sick men were murdered in the hospital; the medical stores were destroyed ; and the wounded who fell into their hands, were not only denied medical aid, but even common sustenance. During two days, did the British thus throw aside, not merely the character of soldiers, but of men; when, fearing an attack from the neighbouring militia, they withdrew with such precipitation, that a considerable quantity of provisions and ammunition, and some of their men, were left behind.

This picture is by no means overcharged. It is founded on authentic evidence submitted to a committee of congress. The feelings of the people of Virginia were, if possible, more excited by this affair, than were those of the citizens of Kentucky at the massacre by Proctor. General Taylor, who commanded the station, addressed a letter to sir Sydney Beckwith, couched in terms of dignified, thrilling eloquence, such as the feelings of an honourable man alone can dictate. After stating the enormities of which the British had been guilty, he desired to be informed of the nature of the war which they intended to carry on against the United States; whether the scenes enacted at Hampton were unauthorised by the British government, or whether that power had entirely thrown aside the usages which govern civilized nations when at variance. "Worthless," said he, " is the laurel steeped in female tears, and joyless the conquests which have inflicted needless woe on the peaceful and unresisting." Sir Sydney replied, that he was sorry for the excesses at Hampton; and hoped that, in future, the war would be carried on with as much regard to humanity as possible. This evasive answer was not deemed satisfactory; and one more explicit was required. He then declared that the excesses committed were in retaliation, for the conduct of the Americans at Craney island in shooting at the seamen who clung to a barge which had overset. General Taylor immediately instituted a court of inquiry, which proved the charge to be without foundation. On the result of this investigation being communicated to sir Sydney, he did not think proper to give a written reply: he promised, verbally, to withdraw his troops from the neighbourhood; excusing himself, on the score of his ignorance of the kind of warfare to which his men had been accustomed in Spain; and alleging, that as soon as he found them engaged in the excesses complained of, he had given orders for them to re-embark. It is unpleasant to implicate admiral Warren and sir Sydney Beckwith in this detestable affair; but there was in the conduct of these two officers a shameful indifference upon a subject which so deeply regarded the character of the British government.

The squadron, during the remainder of the summer, frequently threatened the cities of Washington, Annapolis and Baltimore. Large bodies of militia were on several occasions drawn out, and the country was in consequence much harassed. This was fair and justifiable in the enemy, and is no subject of complaint, and had any of our towns been laid in ashes while attempting a resistance, it would have been regarded only as a misfortune of war which the enemy had a right to inflict. Admiral Cockburn was permitted to pursue his own inclination, in moving to the south with a formidable squadron, to carry on, in the Carolinas and Georgia, the same species of warfare which he had so successfully practised in Chesapeake Bay. In the beginning of July, he appeared off Ocracoke, a village of North Carolina, and shortly after, crossing the bar with a number of barges, attacked two private armed vessels, the Anaconda and the Atlas, which, after a gallant resistance, he captured. The revenue cutter, then in port, made her escape to Newbern, and giving the alarm to the citizens, they assembled in such numbers that the admiral's designs upon that town were frustrated. Landing about three thousand men, he proceeded to Portsmouth, and treated its inhabitants in his usual manner. He returned to his barges with a valuable booty, and a number of slaves. whom he had induced to leave their masters under a promise of freedom, which he afterwards redeemed by selling them in the West Indies.

To the north of the Chesapeake, where fortunately these disgraceful depredations were not committed, the coast was not exempt from the effects of war. The city of New York was strictly blockaded. The American frigates United States and Macedonian, and the sloop Hornet, attempted to sail on a cruise from that port about the beginning of May ; but finding the force at the Hook much superior to theirs, they put back, and passed through Hell Gate, with the intention of getting out by the sound. In this they were also frustrated ; and on the 1st of June, after another attempt, they were chased into New London. Six hundred militia were immediately called in from the surrounding country, for the protection of the squadron ; and commodore Decatur, landing some of his guns, mounted a battery on the shore, and at the same time so lightened his vessels, as to enable them to ascend the river out of the reach of the enemy. This place was so well fortified, however, that no attempt was made upon it, although the blockade was strictly kept up for many months.

It is pleasing to contrast the conduct of commodore Hardy, who commanded the squadron north of the Chesapeake, with that of Cockburn. Although he frequently landed on different parts of the coast ; his deportment was such as might be

M

expected from a manly, humane and generous enemy. If the procedings of Cockburn were authorised by his government, they were dictated by a very mistaken policy; for nothing could more effectually heal political differences, and render the war a common cause with every American.

An act of congress had been passed during the winter, which cannot be mentioned but with feelings of regret. By this act, a reward of half their value, was offered for the destruction of ships belonging to the enemy by means other than those of the armed or commissioned vessels of the United States. This measure was intended to encourage the use of torpedoes, of which so much at that time was said. There is something unmanly in this insidious mode of annoyance. It is not justifiable for defence even against an unsparing foe; and is but little better than poisoning fountains. Valour can claim no share in such exploits; and to the noble mind little pleasure can be derived from the recollection of success over an enemy treacherously vanquished. It had been in the power of general Sinclair, in the war of the revolution, to have poisoned his spirituous liquors at the moment of his defeat, and thus to have destroyed a cruel enemy; but shame would have followed the infliction of such an injury, even upon savages.

Several attempts at blowing up the enemy's vessels were made, in consequence of the law. The most remarkable were those against the Ramillies, the admiral's ship, and the Plantagenet. The schooner Eagle, having been filled with flour barrels, and a quantity of gunpowder, with the latter of which a concealed gun lock communicated, was thrown in the way of the blockading squadron's boats. Fortunately, the seamen, instead of taking her alongside of the Ramillies, determined first to unlade some of the cargo: while employed in doing this, the schooner blew up, and destroyed several of her captors. The next experiment made with the torpedo, was against the Plantagenet, then lying below Norfolk. After four or five attempts, in which the persons engaged could not come sufficiently near the ship without being discovered, the torpedo was dropped at the distance of a hundred yards, and left to be swept down by the tide. On touching the vessel, it exploded in the most awful manner; causing an immense column of water to be thrown up, which fell with vast weight upon the deck of the ship; while a yawning gulf seemed to swallow her up. The crew immediately took to their boats, completely panic struck. Commodore Hardy was justly indignant at this dishonourable species of annoyance, and protested against it in strong terms. It had the effect, however, of compelling the enemy to be extremely cautious in their approach to our harbours; and although the use of torpedoes was relinquished, their apprehensions served to keep them at a greater distance. If any thing could justify this mode of attack, it was the scenes at Hampton, and the deportment of Cockburn and his crew; but commodore Hardy was a generous enemy, and merited different treatment.

CHAPTER X.

Naval Affairs—The Hornet captures the Peacock—Humane and generous Conduct of Captain Lawrence and the Crew of the Hornet—Captain Lawrence appointed to the Chesapeake—The Shannon challenges the Chesapeake—The Shannon captures the Chesapeake—Death of Captain Lawrence—The Pelican captures the Argus—Cruise of Commodore Porter in the South Seas—The Enterprize captures the Boxer—Cruise of Commodore Rodgers—Cruise of the Congress—Conduct of American Privateers—of the Comet—of the General Armstong—The Privateer Decatur captures the Dominica.

It is now time to return to the affairs of our navy. Our vessels continued to annoy the enemy, in spite of the thousand ships with which she pursued them in squadrons through every sea. Instead of courting an engagement with them, she studiously avoided coming in contact, except where her force was greatly superior. The "fir built frigates" of America had suddenly become ships of the line, and Great Britain cut down her seventy-fours, that her vessels might engage with ours on equal terms. The government of the United States had become so sensible of the importance of our marine, that congress, during the last session, had authorised the building of several additional vessels; and it was proposed to continue to augment our navy, by annual appropriations for the purpose. This was undoubtedly wise policy; for whatever we may fear from a standing army, there can be no similar ground of objection to a navy. Besides, it is only on that element that we can come in contact with an enemy of consequence. Fortunately for us, our territory adjoins to that of no power, from which we need apprehend any great danger. while the colonies of England and of Spain might have reason for apprehension, if the genius of our government were not opposed to conquest. On the ocean, however, we must unavoidably come in contact with other nations, so long as we pretend to have commerce ; for without a navy that commerce cannot be protected.

In our last chapter on the naval war, it was mentioned, that the Hornet, captain Lawrence, was left to blockade the Bonne Citoyenne, at St Salvador. This latter vessel was formally challenged by the Hornet : but either from unwillingness to risk the loss of a quantity of specie which she had on board, or because she was not inclined to engage in the combat though of superior force, she thought proper to pay no attention to the challenge. Commodore Bainbridge had parted from the Hornet at this place ; and it will be recollected how gloriously he met the Java and captured her a few days afterwards. The Hornet continued the blockade until the 24th of January, when the Montague seventy-four hove in sight, and compelled her to escape into port. She ran out, however, the same night, and proceeded on a cruise. Her commander first shaped his course to Pernambuco, and on the 4th of February, captured the English brig Resolution, of ten guns, with twenty-three thousand dollars in specie. He then ran down the coast of Maranham, cruised off there a short time ; and thence off Surinam, where he also cruised for some time ; and on the 22d stood for Demerara. The next day, he discovered an English brig of war lying at anchor outside of the bar, and on beating round the Carabana bank, to come near her, he discovered, at half past three in the afternoon, another sail on his weather quarter, edging down for him. This proved to be a large man of war brig, the Peacock, captain Peake, somewhat superior to the Hornet in force. Captain Lawrence manœuvred some time to gain the weather gage of her ; but his efforts proving fruitless, he hoisted the American ensign, tacked about, and in passing her, exchanged a broadside at the distance of pistol shot. The Peacock being then discovered in the act of wearing, Lawrence bore up, received her starboard broadside, ran her close on the starboard quarter, and poured into her so heavy a fire, that in fifteen minutes she surrendered. At the moment of her surrender, she hoisted a signal of distress ; as she was literally cut to pieces, and had already six feet water in her hold.

Lieutenant Shubrick, the gallantry of whose conduct in this affair was not less conspicuous than in the actions with the Guerriere and Java, was despatched to bring the officers and crew of the vanquished vessel on board the Hornet. He found that her captain had been killed, and the greater part of her crew either killed or wounded: and that the vessel was sinking fast, in spite of every effort to keep her above water. Strenuous exertions were made to take off the crew before the vessel sunk: her guns were thrown overboard, the shot holes were plugged; and a part of the Hornet's crew, at the risk of their lives, laboured incessantly in the removal of the prisoners. The utmost efforts of these generous men were vain, she sunk in the midst of them, carrying down nine of her own crew and three of the American. Thus did our gallant countrymen twice risk their lives: 'first in the cause of their country, and next in the cause of humanity; first to conquer their enemies, and then to save them. These are actions, which it unfortunately falls too rarely to the lot of the historian to record. The crew of the Hornet divided their clothing with the prisoners, who were left destitute by the sinking of the ship; and so sensible were the officers of the generous treatment which they experienced from captain Lawrence and his men, that, on their arrival at New York, they expressed their gratitude in a public letter of thanks. "So much," say they, "was done to alleviate the uncomfortable and distressing situation in which we were placed, when received on board the ship you command, that we cannot better express our feelings, than by saying, we ceased to consider ourselves prisoners; and every thing that friendship could dictate, was adopted by you and the officers of the Hornet, to remedy the inconvenience we otherwise should have experienced, from the unavoidable loss of the whole of our property and clothes, by the sudden sinking of the Peacock." This praise is worth more than a victory; and the conduct which elicited it is certainly much more deserving to be termed *glorious* than the destruction of human life, on whatever scale it may be accomplished.

The number of killed and wounded, on board the Peacock, could not be exactly ascertained, but was supposed to exceed fifty; while the Hornet received but little injury. The officers mentioned as having distinguished themselves on this occasion, were lieutenants Conner and Newton, and midshipmen Cooper, Mayo, Getz, Smoot, Tippet, Boerum and Titus. Lieutenant Stewart was unfortunately too ill to take a part in the action.

On the 10th of April, shortly after the return of the Hornet, the Chesapeake arrived at Boston, after a cruise of four months. Her commander, captain Evans, having been appointed to the New York station, she was assigned to captain Lawrence.

The British, whose mortification at their repeated defeats may be easily imagined, and who regarded the reputation of their navy as their great bulwark, had become seriously alarmed.

M*

If the charm of their fancied superiority on this element were once destroyed, other nations, who now yielded to them the palm, might conceive the idea of resistance also. In some recent rencounters, even the French, who had been so unfortunate in their naval combats with the British, had begun to pluck up courage Something immediate must be done to retrieve their character, or all their naval songs must be burnt and their boastings suddenly terminate. The course was naturally fallen upon of selecting one of their best frigates, manned by picked seamen, and exercised with all possible pains, for the special purpose. They deigned to copy every thing which in reality, or which they fancied, prevailed in the American ships. An idle rumour was current, that backwoodsmen were placed in the tops of our vessels, expressly for the purpose of shooting the British officers. Sharpshooters were now carefully trained by the British, and directed to aim only at the officers of the Americans. Thus provided with a chosen ship and crew, captain Brooke appeared with the Shannon on the American coast. In April, off Boston harbour, he sent a challenge to the President, commodore Rodgers, which happened to be there. On the 23d, this vessel, with the Congress, captain Smith, sailed on a cruise ; but the Shannon, then in company with the Tenedos, either intentionally avoided them, or by accident happened to be out of the way. The Shannon some time afterwards returned, and sent a formal challenge to captain Lawrence, who had just taken the command of the Chesapeake, which unfortunately was not received by him.

We are now to relate an occurrence which imparts a melancholy tone to our naval chronicle, thus far so brilliant. Captain Lawrence, on arriving to take command of his ship, was informed that a British frigate was lying before the harbour, apparently courting a combat with an American. Listening only to the dictates of his generous nature, he burned with impatience to meet the enemy, and unfortunately did not sufficiently pause to examine whether the terms were equal. The greater part of the Chesapeake's crew consisted of men who had just been enlisted; several of his officers were sick ; and that kind of mutual confidence, which arises from a long knowledge of each other, was wanting between himself and his men. But he could not brook the thought of being thus defied. On the 1st of June he sailed forth, resolved to try his fortune. When he came in sight of the Shannon, he made a short address to his crew, but found it received with no enthusiasm : they murmured, alleging as the cause of complaint that their prize money had not been paid. He immediately gave them tickets for it, and supposed they were now conciliated; but, unfortunately, they were at this moment almost in a state of mutiny. Several foreigners, who had accidentally found their way into the crew, had succeeded in poisoning their minds. The brave Lawrence, consulting his own heart, looked only to the enemy without, and not to the enemy within.

The Shannon, observing the Chesapeake, put to sea, and was followed by her. At half past five, the Chesapeake closed with the enemy, and gave him a broadside; which was returned. It proved equally destructive on both sides; but the Chesapeake was particularly unfortunate in the loss of officers: the sailing-master, White, was killed; lieutenant Ballard, mortally wounded; and lieutenant Brown of the marines, and Captain Lawrence himself, were severely wounded. The latter, although in great pain, still continued to give orders. A second and a third broadside were exchanged, with evident advantage on the side of the Chesapeake; but the same misfortune in the loss of officers continued: the first lieutenant, Ludlow, was carried below mortally wounded; and three men successively were shot from the wheel. A ball having struck her foresail, so that she could no longer answer her helm; and being disabled in her rigging; the Chesapeake fell with her quarter on the Shannon's starboard anchor. This accident may be considered as having decided the contest; an opportunity being thus given to the enemy to rake the Chesapeake, and, towards the close of the action, to board her. Captain Lawrence, although severely wounded, as before mentioned, still persisted in keeping the deck, and commanded the boarders to be called up: at this moment a musket ball entering his body, he was carried below, having first uttered those memorable words, which have since become the motto of the American navy, Don't give up the Ship. The officers of the Chesapeake being now nearly all killed, the command devolved on lieutenant Budd; who called up the men for the purpose of carrying the order of Lawrence into execution. At this time, captain Brooke, finding that his vessel had received so many shots between wind and water that there was danger of her sinking, and perceiving the confusion which reigned on board the American ship, threw twenty of his marines on board of her, and immediately followed them. Lieutenant Budd endeavoured to shoot his vessel clear of the Shannon; but being soon after wounded, and a part of the crew having mutinied, the scheme entirely failed. A number, however, continued to fight with unalterable resolution. Captain Brooke received a wound in the head, and was carried on board his own ship; and lieutenant Watt, who succeeded him in the command, was killed; but a large reinforcement coming to the assistance of the enemy, they gained possession of the deck, and soon after hoisted the English flag.

In this sanguinary conflict, twenty-three of the enemy were killed, and fifty-six wounded: among the killed, her first lieutenant, her clerk and purser; and among the wounded, her captain. On board the Chesapeake, the captain, the first and fourth lieutenants, the lieutenant of marines, the master, midshipmen Hopewell, Livingston, Evans, and about seventy men were killed; and the second and third lieutenants, midshipmen Weaver, Abbot, Nicholls, Beirv, and about eighty men, wounded. The greater proportion of this loss was sustained after the enemy had gained the deck. The British have been charged with cruel and ungenerous conduct towards the vanquished; and we could wish that this charge, if untrue, had been properly repelled. It is said that, after the Americans had submitted, the work of destruction was continued; and that the treatment of the prisoners was not of that liberal character which might have been expected from manly victors. The generosity of their subsequent conduct leads us to hope that these complaints were unfounded. The bodies of our naval heroes, Lawrence and Ludlow, on their arrival at Halifax, were interred with every honour, civil, naval and military, which could be bestowed; and no testimony of respect that was due to their memories was left unpaid. They were afterwards brought to the United States, by Mr Crowninshield of Boston, at his own expense, in a vessel manned by twelve masters of vessels, who volunteered their services for the occasion; a passport having been readily granted for this purpose by commodore Hardy.

The loss of the Chesapeake has been attributed to the accident of her falling on board the Shannon, and to the mutinous state of her crew. She was somewhat inferior in force also: but this ought not to be taken into consideration; for until the fatal accident, the advantage in the contest was decidedly hers.

Never did any victory—not the victories of Wellington in Spain, nor even those of Nelson—call forth such expressions of joy, on the part of the British; a proof that our naval character had risen somewhat in their estimation. In the United States it was regarded as an occurrence which proved no superiority in the enemy: and it was lamented chiefly for the loss of our brave officers.

The tide of fortune seemed for a short time to set in favour of Great Britain. On the 4th of August, another of our national vessels was captured by the enemy. The Argus, after carry-

ing out Mr Crawford, our minister to France, in the spring of
1813, proceeded, early in June, to cruise in the British channel, where she continued for two months to commit great havock on the British shipping. So much uneasiness did she
cause, that the English merchants were unable to effect an in-
surance on their vessels, under three times the usual premium.
The British government was induced, at last, to adopt measures for driving off this daring enemy. On the 14th, at four
in the morning, the Pelican, a British sloop of war of greater
force than the Argus, obtained sight of her by the light of a brig
then on fire; and immediately prepared to attack her. At five
o'clock, the action commenced at the distance of musket shot;
the Pelican having the weather gage. At the first broadside
captain Allen, of the Argus, fell, severely wounded, but remained
on deck until several broadsides were exchanged, when he was
carried below, leaving the command to lieutenant Watson. At
half past six, the rigging of the Argus was so cut up, as to render her almost unmanageable; and the lieutenant was severely
wounded in the head. The command now devolved on lieutenant
William H. Allen, Jun., who for some time, by great exertion,
defeated the attempts of the Pelican to gain a raking position.
At thirty-five minutes past six, the Argus, having lost her wheel
ropes and running rigging could no longer be manœuvred; and
the Pelican having chosen a position in which none of the guns
of the Argus could be brought to bear upon her, the latter had nothing but musketry to oppose to the raking broadsides of the other.
At forty-seven minutes past six, she surrendered, with the loss
of six killed and seventeen wounded. On board the Pelican,
there were three killed, and five wounded. Captain Allen, and
midshipmen Delphy and Edwards, died soon afterwards in
England, and were all interred with the honours of war. The
Pelican was a sloop of twenty guns, the Argus of eighteen; but
the victory, in this instance, may fairly be awarded to the
English. Our officers and men did their duty; but were compelled to submit to a more fortunate adversary. Captain Allen
was justly a favourite in this country, and his memory is dear
to his countrymen.

By letters dated early in July, news reached the United States
from captain Porter, that he had captured several British vessels
in the South Seas, and was then cruising with great success.
He had actually created a fleet of nine sail, by means of vessels
captured on those seas, eight of which had been letters of
marque, and was completely master of the Pacific ocean. This
may be regarded as a novelty in naval history; and there is little doubt, had it been performed by an English naval com-

mander, that it would have been applauded to the skies. By none of our commanders was there so much injury done to British commerce; and against none of them were our enemies so profuse in their invectives. On the list of his captures were two fine English ships, pierced for twenty guns and carrying between them sixteen, with fifty-five men, and having on board a considerable sum in specie. On the 26th of March, he fell in with a Spanish ship, the Nereyda, which had been engaged in capturing American ships: he took the liberty of throwing her guns overboard, and liberating the ships and prisoners which the pirate had captured. This is probably one of the grounds upon which commodore Porter was denominated a bucanier by the British.

The enemy were not long permitted to rejoice in the conquest of the Argus: victory once more returned to the side of justice, "free trade and sailors' rights." The American brig Enterprize, Lieutenant commandant William Burrows, sailed from Portsmouth on a cruise, about the 1st of September. On the 5th, a large man of war brig was discovered, to which she gave chase. The enemy, after firing some guns, stood for the Enterprize with several ensigns hoisted. She proved to be the Boxer, of a force somewhat superior to that of the Enterprize. A little after three, the firing commenced on both sides, within pistol shot. After the action had continued fifteen minutes, the Enterprize ranged ahead, and raked her for the space of twenty minutes. At the end of this period, the enemy ceased firing, and cried for quarter; being unable to haul down her flag, as it had been nailed to the mast. The Enterprize had thirteen wounded and one killed, but that one was the lamented Burrows. He fell at the commencement of the action, but refused to quit the deck. He had requested that the flag might never be struck; and when the sword of the enemy was presented to him, he clasped it to his breast, and exclaimed with enthusiasm, "I die contented." Then, and not till then, would he permit himself to be carried below. The British loss was much more considerable, but was not properly ascertained: it was supposed, however, that between thirty and forty of the crew of the Boxer were killed and wounded; among the former her commander, captain Blythe. The bravado of nailing the flag to the mast was an additional proof of the new light in which the Americans were now held by an enemy, which before affected to despise them. The two commanders, both most promising young men, were interred beside each other, at Portland, with military honours.

On the 26th of September, the President, commodore Rod-

gers, arrived at Newport, Rhode Island, after a cruise of unusual length. He had put to sea on the 30th of April, in company
with the Congress, captain Smith. After cruising off our coast
without any important occurrence, the commodore parted from
the Congress on the 8th of May, and shaped his course so as
to intercept the British trade in the West Indies. Meeting with
no success, he stood towards the Azores. where he continued
until the 6th of June, without encountering any of the enemy's
vessels. He now sailed in the direction of England; and
made four captures between the 9th and 13th of June He
next cruised in the track from Newfoundland to St George's
Channel, without meeting a single vessel; and being short
of provisions, put into North Bergen on the 27th of June.
Thence he steered towards the Orkneys, to intercept a convoy
from Archangel; but about the middle of July, when in momentary expectation of meeting with it, he was chased by a
ship of the line and a frigate for several days. Having effected
his escape, he next placed himself in the direction of the trade
passing out of and into the Irish Channel. In this position he
made three captures; when finding that the enemy had a superior force near at hand, he made a circuit round Ireland, and
steering for the Banks of Newfoundland, made two captures
there. On the 23d of September he captured, in a singular
manner, the British schooner Highflyer, tender to admiral Warren. On her approach to the President, she hoisted a private
signal, which was answered by one that chanced to be the
British signal for that day: she accordingly bore down and
was captured. By this means the British private signals,
and admiral Warren's instructions, were obtained : and the
commodore was enabled to avoid their squadrons on the coast.
He soon after arrived at Newport.

The Congress, after parting from the President, continued
at sea until the 12th of December, when she arrived at
Portsmouth, New Hampshire. She had cruised chiefly on the
coast of South America, and had captured a number of the
enemy's vessels, among which were two armed brigs of ten
guns each.

It has already been said, that the character of our flag at
sea, was supported not merely by our national vessels· there
were numerous instances in which our private cruisers acquitted themselves in a manner which entitled them to honourable
notice. The public attention, however, was so much occupied
with the former, that the latter perhaps did not receive a due
share of applause. A few instances may now be selected from
among many. Perhaps no action during the war displayed

more daring courage, and greater superiority of seamanship, than the engagement of captain Boyle, of the Comet, with a Portuguese brig, and three armed merchantmen. After encountering them all, and fighting them for several hours, he compelled one of the merchantmen to surrender, and the brig to sheer off, although of double the force of the Comet. This would appear almost incredible, if the details were not perfectly authenticated.

On the 11th of March, off Surinam, the General Armstrong discovered a sail which she supposed to be a letter of marque, and after giving her a broadside, and wearing to give another, to her surprise she found herself alongside of a frigate, which soon opened such a heavy fire, as would have sunk the schooner, had she not succeeded in making her escape.

On the 15th of August, the privateer Decatur, being on a cruise, discovered a ship and a schooner : the first proved to be the British packet, the Princess Charlotte; the other the British vessel of war, the Dominica. She immediately stood towards them, and soon found herself abreast of the schooner. Both vessels continued to manœuvre for two or three hours; the Dominica endeavouring to escape, and the Decatur to board : during which time several broadsides were fired by the former, and some shot from the large gun of the latter. The Decatur at last succeeded in boarding; a number of her men passing by means of her bowsprit into the stern of the enemy. The fire from the artillery and musquetry was now terrible, being well supported on both sides. The Dominica not being able to disengage herself, dropped alongside, and was boarded by the whole crew of the Decatur. Firearms now became useless, and the crews fought hand to hand with cutlasses. The officers of the Dominica being all killed or wounded, she was forced to surrender. As soon as the combat was over, the Princess Charlotte tacked about and escaped.

The Decatur was armed with six twelve-pound carronades, and one eighteen-pounder on a pivot, with one hundred and three men. Her loss was three killed, and sixteen wounded. The Dominica had twelve twelve-pound carronades, two long sixes, one brass four-pounder, and one thirty-two pound carronade on a pivot, with eighty-three men. She had thirteen killed, and forty-seven wounded. The surviving officers of the Dominica attributed their defeat to the masterly manœuvring of the Decatur, and the superior skill of her crew in the use of musketry. The captain of the Dominica, a young man of about twenty-five years of age, was wounded early in the action; but he fought to the last moment, declaring that he would surrender his vessel only with his life.

The Decatur arrived at Charlestown with her prize, on the
20th of August. It is pleasing to record, that in this instance
our brave tars did not depart from their accustomed generosity.
The surviving officers of the Dominica spoke in the highest
terms of the humanity and attention which they experienced
from the victors.

CHAPTER XI.

In the midst of the various occurrences of the war on the
northern frontier, on the seaboard and on the ocean, important
preparations were making to the westward, and although the
spring and summer had elapsed without the occurrence of any
incident in this quarter worthy of record, they had not passed
inactively. The general attention was now turned towards it
with much anxiety; and the armies of the Niagara and the St
Lawrence remained almost with folded arms, awaiting the respective results of Harrison's campaign, and of the contest for the
command of Lake Erie. The British, aware of the consequences of defeat, laboured with great assiduity to strengthen
themselves; and the reinforcements continually arriving at Fort
George, were evidently destined to follow up the advantages
which Proctor, in conjunction with the commander on the lake,
might gain.

In the meanwhile, the people of the neighbouring states
of Kentucky and Ohio were excited in a surprising degree.
Had it been necessary, they would have risen *en masse;* for
almost every man capable of bearing a musket, was ready to

N

march. The governor of Ohio had scarce issued his proclamation for volunteers (for the legal obligation to render military
service was no longer enforced), when fifteen thousand men,
completely armed and equipped—a number five times greater
than was required—presented themselves.   The venerable
governor of Kentucky, Shelby, a revolutionary hero, and the
Nestor of the war, made it known that he would put himself
at the head of the injured citizens of that state, and lead them
to seek revenge for the murder of their relatives and friends ;
but he limited the number of volunteers to four thousand.
The territory embraced by the state of Kentucky, called by
the natives " the dark and bloody ground," sixty years ago was
an uninhabited forest; and had been, from time immemorial, the
theatre of sanguinary Indian wars.   At this day, it blooms beneath the hand of agriculture ; and is filled with beautiful towns
and villages—the abodes of peace and opulence.   The inhabitants are derived principally from those of Virginia and
North Carolina.   Living in abundance and at their ease, and
remote from the seats of commerce, they had imbibed less of
foreign attachments and feelings, than any of our people ; and
were imbued with a purer enthusiasm for the institutions of
freedom.   To an enlightened manliness of mind, they united a
romantic cast of character, arising from the independence of
their situation and the absence of too close an intercourse with
the sordid world.   Possessing not a little of the chivalric in their
generous and hospitable deportment, and fearing dishonour more
than danger; they were benevolent and disinterested in the
extreme.   Had the elder brethren of our confederacy acted in
any respect as did this younger member, the Canadas would
have been ours.

The transactions which are now to be related, may justly be
ranked among the most pleasing to our national pride, of any
which took place during the war.   The campaign opened with
an affair, which, though comparatively of small consequence,
was characterized by the most brilliant bravery.   This was the
unparalleled defence of Fort Sandusky, by a youth of twenty-one
years of age.   In August, and before the arrival of the Ohio
and Kentucky volunteers, which did not take place until the
following month, threatening movements had been made upon
all the different forts established by the Americans on the rivers
which fall into Lake Erie.   After the siege of Fort Meigs, the
British had received considerable reinforcements of regular
troops, and also of Indians under their great leader Tecumseh.
It was all important to reduce these forts before the arrival of the
American volunteers.   Major Croghan, then commanding at Up-

per Sandusky, having received intimations that the enemy were
about to invest the fort of Lower Sandusky, marched to this
latter place with some additional force. He occupied himself
with great assiduity in placing it in the best posture of defence;
but the only addition of importance, which the time would
allow him to make, was a ditch six feet deep and nine feet wide,
outside the stockade of pickets by which the fort was enclosed.
He had but one six-pounder; and about one hundred and sixty
men, consisting of some regulars, and of detachments of the
Pittsburgh and Petersburgh volunteers: while his slight and
hastily constructed fortifications afforded but a weak defence
against artillery. General Harrison, not conceiving it practicable to defend the place, ordered young Croghan to retire on
the approach of the enemy, after destroying the works. By a
despatch, which was intended to fall into the hands of the enemy, the latter declared his unwillingness to obey, as he was
able to defend the fort. This reaching the general, he sent for
Croghan, and, on receiving satisfactory explanations, fully
authorised him to make the attempt.

On the 1st of August, general Proctor, having left a large
body of Indians under Tecumseh to keep up the appearance
of a siege of Fort Meigs, arrived at Sandusky with about five
hundred regulars, seven hundred Indians, and some gun boats.
After he had made such dispositions of his troops as rendered
the retreat of the garrison impracticable, he sent a flag by colonel Elliot and major Chambers, demanding a surrender, accompanied with the usual threats of butchery and massacre if the
garrison should hold out. Croghan, who found that all his companions, chiefly striplings like himself, would support him to
the last, returned a spirited answer: to the effect that, "when
the fort should be taken, there would be none left to massacre;
as it would not be given up while a man was able to fight."

When the flag returned, a brisk fire was opened from six-
pounders in the boats and a howitzer, which was kept up during
the night. In the morning, it was discovered that three sixes
had been planted, under the cover of the night, within two hundred and fifty yards of the pickets; which shortly after commenced firing, but with little effect. About four o'clock in the
afternoon, the enemy having concentrated his fire against the
northwest angle of the fort, with the intention of making a breach,
it was immediately strengthened by means of bags of flour and
sand. At the same time, the six-pounder, the only piece of
artillery in the fort, was carefully concealed in the bastion which
covered the point to be assailed, and loaded with slugs and
grape. About five hundred of the enemy now advanced to

assail the part where it was supposed the pickets had been injured : at the same time making several feints, to draw the attention of the besieged from the real point of attack. Their force being thus disposed, a column of three hundred and fifty men, which were so enveloped in smoke as not to be seen until they approached within twenty paces of the lines, advanced rapidly to the assault. A fire of musquetry from the fort, threw them for a moment into confusion , but they were quickly rallied by colonel Short their commander, who sprung over the outer works into the ditch, and commanded his men to follow, crying out, " Give the d——d Yankees no quarter !" Scarcely had these words escaped his lips, when the six-pounder opened upon them a most destructive fire ; killing their barbarous leader and twenty others, and wounding as many more. A volley of musketry was, at the same time, fired upon those who had not descended. The officer who succeeded Short, exasperated at being thus treated by a few boys, formed the broken column anew, and again rushed to the ditch. The six-pounder was a second time played on them with the same success as before ; and the small arms were discharged so rapidly, that they were again thrown into confusion, and, in spite of the exertions of their officers, fled to an adjoining wood, whither they were soon followed by the Indians. Shortly afterwards, the assailants abandoned the attack. Panic-struck, they retreated to their boats, in sullen silence ; scarcely daring to cast their eyes towards the fatal spot, where they had been so signally chastised by a force scarce a tenth of theirs in number.

If this gallant defence deserved the applause of the brave, the subsequent conduct of the besieged was well entitled to the praise of every friend of humanity. Forgetting in a moment that they had been assailed by merciless foes, who sought to massacre them without regarding the laws of honourable war, the little band felt only the desire of relieving the wounded men who had been left behind by the enemy. During the night, provisions and buckets of water were handed over the pickets ; and, by an opening which was made, many of the sufferers were taken in and immediately supplied with surgical aid : and this, although a firing was still kept up with small arms by the enemy for a part of the time.

The loss of the garrison amounted to one killed and seven wounded. That of the enemy could not have been less than one hundred and fifty : upwards of fifty were found in and about the ditch. It was discovered next morning, that the enemy had hastily retreated ; leaving a boat, a considerable quantity of military stores, and upwards of seventy stand of arms. The

Americans were engaged, during the day, in burying the dead with the honours of war, and providing for the wounded.

This exploit called forth the admiration of all parties throughout the United States. Croghan, together with his companions, captain Hunter, lieutenants Johnson and Baylor, and ensigns Shipp and Duncan (the present governor of Illinois) of the Seventeenth regiment; Anthony and Anderson, of the Twenty-fourth; and Meeks, of the Seventh; and the other officers and volunteers, were highly complimented by general Harrison. They afterwards received the thanks of congress. Croghan was promoted to the rank of lieutenant-colonel, and was presented with an elegant sword by the ladies of Chillicothe.

Soon after this affair, Tecumseh, having raised the siege of Fort Meigs, followed Proctor to Detroit; and all hope was given up by the enemy of reducing the American forts, until they could gain the ascendency on the lake.

The utmost exertions had been made, in the meanwhile, by captain Perry, to complete the naval armament on Lake Erie. By the 2d of August, the fleet was equipped; but some time was lost in getting several of the vessels over the bar at the mouth of the harbour of Erie. On the 4th, he sailed in quest of the enemy; but not meeting him, he returned on the 8th. After receiving a reinforcement of sailors brought by captain Elliot, he again sailed on the 12th, and on the 15th anchored in the bay of Sandusky. Here he took in about twenty volunteer marines, and again went in search of the enemy; and after cruising off Malden, retired to Put-in-Bay, a distance of thirty miles. His fleet consisted of the brig Lawrence, his flag vessel, of twenty guns; the Niagara, captain Elliot, of twenty; the Caledonian, lieutenant Turner, of three, the schooner Ariel, of four: the Scorpion, of two; the Somers, of two guns and two swivels; the sloop Trippe, and schooners Tigress and Porcupine, of one gun each: amounting in all to nine vessels, fifty-four guns and two swivels. On the morning of the 10th of September, the enemy was discovered bearing down upon the American squadron, which immediately got under weigh, and stood out to meet him. The Americans had three vessels more than the British; but this advantage was fully counterbalanced by the size, and the number of guns. of those of the enemy. The fleet of the latter consisted of the Detroit, commodore Barclay, of nineteen guns and two howitzers; the Queen Charlotte, captain Finnis, of seventeen guns; the schooner Lady Prevost, lieutenant Buchan, of thirteen guns and two howitzers; the brig Hunter, of ten guns; the sloop Little Belt, of three guns; and

N*

the schooner Chippewa, of one gun and two swivels : in all, six vessels, sixty-three guns, four howitzers and two swivels.

When the Americans stood out, the British fleet had the weather gage ; but the wind soon after changed, and brought the American fleet to windward. The line of battle was formed at eleven ; and at fifteen minutes before twelve, the enemy's flag ship, and the Queen Charlotte, opened their fire upon the Lawrence ; which she sustained for ten minutes, before she was near enough for her guns, which were carronades, to return it. She continued to bear up, making signals for the other vessels to hasten to her support; and at five minutes before twelve, brought her guns to bear upon the enemy. Unfortunately, the wind being light, the smaller vessels of the squadron could not come up to her assistance ; and she was compelled to contend, for two hours, with two ships each nearly equal to her in force. The contest was, notwithstanding, maintained by her with unshaken courage, and with a coolness which deserves the highest admiration. By this time the Lawrence had become entirely unmanageable. Every gun in the brig being dismounted ; and with the exception of four or five, her whole crew either killed or wounded ; Perry determined to leave her. With a presence of mind which drew forth the praise of the gallant officer to whom he was opposed, he sprung into his boat, and heroically waving his sword, passed unhurt to the Niagara, carrying his flag with him. At the moment he reached the Niagara, the flag of the Lawrence came down. She was utterly unable to make further resistance ; and it would have been a wanton waste of the remaining lives, to continue the contest. Captain Elliot now left the Niagara, with the view of bringing up the rest of the fleet ; while Perry again bore down among the enemy in a ship which had as yet taken no share in the action. As he passed ahead of the Detroit, Queen Charlotte and Lady Prevost, he poured into each a broadside from his starboard side ; and from his larboard fired into the Chippewa and Little Belt. To one of the vessels—the Lady Prevost, which he approached within half pistol shot, the fire was so destructive, that her men were compelled to run below. At this moment the wind freshening, the Caledonia came up, and opened her fire ; and several others of the squadron were enabled soon after to do the same. For a time, this novel and important combat raged with indescribable violence and fury. The result of a campaign, the command of a sea, the glory and renown of two rival nations matched for the first time in squadron, were at issue. The contest was not long doubtful. The Queen Charlotte, having lost her captain and all her principal officers, by some mischance ran foul of the Detroit. By this accident the greater part of their guns were rendered useless; and the two ships were now in turn compelled to sustain an incessant fire from the Niagara, and the other vessels of the American squadron. The flag of captain Barclay soon struck; and the Queen Charlotte, the Lady Prevost, the Hunter and the Chippewa surrendered in immediate succession: the Little Belt attempted to escape, but was pursued by two gun boats and captured.

Thus, after a contest of three hours, was a naval victory achieved, in which every vessel of the enemy was captured. If any thing could enhance its brilliancy, it was the modest manner in which it was announced by the incomparable Perry: WE HAVE MET THE ENEMY, AND THEY ARE OURS, were his words. Great Britain had already been defeated in single combat; she was now beaten in squadron. The carnage in this affair was very great in proportion to the numbers engaged. The Americans had twenty-seven killed, and ninety-six wounded: among the former, were lieutenant Brooks of the marines, and midshipman Laub; among the latter, lieutenant Yarnall, sailing-master Taylor, purser Hamilton and midshipmen Claxton and Swartwout. The loss of the British was about two hundred in killed and wounded; many of whom were officers: and the prisoners, amounting to six hundred, exceeded the whole number of the Americans. Commodore Barclay, a gallant sailor, one of whose arms had been shot off at the battle of Trafalgar, was severely wounded in the hip, and lost the use of his remaining arm.

The news of this event was received with unbounded demonstrations of joy. All party feelings were for a moment forgotten; and the glorious occurrence was celebrated by illuminations and festivals, from one end of the continent to the other.

It is highly gratifying to know, that the treatment of the British prisoners was such, as to call forth their thanks. Captain Barclay declared, that " the conduct of commodore Perry towards the captive officers and men, was sufficient, of itself, to immortalize him."

The Americans having thus obtained possession of the lake, active preparations were immediately made for expelling Proctor from Malden and for the recovery of Detroit. General Harrison now called on governor Meigs for a portion of the Ohio militia, spoken of in a former page; the whole of which had not as yet been disbanded. On the 17th of September, four thousand volunteers, the flower of Kentucky, with the venerable governor of that state, Isaac Shelby, the hero of King's Mountain, at their head, arrived at the camp. Thus reinforced, general Harrison determined to embark the infantry on board the fleet for Malden; and directed colonel R. M. Johnson to proceed with his mounted regiment of Kentuckians to Detroit by land. The latter accordingly marched, but on approaching the river Raisin, they halted some time to contemplate the tragic spot. The feelings which they experienced on this occasion cannot be described; for many of them had lost friends and relations here. The mourners collected the still unburied bones of the victims, and consigned them to one common grave, with the most affecting demonstrations of grief.

On the 27th, the troops were received on board, and on the same day reached a point below Malden. The British general had in the meanwhile destroyed the fort and public stores, and had retreated along the Thames, towards the Moravian villages, together with Tecumseh's Indians. When the American army arrived at Malden, a number of females came out to implore the protection of their general. This was unnecessary; for general Harrison had given orders that even Proctor, if taken, should not be hurt; and governor Shelby had issued an address to the Kentucky volunteers, in which he said, " while the army remains in this country, it is expected that the inhabitants will be treated with justice and humanity, and their property secured from unnecessary and wanton injury."

On the 29th, the army reached Detroit, where it was joined on the following day by colonel Johnson's regiment. It was now resolved by Harrison and Shelby, to proceed immediately in pursuit of Proctor. On the 2d of October, they marched, with about three thousand five hundred men, selected for the purpose, consisting chiefly of colonel Ball's dragoons, colonel Johnson's regiment, and other detachments of Governor Shelby's volunteers. The heroic Perry and general Cass accompanied general Harrison as volunteer aids. They moved with such rapidity, that on the first day they travelled the distance of twenty-six miles. The next day they captured a lieutenant of dragoons and eleven privates, from whom they learned that Proctor had no certain knowledge of their approach. On the 4th, having reached Chatham, seventeen miles above Lake St Clair, they were detained some time by a deep creek, one of the branches of the river Thames, the bridge over which had been partly destroyed by the retreating enemy. While the bridge was being repaired, some Indians commenced an attack from the opposite bank; but were soon dispersed by colonel Johnson, and the artillery of colonel Wood. Here, the Americans found two thousand stand of arms and a quantity of clothing; and, crossing the creek, pursued the enemy four miles up the Thames, took several pieces of cannon, and obliged them to destroy three vessels containing public stores. On the 5th, the pursuit was renewed, when, after capturing provisions and ammunition to a considerable amount, they reached the place where the enemy had encamped the night before. Colonel Wood was now sent forward by the commander in chief, to reconnoitre the British and Indian forces; and he very soon returned with information, that they had made a stand a few miles distant, and were ready for action. General Proctor had drawn up his regular forces, across a narrow strip of land covered with beach trees, flanked on one side by a swamp and on the other by the river, their left resting on the river supported by the larger portion of their artillery, and their right on the swamp. Beyond the swamp, and between it and another morass still further to the right, were the Indians under Tecumseh. This position was skilfully chosen by Proctor, with regard to locality, and the character of his troops; but he committed an irreparable oversight in neglecting to fortify his front by a ditch or abatis, and in drawing up his troops " in open order, that is, with intervals of three or four feet between the files"—a mode of array which could not resist a charge of cavalry. His whole force consisted of about eight hundred regular soldiers and two thousand Indians.

The American troops, amounting to something more than three thousand men, were now disposed in order of battle. General Trotter's brigade constituted the front line; general King's brigade formed a second line, in the rear of general Trotter; and Chiles's brigade was kept as a corps of reserve. These three brigades were under the command of major general Henry. The whole of general Desha's division, consisting of two brigades, was formed en potence on the left of Trotter's brigade. Each brigade averaged five hundred men. The regular troops, amounting to one hundred and twenty men, were formed in columns, and occupied a narrow space between the road and the river, for the purpose of seizing the enemy's artillery, should opportunity offer. General Harrison had at first ordered colonel Johnson's mounted men to form in two lines, opposite to the Indians; but he soon observed that the underwood here was too close for cavalry to act with any effect. Aware of the egregious error committed by Proctor as above mentioned; and well knowing the dexterity of backwoodsmen in riding, and in the use of the rifle, in forest ground: he immediately determined that one battalion of the mounted regiment should charge on the British regulars. The other, under the immediate command of colonel Johnson, was left to confront the Indians. The requisite arrangements having been made, the army had moved forward but a short distance, when the enemy fired. This was the signal for our cavalry to charge; and although the men and horses in the front of the column at first recoiled, they soon recovered themselves, and the whole body dashed through the enemy with irresistible force. Instantly forming in the rear of the British, they poured on them a destructive fire, and were about to make a second charge; when the British officers, finding it impossible, from the nature of the ground and the panic which prevailed, to form their broken ranks, immediately surrendered.

On the left, the battle was begun by Tecumseh with great fury. The galling fire of the Indians did not check the advance of the American columns; but the charge was not successful, from the miry character of the soil and the number and closeness of the thickets which covered it. In these circumstances, colonel Johnson ordered his men to dismount, and leading them up a second time, succeeded, after a desperate contest, in breaking through the line of the Indians and gaining their rear. Notwithstanding this, and that the colonel now directed his men to fight them in their own mode, the Indians were unwilling to yield the day; and quickly collecting their principal strength on the right, attempted to penetrate the line of infantry commanded by general Desha. At first they made an impression on it; but they were soon repulsed by the aid of a regiment of Kentucky volunteers led on by the aged Shelby, who had been posted at the angle formed by the front line and Desha's division. The combat now raged with increasing fury; the Indians, to the number of twelve or fifteen hundred, seeming determined to maintain their ground to the last. The terrible voice of Tecumseh could be distinctly heard, encouraging his warriors : and although beset on every side except that of the morass, they fought with more determined courage than they had ever before exhibited. An incident, however, now occurred which eventually decided the contest. The gallant colonel Johnson having rushed towards the spot where the Indians, clustering around their undaunted chief, appeared resolved to perish by his side; his uniform, and the white horse which he rode, rendered him a conspicuous object. In a moment his holsters, dress and accoutrements were pierced with a hundred bullets; and he fell to the ground severely wounded. Tecumseh, meanwhile, was killed in the melee. After the rescue and removal of the wounded colonel, the command devolved on major Thompson. The Indians maintained the fight for more than an hour; but no longer hearing the voice of their great captain, they at last gave way on all sides. Near the spot where this struggle took place, thirty Indians and six whites were found dead.

Thus fell Tecumseh, one of the most celebrated warriors that ever raised the tomahawk against us; and with him faded the last hope of our Indian enemies. This untutored man was the determined foe of civilization, and had for years been labouring to unite all the Indian tribes in resisting the progress of our settlements to the westward. Had such a man opposed the European colonists on their first arrival, this continent might still have been a wilderness. To those who prefer a savage, uncultivated waste, inhabited by wolves and panthers, and by men more savage still, to the busy city; to the peaceful hamlet and cottage; to Christianity, science and the comforts of civilization: to such, it may be a source of regret that Tecumseh came too late. But to all others, it must be a just cause of felicitation, that he was the champion of barbarism at a period when he could only draw down destruction on his own head. Tecumseh fell respected by his enemies, as a great and magnanimous chief. Although he seldom took prisoners in battle, he was merciful to those that had been taken by others; and, at the defeat of Dudley, actually put to death a chief whom he found engaged in the work of massacre. He had been in almost every engagement with the whites since Harmer's defeat in 1791, although at his death he scarcely exceeded forty years of age. Tecumseh had received the stamp of greatness from the hand of nature; and had his lot been cast in a different state of society, he would have shone as one of the most distinguished of men. He was endowed with a powerful mind, and with the soul of a hero. There was an uncommon dignity in his countenance and manners: by the former he could easily be discovered, even after death, among the rest of the slain, for he wore no insignia of distinction. When girded with a silk sash, and told by General Proctor that he was made a brigadier general in the British service for his conduct at Brownstown and Magagua, he refused the title. Born without title to command; such was his native greatness, that every tribe yielded submission to him at once, and no one ever disputed his precedence. Subtle and fierce in war, he was possessed of uncommon eloquence. Invective was its chief merit, as we had frequent occasion to experience. He gave a remarkable instance of its power in the reproaches which he applied to general Proctor, in a speech delivered a few days before his death; a copy of which was found among the papers of the British officers. His form was uncommonly elegant. His stature was about six feet, and his limbs were perfectly proportioned.

In this engagement, the British loss was, nineteen regulars killed, fifty wounded, and about six hundred taken prisoners. The Indians left one hundred and twenty on the field. The American loss, in killed and wounded, amounted to upwards of fifty; seventeen of the slain were Kentuckians, and among them was colonel Whitely, a soldier of the revolution, who served on this occasion as a private. He by some was supposed to have killed Tecumseh; while others affirmed that colonel Johnson was the person. Several pieces of brass cannon, the trophies of our revolution, and which had been surrendered by Hull at Detroit, were once more restored to our country. General Proctor had basely deserted his troops as soon as the charge was made; and though hotly pursued, was enabled, by means of swift horses and his knowledge of the country, to escape down the Thames. His carriage, with his private papers, however, was taken.

By this splendid achievement, general Harrison rescued the whole northwestern frontier from the depredations of the savages and the horrors of war   The national gratitude burst out in one loud voice of applause.   He was complimented by congress and by various public bodies; and a distinguished public man asserted, on the floor of the national house of representatives, that his victory " was such as would have secured to a Roman general, in the best days of the republic, the honours of a triumph "

The time had now come, which would prove whether the stigma cast upon the chivalrous people of Kentucky by Proctor, in order to hide his own conduct, was founded in truth.   It was now to be seen whether, to use the words of Proctor, they were a " ferocious and mortal foe, using the same mode of warfare, with the allies of Britain."   The recollection of the cruelties at the river Raisin might have justified revenge; and the instruments of those deeds were now at their disposal : for, bereft of hope by this signal defeat and the loss of their great leader, the savages had sued for peace, and as an earnest of their sincerity, offered to raise their tomahawks on the side of the United States, and to execute on the British captives the same atrocities they had perpetrated on the Americans.

But the Kentuckians, as might have been expected, forbore even a word or a look of reproach to their prisoners.   The latter were distributed in small parties in the interior towns; and although extremely insulting in their deportment, were not only treated with humanity, but in many places actually fed with dainties by the humane inhabitants.   This treatment was carried to an extreme which might properly have been termed foolish, had it not been a noble retaliation for what our countrymen were at that moment enduring in the British dungeons on the land, and in their floating prisons on the sea.

Nor was the treatment of the conquered savages less generous.   Peace was granted to them, and during the succeeding winter they were actually supported at the public expense. They were obligated to raise the tomahawk against their former friends, but were forbidden to assail the defenceless and the noncombatant.

Security having thus been restored to our frontier, the greater part of the volunteers were permitted to return home; and Harrison, after stationing general Cass at Detroit with about one thousand men, on the 23d of October proceeded, according to his instructions, with the remainder of his force, to join the Army of the Centre at Buffalo.   Shortly before his departure an interesting correspondence took place between him and general Vincent, growing out of a request by the latter, that the British prisoners in his possession might be treated with humanity. General Harrison, after assuring him that such a request was unnecessary, referred him to the prisoners themselves for information on this score.   He then took occasion to go into a minute detail of the violations of the laws of civilized warfare committed by the British and Indians.   He painted the scenes of the river Raisin, the Miami, and other places, the atrocity of which general Proctor had attempted to palliate by the utterance of a slander on the Western people: and at the same time stated, that in no single instance had the British had occasion to complain of a deviation from civilized warfare on our part.   For the truth of these facts, he appealed to the personal knowledge of general Vincent.   General Harrison said, that, in his treatment of British prisoners, he acted purely from a sense of humanity, and not on the principle of reciprocity; and as there were still a number of Indians in the employment of the British, he begged to be informed explicitly, whether these allies would be kept in restraint for the future, or whether general Vincent would still permit them to practise their usual cruelties.   "Use, I pray you," said he, "your authority and influence to stop the dreadful effusion of innocent blood which proceeds from the employment of those savage monsters, whose aid, as must now be discovered, is so little to be depended on when most wanted, and which can have so trifling an effect on the issue of the war."

The reply of general Vincent, like that of sir Sydney Beck-

o

with, was vague and evasive. He expressed himself perfectly satisfied with the assurances as to the treatment of the prisoners, but declined saying any thing on the other topics; it was beyond his power to give an *explicit answer ;* but he pledged his honour, that, to the utmost of his power, he would join with general Harrison in alleviating the calamities of the war.

CHAPTER XII.

Preparations for invading Canada—General Armstrong appointe   cretary of War —General Wilkinson takes command of the Troops on the Niagara, and General Hampton of those at Plattsburg—Rendezvous of the American Forces at Grenadier Island—General Wilkinson descends the St Lawrence—British harass the American Army—Battle of Chrystler's Field—General Hampton descends the Chateaugay River—Is attacked by the British—Repulses them and retreats—His Inability or Unwillingness to co-operate with General Wilkinson—Both American Armies go into Winter Quarters—Failure of the Expedition against Montreal—Cruise of Commodore Chauncey on Lake Ontario—He captures five armed British Schooners—Burning of Newark by the Americans—British Retaliation—Fort Niagara surprised—Destruction of Lewistown, Buffalo and other places.

THE glorious result of the operations of the Northwestern army, and the splendid victory on the lake, opened the way to a more effectual invasion of Canada. We were now in the situation in which we should have been at the commencement of the war, had Hull's expedition proved successful; with this difference, however: that the British had been enabled to provide for defence, by collecting troops, disciplining militia and fortifying the borders of the St Lawrence; while, on the other hand, the American force on the frontier was more formidable than it had been at any time previously during the war, and was commanded by officers whose merits had been tried in actual service—in addition to which, the greater part of the neighbouring Indians had declared against the British. The public mind was now so elated by the brilliant victories to the westward, that it was thought the tide of fortune had at last turned in our favour, and confidently expected that the administration would attempt the conquest of Canada in good earnest.

At the head of the war department now, was a man of energy and talents, who had resided a considerable period in Europe;

and, from the known bias of his mind to military affairs, it was presumed that he had availed himself to the utmost of the opportunities there within his reach of increasing his military knowledge. Much was expected from him; and it was soon acknowledged that some improvements had been introduced into his department. General Armstrong, knowing the sanguine anticipations which prevailed through the country, proceeded to the northern frontier, with a plan of operations digested in the cabinet, which he intended to have carried into effect under his own eye. The plan, as afterwards developed, was in itself judicious; but there was not perhaps, in its execution, sufficient allowance for a change of circumstances. Although the season was far advanced, much might yet be done: but, to satisfy the public expectations, to the extent to which the successes of Harrison had raised them, was scarcely possible. Little short of the complete conquest of Canada would suffice; while but vague ideas of the nature of the enterprise, and of the difficulties to be encountered, prevailed through the great body of the nation. The people in this country, like other sovereigns, regarding only the success or failure of their agents, seldom weigh the peculiar circumstances under which they may have acted. To the desire of doing too much, may perhaps be attributed the misfortunes experienced in a campaign, the chief incidents of which are now about to be related.

On the resignation of general Dearborne, general Wilkinson then in the southern section of the union, was appointed to succeed him as commander-in-chief of the American forces. Public opinion was much divided, as to some points in the previous character and conduct of this officer; but it was generally admitted, that he possessed a greater share of military science than any one in the army. The general, on taking the command, issued an order which gave universal satisfaction; and it was expected that, for the sake of firmly establishing his reputation, he would endeavour to render some signal service to his country. The force under his command on the Niagara, amounted to eight thousand regulars, besides those under Harrison,* which were expected to arrive in the course of the month of October. General Wade Hampton, a distinguished

* This officer shortly afterwards retired from the army, in consequence of being placed in an inferior command; and his services were thus lost to the country for the remainder of the war. For the act which induced general Harrison to take this step, the administration, and particularly the secretary of war, were much and justly blamed.

revolutionary officer, also called from the south, was appointed
to the command of the Army of the North, then encamped
at Plattsburg, on Lake Champlain, and amounting to about four
thousand men. As the season for military operations was
rapidly drawing to a close, it was important that no time
should be lost, and measures were immediately taken for carrying into effect the projected invasion. The outline of the
plan which had been adopted, was: to descend the St Lawrence, passing the British posts without attempting their capture; to form a junction with general Hampton at some designated point on the river; and then with the united forces to
proceed to the Island of Montreal. After which, to use the
language of general Wilkinson, "their artillery, bayonets and
swords must secure them a triumph, or provide for them honourable graves." It is said that a difference of opinion existed
between the general-in-chief and the secretary at war, on this
subject · the former not considering it prudent to leave Kingston and other British garrisons in the rear; and the latter
seeming to think, that as there was no doubt of taking Montreal, all the posts on the river and lakes above that place
must fall of course. The correctness of this conclusion could
not be denied: but as there is a degree of uncertainty in every
human undertaking, it is unwise to make no allowance for
some possible failure; except, indeed, where the party, like
Cæsar, resolves to be great or dead.

The army, which had been distributed in different corps,
and stationed at various points, was now to be concentrated at
some place convenient for its embarkation. For this purpose,
Grenadier Island, which lies between Sackett's Harbour and
Kingston, was selected, on account of its contiguity to the St
Lawrence. On the 2d of October, general Wilkinson left
Fort George, with the principal body of the troops, and soon
after reached the island. Here he occupied himself incessantly in making preparation for the prosecution of his enterprise. He several times visited Sackett's Harbour, the point
at which the troops first arrived, and whence, after receiving the
necessary supplies, they proceeded to the place of rendezvous. Colonel Scott, whom he had left in command of Fort
George, was ordered to embark, with his regiment of artillery, and colonel Randolph's infantry, and proceed to the
island; while colonel Dennis was left in charge of Sackett's
Harbour. The general having provided boats to transport the
artillery through the St Lawrence, proceeded to put his troops in
motion. By the 23d, the forces thus collected exceeded seven

thousand men, and were composed of colonel Porter's light artillery, a few companies of colonel Scott's, and the whole of colonel Macomb's regiment of artillery, twelve regiments of infantry, and Forsyth's rifle corps. In consequence of the high winds on the lake, which prevailed for several days, it was not until the 25th that the army could get under weigh ; and although the general was suffering from a disorder which rendered his health very precarious, his anxiety induced him to superintend the embarkation in person.

A few days before, intelligence had been received from colonel Scott, that the enemy, in consequence of the departure of the American army from Fort George, had also abandoned that neighbourhood, and was occupied in concentrating his forces at Kingston, in the belief that the latter place was the object of attack. General Wilkinson, to favour this idea, fixed on French Creek, which lay opposite the most proper point of debarkation on the Canada side, as the place of rendezvous for the troops after their entrance into the St Lawrence. Brigadier general Brown, of the regular service of the United States, was ordered forward to take the command of the advance of the army at this place. On the 1st of November, a British squadron made its appearance near French Creek, with a large body of infantry, and attacked the American detachments there ; but a battery of three eighteen-pounders, skilfully managed by captains M'Pherson and Fanning, soon forced them to retire. The attack was renewed the next morning, but with no better success , and as the other corps of the army were now daily arriving, the enemy thought proper to move off. On the 6th, the army was embarked on the river, and in the evening landed a few miles above the British Fort Prescott. After reconnoitering the passage at this place and finding that the fort commanded the river, general Wilkinson directed the powder and fixed ammunition to be transported by land to a safe point below. The troops were also debarked, and marched to the same point ; and it was determined to take advantage of the night to pass with the flotilla, on board of which a sufficient number of men to navigate it had been left. Availing himself of a heavy fog which came on in the evening, the commander-in-chief endeavoured to pass the fort unobserved ; but the weather clearing up, and the moon shining, he was discovered and fired upon by the enemy. General Brown, who was in the rear with the flotilla, thought it prudent to halt, until the night should grow darker. On the setting of the moon, he proceeded down the river, and being again discovered, was exposed to a severe cannonade of three hours. During all this time not one

o*

out of three hundred boats suffered the slightest injury ; and before ten o'clock of the next day, they had all safely arrived at the place of destination. A messenger was now despatched to general Hampton, informing him of the movements of the army, and requiring his co-operation.

The enemy, having by this time penetrated the design of the Americans, endeavoured, assiduously, to counteract it. The descent of our troops was now found to be impeded by considerable bodies of the British, stationed at narrow parts of the river, whence they could annoy our boats within musket shot , and the embarrassment thus occasioned was increased by the illness of the commander-in-chief, which had augmented in the most alarming degree. The army was also delayed for half a day in extricating two schooners loaded with provisions, which had been driven into a part of the river near Ogdensburg, by the enemy's fire. On the 7th, in the morning, a corps of twelve hundred men, under colonel Macomb, was despatched to remove the obstructions to the descent of the army; and at three o'clock he was followed by the main body. On passing the first rapids of the St Lawrence, the barge of the commander-in-chief was assailed by two pieces of artillery, which had not been perceived by colonel Macomb in his march. No injury was done except to the rigging : and the attention of the enemy was soon diverted by lieutenant-colonel Eustis, who returned their fire from some light barges ; while major Forsythe, landing some of his riflemen, attacked them unexpectedly, and compelled them to retreat. The flotilla came-to about six miles below Hamilton ; where the general received intelligence that colonel Macomb had routed the enemy at a block-house two miles below, and that the dragoons attached to the first division of the enemy had been collected at a place called the White House, at a contraction of the river. On the arrival of the flotilla at this place on the 8th, general Brown was ordered to go forward with his brigade, to reinforce colonel Macomb and to take command of the advance ; while the commander-in-chief directed the transportation of the dragoons across the St Lawrence. This latter business was effected during the night.

The British troops which had been concentrated at Kingston, being released from the apprehension of an attack on that place, immediately followed the American army. On the 9th, they had so far gained upon it, that a skirmish was brought on between the American riflemen, and a party of militia and Indians. To be thus harassed by a large body of troops hanging on the rear of an army, is a situation which military men have always carefully avoided; and this, in the present case, was the necessary consequence of withdrawing the troops from above which might have kept the enemy in check. Had two thousand men been stationed in the vicinity of Kingston to threaten it, the enemy would have been compelled to retain a large force at that place; by which means the main body of our army might have passed on in greater safety. In the course of the day, the cavalry, and four pieces of artillery under captain M'Pherson, were ordered to clear the coast below as far as the head of the *Longve Saut*, a rapid eight miles long; and in the evening the army arrived at a place called the Yellow House, which stands near the Saut. As the passage here would be attended with considerable difficulty, from the rapidity and length of the current, it was deemed prudent to wait until the next day; and in the meanwhile it became necessary to use the utmost vigilance.

On the morning of the 10th, general Brown, with the troops under his command, excepting two pieces of artillery and the second regiment of dragoons, was ordered to continue his march in advance of the army. A regard for the safety of the men had induced the commander in-chief to retain as few of them in the boats as possible, during the long and dangerous passage of the rapid, on account of the fire to which they would be subject from the batteries which the enemy had in all probability established along it. The second regiment of dragoons, and all the men of the other brigades, with the exception of a number sufficient to navigate the boats, were placed under the command of general Boyd, and ordered to prevent the enemy, who were still hanging on the rear, from making any advantageous attack. General Brown now commenced his march at the head of his troops, consisting principally of colonel Macomb's artillery, some companies of colonel Scott's regiment, part of the light artillery, the riflemen, and the Sixth, Fifteenth and Twenty-second regiments. It was not long before he found himself engaged with a strong party at a block-house near the Saut, which, after a contest of a few minutes, was repulsed by the riflemen under major Forsythe. In this short engagement, the latter was severely wounded. About the same time some of the enemy's galleys approached the flotilla, then lying at the shore, and commenced a fire upon it, by which a number of the boats were injured; two eighteen-pounders, however, being hastily placed on the land, the fire from them soon compelled the assailants to retire. The day being now too far spent to attempt the passage of the Saut, it was resolved to postpone it until the following morning.

At ten o'clock on the 11th, at the moment that the flotilla was about to proceed, and when at the same time the division under general Boyd, consisting of his own and the brigades of generals Covington and Swartwout, was drawn up in marching order, an alarm was given that the enemy were approaching in column. The commander-in-chief and general Lewis being both too much indisposed to take the command, general Boyd was ordered to face about and attack the advancing foe. The enemy's galleys were at the same time coming down, for the purpose of assailing the rear of the American flotilla. General Boyd now led on his detachment formed in three columns, and ordered a part of general Swartwout's brigade to move forward and bring the enemy into action. Colonel Ripley, accordingly, at the head of the Twenty-first regiment, passed the wood which skirts the open ground called Chrystler's Field, and drove in several of the enemy's parties. On entering the field, he met the advance of the British, consisting of the Forty-ninth and the Glengary regiments ; and immediately ordered a charge. This was executed with such surprising firmness, that these two regiments, nearly double his in number, retired precipitately ; and on making a stand, were a second time driven before the bayonet, and compelled to pass over the ravines and fences by which the field was intersected, until they fell on their main body. General Covington had, before this, advanced upon the right, where the enemy's artillery was posted ; and at the moment that colonel Ripley had assailed the left flank, he forced the right by a determined onset. Success appeared scarcely doubtful ; when, unfortunately, general Covington, whose activity had rendered him conspicuous, became a mark for the sharp-shooters which the enemy had stationed in Chrystler's house, and was shot from his horse. The fall of this gallant officer arrested the progress of the brigade ; and the artillery of the enemy threw it into confusion, and caused it to fall back in disorder. The British commander now wheeled part of his line into column, with the view of capturing some pieces of artillery, which were left unprotected by the Americans. A body of dragoons, under adjutant general Walbach, attempted, in a very gallant manner, to charge the British column ; but from the nature of the ground were not successful. At this critical moment, colonel Ripley, who had been engaged with the enemy's left flank, threw his regiment between the artillery and the advancing column, and frustrated their design. The British fell back with precipitation. The American regiments which had broken had not retired from the field, but still continued to maintain an irregular fight with various success. The Twenty-first having by this time expended its ammunition, and being in an exposed situation, was withdrawn from the position in which it had been placed by colonel Ripley ; and the enemy again attempted to possess themselves of the artillery.   One piece was unfortunately captured by them, in consequence of the death of lieutenant William S. Smith, who commanded it: the rest were brought off by the coolness and bravery of captain Armstrong Irvine.   The action soon after ceased, having been kept up for two hours by undisciplined troops against an equal number of veterans.   The British force consisted of detachments from the Forty-ninth, Eighty-fourth, and One hundred and fourth regiments of the line, and of three companies of the Voltigeur and Glengary corps.   The enemy soon after retired to their camp, and the Americans to their boats.

In this battle the loss of the Americans amounted to three hundred and thirty-nine wounded, and one hundred and two killed.   Among the killed were lieutenants Smith, Hunter and Holmstead: among the wounded, were general Covington, who died two days afterwards ; colonel Preston ; majors Chambers, Noen and Cummings ; captains Townsend, Foster, Myers, Campbell and Murdock ; and lieutenants Heaton, Williams, Lynch, Pelham, Brown and Creery.   The British loss could not have been less than that of the Americans.

Both parties claimed the victory on this occasion : but it was properly a drawn battle ; the British retiring to their encampments, and the Americans to their boats.   Perhaps, from the circumstance that the enemy never again assailed the American army, it may be assumed, that they were defeated.   General Brown had, in the meanwhile, reached the foot of the Rapid, and awaited the arrival of the army.   On the 11th, the army proceeded on its route, and joined the advance near Barnhart.   At this place, information was received which at once put an end to the further prosecution of the design on Montreal.

On the 6th, a few days before the battle of Chrysler's Field, the commander-in-chief had sent orders to general Hampton, to meet him at St Regis.   A letter in reply was received from general Hampton, in which he stated, that owing to the disclosure of the scantiness of general Wilkinson's supply of provisions, and the condition of the roads to St Regis which rendered it impossible to transport a quantity greater than could be carried by a man on his back, he had determined to open a communication with the St Lawrence at Coghnawago. About the time that general Wilkinson was concentrating the

army at Grenadier island, preparatory to the descent of the
St Lawrence, general Hampton, with a view to a readier
co-operation in the contemplated attempt on Montreal, had descended the Chateaugay river from Plattsburg, with the forces
under his command. The British general, perceiving this movement towards Montreal, had collected all his force to oppose it.
On the 21st of October, General Hampton found his road obstructed by fallen timber, and ambuscades of the enemy's militia
and Indians.   A wood of considerable extent lay in advance,
through which it was necessary to pass ; and while the engineers
were engaged in cutting a way through, colonel Purdy, with the
light troops and one regiment of the line, was detached, with
directions to turn the enemy's flank, and then seize on the open
country below.   In this he succeeded, and the army by the
next day reached the position of the advance.   About seven
miles further on the route, was another wood, which the enemy
had felled and formed into an abatis, and filled with a succession of breast-works, the rearmost of which was well supplied with artillery.   General Prevost was understood to have
command of the forces which had these works in charge.   On
the 25th, colonel Purdy, with the first brigade, was ordered to
cross the river and march down on the opposite side, until he
should have passed the enemy, when he was to re-cross and
attack him in his rear; whilst the brigade under general Izard
would assail him in front   Colonel Purdy accordingly crossed
the river; but he had not marched far, when his orders were
countermanded.   On his return, he was attacked by the enemy's
infantry and Indians ; and repelled them, after a short contest
in which they threw his column into some confusion.   At the
same moment they came out of their works in front, and attacked general Izard, but were soon after compelled to retire
behind their defences.   General Hampton, now receiving information that the enemy were obtaining accessions continually,
resolved, by the advice of his officers, to retreat to a position,
which he had occupied some days before, called the Four Cor-
ners.   Here he arrived on the last day of the month.   The
British claimed a victory for this affair; which, they said, was
gained with a very inferior force.   It was not, however, the
intention of general Hampton to penetrate to Montreal, but
merely to divert the attention of the British from the army of
general Wilkinson.   Having accomplished this object, he fell
back to a position whence he could, with greater facility, make
his way to some point on the St Lawrence.   It was then that,
in reply to the order of the commander-in-chief, he despatched

the letter already mentioned, stating the impracticability of a compliance with it. On the receipt of general Hampton's communication, a council of the principal officers was called, at which it was determined that the objects of the campaign were no longer attainable. It was therefore resolved that the army should quit the Canadian side of the St Lawrence, and retire into winter quarters at French Mills on Salmon river. General Hampton, with his troops, soon after followed this example; and, in consequence of indisposition, resigned the command of them to general Izard. Thus terminated a campaign, the issue of which gave rise to dissatisfaction proportioned to the sanguine anticipations which had been indulged.

This unexpected turn of affairs appeared to cast a shade upon all the brilliant successes which had preceded. Much diversity of opinion prevailed as to the causes of the failure, and the parties who ought to bear the blame. General Wilkinson, after the disappointment which he met with in his reinforcement and supplies, could not perhaps with prudence have persevered in the prosecution of the original object of the campaign; and besides, from the state of his health, he was not qualified to carry into execution what would have required the utmost vigour of mind and body. With respect to Hampton, military men will probably say, that it was his duty to have obeyed; but if we place implicit reliance upon the correctness of the facts which he alleged, it will be difficult to condemn his conduct. The presence of the secretary at war, for the purpose of superintending the operations of the campaign, was perhaps more injurious than serviceable. He was by no means in a situation in which he could be considered responsible for the failure of the plan; and yet, in the event of success, he might have claimed the merit of it for his own. It was an unfair and improper interference which ought to be condemned.

While these things were taking place on the land, the commander of our squadron on Lake Ontario was not idle. Commodore Chauncey, it has been seen, after his first attempt to bring the enemy to action, returned to Sackett's Harbour. Being reinforced by an additional schooner, he again sailed on a cruise. On the 7th of September, he discovered the British squadron near the Niagara, and immediately stood for it. Sir James Yeo, on perceiving the Americans, made sail to the northward. He was pursued during four days and nights; but owing to the dull sailing of most of the pursuing vessels, he contrived to keep out of their reach. On the fourth day, off Genesee river, commodore Chauncey took advantage of a breeze which arose, and endeavoured, while sir James lay becalmed, to close with him; but he was not able to accomplish this, as the breeze came up with the enemy when the American squadron was still distant half a mile. After a running fight of more than three hours, the British escaped; and the next morning ran into Amherst Bay. The American commodore, having no pilot, did not think it prudent to follow them; and contented himself with forming a blockade. In this skirmish, the British sustained considerable injury; while that of the Americans was very trifling. The blockade was continued until the 17th of September, when, in consequence of a heavy gale from the westward, the British escaped into Kingston, and the American fleet returned to Sackett's Harbour.

After a few hours delay at Sackett's Harbour, commodore Chauncey again sailed towards Niagara, where he arrived on the 24th of September. On the 19th, he passed sir James Yeo at the False Ducks, but took no notice of him; hoping thereby to draw him out into the lake. On the 26th, the American commodore received information, that the enemy was in York Bay. He therefore made for that place, as fast as his dull sailing schooners would permit; and on the 28th, early in the morning, discovered the enemy in motion in the bay, and immediately run down for his centre. This being perceived by sir James, he stood out and endeavoured to escape to the southward; but finding that the American fleet was closing upon him, he ordered the vessels of his squadron to tack in succession, and commenced a well directed fire at the General Pike, commodore Chauncey's flag ship, with the view of covering his rear. As he passed to leeward, he attacked the American rear; but this part of his plan was frustrated by the skilful manœuvring of Chauncey. By bearing down in line on the centre of the enemy's squadron, he threw them into such confusion, that Yeo immediately bore away, but not before his flag ship, the Wolf, had been roughly handled by that of the commodore. In twenty minutes, the main and mizen top-masts and main yard of the Wolf were shot away; but the British commander, by setting all sail on his mainmast and keeping dead before the wind, was enabled to outstrip the greater part of Chauncey's squadron. The chase was continued until three o'clock, P. M.; the General Pike having the Asp in tow, and, during the greater part of the time, being within reach of the enemy's shot. Captain Crane, in the Madison, and lieutenant Brown, of the Oneida, used every exertion to close with the enemy, but without success. The pursuit was at length reluctantly given up; as it came on to blow almost a gale, and there was no hope of closing with the enemy before he could reach the British batteries, nor without great risk of running ashore. The commodore was justly entitled to claim a victory in this affair. Although the enemy were not captured, they were certainly beaten; two of their vessels had at one time been completely in the commodore's power; and but for his eagerness to close with the whole fleet, they could not have effected their escape. The loss on board the General Pike was considerable, owing to her long exposure to the fire of the enemy's fleet; which was seriously increased by the bursting of one of her guns, an accident by which twenty-two men were killed or wounded. The vessel also was a good deal cut up in her hull and rigging.

Commodore Chauncey, shortly after this affair, communicated with general Wilkinson on the subject of the expedition then on foot; and was advised to continue his watch of the enemy's squadron, and, if possible, to prevent its return to Kingston. In the beginning of October, he again pursued the hostile fleet for several days, and forced it to take refuge in Burlington Bay; and, the next morning, on sending the schooner Lady of the Lake to reconnoitre, he found that sir James had taken advantage of the darkness of the night, and escaped towards Kingston. Much pleasantry was indulged in, at the shyness of the British knight, and his ungallant escape from the Lady of the Lake. The chase was now renewed, and, favoured by the wind, the commodore came in sight of seven schooners belonging the enemy. Before sun-down, three of them struck to the General Pike; another to the Sylph and the Lady of the Lake: and afterwards a fifth to the Sylph. They turned out to be gun vessels, bound to the head of the lake as transports. Two of them were the Julia and Growler, which had been taken from the Americans by the enemy, as mentioned in a previous chapter. On board of the captured schooners were three hundred soldiers, belonging to De Watteville's regiment. It was ascertained that the ship of sir James Yeo, and the Royal George, had suffered very considerable injury, as well as loss in killed and wounded. The enemy's fleet were seen going into Kingston the same evening; and commodore Chauncey remained master of the lake during the remainder of the season.

The consequences of leaving a large force in the rear, and withdrawing the troops from the Niagara, soon began to be felt. General Harrison reached Buffalo some days after the departure of the commander-in-chief; and although directed to follow immediately, he was compelled to wait until sometime in November, in consequence of the deficiency of transports. It was not until general Wilkinson had gone into winter quarters

P

that Harrison embarked; orders having previously been sent for him to remain at Buffalo, which unfortunately did not arrive until after his departure. Fort George was left under the command of general M'Clure, with troops consisting entirely of militia whose term of service had nearly expired. By the 10th of December, his force being reduced to a handful of men, and a considerable body of the enemy being within a few miles of him, he called a council of officers, at which it was unanimously agreed, that the place was no longer tenable. Scarcely had the general time to blow up the fort and pass the river, before the British appeared. His retreat was preceded by an act which excited universal dissatisfaction throughout the United States. On the Canadian side of the Niagara and situated immediately below where Fort George stood, was a handsome village, called Newark. As this place, from its situation, would greatly favour the besiegers, authority had been given by the secretary of war, in case it became necessary for the defence of the fort, to destroy the village. The general, misconceiving these orders, gave twelve hours' notice to the inhabitants to retire with their effects, fired the buildings, and left the village in flames. This act was no sooner known to the American government, than it was promptly disavowed. On the 6th of January following. the order under which general M'Clure conceived himself to have acted, was enclosed to sir George Prevost, with a formal intimation that the act was unauthorised. To this an answer dated the 10th of February was returned by the governor of Canada, in which he expressed " great satisfaction, that he had received assurance that the perpetration of the burning of the town of Newark was both unauthorised by the American government, and abhorrent to every American feeling ; that if any outrages had ensued the wanton and unjustifiable destruction of Newark, *passing the bounds of just retaliation*, they were to be attributed to the influence of irritated passions, on the part of the unfortunate sufferers by that event."

The difference of the principles, on which the war was carried on by the Americans, and by the British, was very striking. The former, uniformly disavowing the system of retaliation, considered the outrages committed by British officers unauthorized, until expressly acknowledged by the British government: while the British, on the contrary, proceeded at once to retaliate any violation of the laws of war, without waiting to inquire whether it was disapproved or sanctioned by our government. Had the Americans followed the example of their enemies, the burning of Newark would have been amply justified by the outrages which had been wantonly committed on Lake Champlain and on the sea-bord; and yet, shortly after the massacre and conflagration of the village of Hampton, when the captain of an American privateer had destroyed some private property in the West Indies, on the score of retaliation, his commission was instantly taken from him, and the act publicly disapproved. Their high sense of honourable warfare, was indeed manifested by the American government in a very remarkable manner. Our humane treatment of British prisoners was acknowledged in the British house of commons even by lord Castlereagh; but he meanly attributed it to fear.

Sir George Prevost, however, without waiting for the disapproval by the American government of the burning of Newark, had proceeded to inflict a retaliation sufficient to satiate the vengeance of the fiercest enemy. At daylight, on the 19th of December, Fort Niagara was surprised by colonel Murray, with about four hundred British regulars, militia and Indians; and the garrison, nearly three hundred in number and principally invalids, was put to the sword. Not more than twenty effected their escape. The commanding officer, captain Leonard, appears to have been shamefully negligent, or perhaps he had been bought by the enemy. He was absent at the time, and had used no precautions against an assault. Having possessed themselves of this post, the British soon after increased their force, and began to lay waste the Niagara frontier with fire and sword. A spirited, but unavailing attempt was made by major Bennett to defend Lewistown from the enemy. This place, together with the villages of Manchester, Youngstown, and the town of the Tuscarora Indians, was speedily reduced to ashes; and many of the inhabitants were butchered. Major Mallory advanced from Schlosser, to oppose the invaders; but was compelled by superior numbers to retreat. On the 30th, a British detachment landed at Black Rock, and proceeded to Buffalo. General Hall had organized a body of militia for the defence of the place, but on the approach of the enemy, they could not be induced to hold their ground, although great exertions were made by majors Staunton and Norton and lieutenant Riddle. This village also was reduced to ashes. The whole frontier, indeed, for many miles, exhibited a scene of ruin and devastation.

Thus was ample vengeance taken for the burning of Newark. Even the British general was satisfied. In his proclamation of the 12th of January, he said, "the opportunity of punishment has occurred, and *a full measure of retribution has taken place;*" and he declared his intention of "pursuing no further a system of warfare so revolting to his own feelings, and so

little congenial to the British character." It would have been
well to ask, whether the conflagrations and pillaging antece-
dently committed on Lake Champlain, and the horrid outrages
in Chesapeake Bay, in the course of the previous summer, were
not an ample set-off for the burning of Newark? Would that
the enemy had so deemed them! The affair continued to be
followed up by subsequent retaliatory measures in other quarters of our extended territory. The devastating decree of admiral Cochrane was founded, in part, on the destruction of
Newark, and the charge that the Americans had burnt a brick
house in Upper Canada, in which they found a human scalp.
It was not enough that the burning of this unfortunate village
should have been reprobated and disavowed by our government; it was not enough that it should be expiated by an extensive course of murder and conflagration, which, according
to the admission of sir George Prevost, amply glutted the vengeance of Britain; but our extensive sea-coast of fifteen hundred miles, and our populous and flourishing cities, must be
given up to destruction and pillage, to fill up the measure of
British retaliation. These events will, however, be detailed in
their proper place.

CHAPTER XIII.

Meeting of Congress—Violence of Party Spirit—Unfriendly deportment of the New
England States—Measures for carrying on the War—Recourse to Taxation—Adop-
tion of means for recruiting the Army—Interesting case of twenty-three American
Prisoners—Arrogance of the British Government—Debates in Congress on the subject
—Result of the Debates—Inquiry by Congress into the manner in which the War had
been carried on by the Enemy—American Commissioners of Peace sent to Gottenburg
—The War gains ground in Public Opinion

ON the 6th of December 1813, the congress of the United
States again assembled. The fever of party spirit had almost
reached its crisis, and the debates in that body were characterized by a virulence and animosity which had never before been
witnessed since the foundation of our government. It would
be improper, at this date, to enter minutely into the discussion
of a subject which at any rate had better be forgotten; and in a

narrative of the events of the war, there is scarcely room for it. On the one side, we find the opposition accused of manifesting a spirit of hostility to their country, and a determined resistance to every measure for carrying on the war, although from the peremptory rejection by Great Britain of the Russian mediation, there existed no hope of peace. On the other hand, the party in power were charged with having ruined the country, destroyed its commerce, involved it in debts which it could never pay, and with being engaged in a guilty project of conquest, under the pretext of vindicating national rights. Every measure with respect to the war was sure to involve in it a consideration of its causes, and the same discussions were renewed until they grew stale by repetition. The opposition to every measure proposed for the prosecution of hostilities turned upon the injustice and wickedness of the war. By some it was denied that any cause of war existed; and by others it was alleged, that although we had cause, the time chosen for declaring it was improper. Among the members in opposition was Mr Webster, of whom it is but justice to say, that his sentiments were uniformly national. The splendid abilities of this gentleman, and the no less splendid but more popular career of Mr Calhoun, first became conspicuous about this period. The opposition of Mr Webster was manly and generous. The support given to the administration by Mr Calhoun, was fervid and powerful. Notwithstanding the warm and often intemperate debates to which these subjects gave rise, the different measures in support of the war continued to be carried by large majorities.

In some of the New England states, the opposition was carried on in a spirit of animosity, which occasioned serious regret in the breasts of the more considerate. Such conduct did not, by any means, meet with the concurrence of the opposition party in other parts of the United States, and certainly not of the great mass of the population of the states in which it was exhibited. The effects of the embargo, which was about this time adopted, and the non-intercourse, it was said, were felt much more severely by the people of New England, than in the southern districts; and the administration was accused of partiality. It was alleged in reply, that the smuggling on the Canada line, and the trade from the northern ports with the British, was carried on to such an extent, as almost to put the government at defiance; and that the British squadron, which had so much harassed the southern coasts, had been in a great measure supplied to the northward, when without such assistance it would have been difficult, if not impossible, for it to remain on our shores.

P*

The war had hitherto been supported by means of loans; as the resources of the government, which were derived exclusively from sales of public lands and from imposts, were altogether inadequate. It was now perceived that even as the security upon which to support a credit these were insufficient; and it was therefore determined to create an internal revenue. This measure, it may said, ought to have been coeval with the war: but the unwillingness of the people to submit to taxation, had already been seen; and hence it was the wish of the administration to avoid it as long as possible. At the declaration of war, it was believed that England would scarcely require us to give proof of our ability to carry it on. The proposals for a cessation of hostilities, and the proffered Russian mediation, kept up the hopes of peace for a time; and a measure disagreeable to the people was therefore delayed until it had become unavoidable, or rather until it was called for by themselves. The expenses of the war had also unexpectedly increased, from the unlooked-for reverses of our arms to the westward, and the consequent necessity for the creation of fleets on the lakes; while the means of meeting them were diminished by the unwillingness of the New England people to join heartily in its prosecution. Had we possessed ourselves of Upper Canada, there is very little doubt that we should have had peace the first year of the war; for it was not until she discovered our weakness on our northern and western frontiers, that England rejected the Russian mediation. Not that the loss of Canada would have been a matter of so much consequence to Great Britain; but that it would have furnished her with conclusive proof, that she could have no hope of severing the union by sowing dissensions between the different states.

The next thing with which the national legislature occupied itself, was the provision of means for filling the ranks of the army. The difficulty of inducing men to enlist continued to increase, and even furnished an argument to prove that the war was not popular. But this could be easily accounted for, from the natural reluctance of all men, not actually urged by their necessities, to enter into a positive engagement to serve as common soldiers for a number of years. Besides, the profession of the common soldier, during our long peace, and on account of the inconsiderable force kept on foot, had sunk very low in the estimation of the people: an enlisted soldier was almost a proverbial name for a lazy, worthless fellow. An idea was also prevalent, that the obligations of the enlisted soldier created a species of slavery; or, at least, were incompatible with repub-

lican freedom : this was sufficient to prevent a great number
of spirited and enterprising young men from entering the army.
The sons of farmers, and young mechanics, were willing
enough to engage as volunteers, or to turn out on a tour of
militia duty ; but to enter into engagements which were permanent, or which they regarded as disreputable, was a very different
matter. The only mode of combating this aversion, was the
offering of extravagant bounties ; not so much with the view of
holding out a bait to cupidity, as to overcome the popular prejudice against this mode of serving the country. A law was
passed, increasing the pay of privates, and giving them bounties
in money and lands to a considerable amount. This, it was
confidently hoped, would produce the desired effect.

During this session a very interesting subject was submitted
to the consideration of congress. Twenty-three American soldiers, taken at the battle of Queenstown in the autumn of 1812,
were detained in close confinement on the charge of being
native-born British subjects, and afterwards sent to England to
undergo a trial for treason. On this being made known to our
government, orders were given to general Dearborne to confine
a like number of British prisoners taken at Fort George, and
to keep them as hostages for the safety of the Americans; instructions which were carried into effect, and soon after made
known to the governor of Canada. The British government was no sooner informed of this, than governor Prevost
was ordered to place forty-six American commissioned and
non-commissioned officers in confinement. Governor Prevost,
in his letter to general Wilkinson upon this subject, stated,
that he had been directed to apprise him, that if any of the
British prisoners should suffer death, in consequence of the
twenty-three American soldiers above mentioned being found
guilty and the known law of Great Britain and of every other
country in similar circumstances being executed on them, double
the number of American officers should suffer instant death : he
further notified the general, for the information of his government, that orders had been given to the British commanders to
prosecute the war with unrelenting severity, if unhappily, after
this notice, the American government should not be deterred
from putting to death the British soldiers now in confinement.
General Wilkinson, in his reply, forbore to animadvert on the
nature of the procedure, but could not help expressing his surprise at the threat by which the British government supposed
the United States could be awed into submission. "The government of the United States," said he, " cannot be deterred by
any considerations of life or death, of depredation or conflagra-

tion, from the faithful discharge of its duty towards the American people." The arrogance and haughtiness of the British officer in holding this language, so far from intimidating a people who are proud of their independence and jealous of their national honour, was only calculated to render resistance more obstinate; and justly excited the indignation of every American. General Wilkinson soon after informed governor Prevost, that, in consequence of orders he had received from his government, he had put forty-six British officers in confinement, to be there detained until it should be known that the American officers were released. On the receipt of this intelligence, the Canadian governor ordered all the American prisoners into close confinement; and a similar step was soon after taken by our government.

This interesting subject gave rise to warm debates in congress. One party insisted that Great Britain had a right to her subjects, in all situations and under all circumstances; that they were in fact her property, and without her consent they never could free themselves from her authority. They contended further, that a man cannot divest himself of his allegiance to the government of the country in which he happens to be born; that although he may leave the country of his birth for a time, he never can expatriate himself. The procedure of our administration, in attempting to prevent the British government from punishing natives of Great Britain naturalized in this country for taking up arms against that power, was condemned. It was immaterial, it was asserted, that such persons had resided among us ten or even twenty years before the war; they must be regarded in the same light as deserters from the British armies. It was answered on the other side, that it ill became Americans to deny the right of expatriation on principle; however we might from necessity yield to the unjust laws of other nations, where the subject is regarded as a slave—for he that has an *owner* whom he cannot change, is indeed a slave. Can it be possible, it was asked, for an American to contend on principle, that a free man cannot change his allegiance, and attach himself to the country of his choice, but that he must for ever drag a chain after him at every remove? Such a doctrine could only originate in that species of slavery called the feudal system; and was indeed closely allied to that of the divine right of kings, or rather of legitimate sovereigns; which goes so far as to assert that no government is lawful, unless it exists in the hands of some one who claims it by birthright—or at least, that this is the only just foundation of European dynasties. If we ought not to reprobate such systems of government, it is permissible to view them with compassion ; for we cannot admire them, without at the same time despising our own noble institutions' The principle of American liberty is, that allegiance is a matter of choice, not force ; and however we may unavoidably give way, where we interfere with the usages of other nations, we ought never to approve the principle. But, it was further contended, that, according to the law and the uniform practice of nations, the right of expatriation was acknowledged. Numerous instances were cited, where the subjects of a nation taken in arms against her, were regularly exchanged. The practice of Great Britain in naturalizing foreigners was also shown : by which they were placed on the same footing with her native citizens, and equally entitled to protection. She could not object to our practice of naturalizing her subjects, as she did the same thing with respect to our citizens. Would *she* not think herself bound to protect her adopted subjects ? If the United States alone naturalized foreigners, the case might then rest on its principles; but when the same thing is done everywhere, who has a right to complain ? A case in point was adduced, to show the practice of the British government, where she was differently situated. She had engaged in her service a regiment of French emigrants, to serve against France; and the question was agitated in the house of commons, whether she should proceed to retaliate, in case the French should put any of them, if captured, to death: and it was agreed that such would have been her duty. She went much further than the American government: lord Mulgrave declared in debate, that, " while he had the command of the British troops at Toulon, and of the French who voluntarily flocked to their standard, under the authority and invitation of his Britannic majesty's proclamation, he had always considered the latter entitled to the same protection in every respect as the British troops." Thus it appeared, that, both in principle and practice, the conduct of Great Britain had been similar to that of the United States.

The result of this debate was a determination to maintain with firmness the position which the administration had taken ; and if Great Britain persisted in the unhappy resolution of rendering the war bloody beyond the example of modern times, as they had already rendered it most barbarous and ferocious, the United States must reluctantly pursue a course to be lamented by every man of common humanity.

Somewhat connected with this. was an investigation, which was set on foot, of the spirit in which the war had been carried on by the enemy. The report of the committee charged with it enumerated the various instances, in which the British military and naval officers had violated all the known usages of civilized nations, in their manner of conducting the war against the United States. The massacres on the river Raisin, the depredations and conflagrations along the lakes before there existed any pretext for retaliation, and the barbarous warfare of the sea coast were spoken of in terms of the strongest reprobation. The war, on the part of Great Britain, had been carried on nearly in the same spirit as at the commencement of our struggle for independence. she appeared to be actuated by a belief that she was chastising rebellious subjects, and not contending with an independent nation. The treatment of American prisoners was the most cruel that can be imagined: several hundred unhappy wretches were shut up, without light or air, in the holds of ships, and in this manner were carried across the Atlantic. In this cruel and unnecessary transportation many of our countrymen perished, and all experienced sufferings almost incredible. Such treatment was contrasted with that received by British prisoners in this country, who in fact were treated more like guests than prisoners. The committee declared itself satisfied, from the evidence submitted to it, that Great Britain had violated the laws of war in the most flagrant manner; and submitted to congress the propriety of devising some mode of putting a stop to such disgraceful conduct. Among the most extraordinary of the enemy's acts, was the putting in close confinement the unfortunate Americans who had been kidnapped by her before the war and compelled to fight her battles. *About two thousand*, who were acknowledged to be Americans, on refusing to fight against their country, were compelled to undergo the same treatment as if they had been prisoners of war. This was indeed accumulating outrage upon outrage. It were well if this had been the whole number; but there was every reason to believe, that by far a larger number were still compelled to obey the officers who had enslaved them, under the pretence that they were not Americans.

It has been mentioned, that Russia had offered her mediation. Under the flimsy pretext of being unwilling to submit her rights to the decision of an umpire, this was declined by Great Britain; although nothing of the kind was proposed, the interference of the emperor of Russia terminating when the contending parties had been brought together. The Prince Regent, however, offered a direct negotiation at London or Gottenburg. This was no sooner made known to our government, than it was accepted. In addition to the commissioners already in Europe under the Russian mediation, the president nominated Henry Clay, Jonathan Russel and Albert Gallatin as commissioners of peace, and they soon after left this country for Gottenburg. Little more was expected, however, from this, than to make apparent the sincerity of the United States in desiring peace; and the conduct of Great Britain soon proved, that her only wish was to keep open a door for negotiation. Subsequent transactions sufficiently proved, that she rejected the Russian mediation solely with the view of gaining time.

Notwithstanding the strength of the opposition on the floor of congress, the war was evidently gaining ground in the estimation of the people. The conduct of the enemy in the prosecution of hostilities had been such as to awaken the patriotism of every American; and his rejection of the Russian mediation surprised many who had confidently predicted a prompt acceptance of it. The victories, which we had obtained at sea, came home to the feelings of the whole nation; and were particularly acceptable to the opposition, who claimed the exclusive merit of them, as having always been the best friends of the navy. Great Britain actually complained, that those whom she had considered her friends in America rejoiced in her naval defeats; and accused them of faithlessness and inconstancy, because they permitted their love of country to overcome their hatred for the men in power. The sentiment, that it becomes every virtuous man to rejoice in the good fortune of his country, however he may dislike the rulers for the time being, was gradually gaining ground. The warlike aspect of every thing around them, interested the ardent minds of the young and enterprizing; the feats of arms daily recounted, awakened a desire for distinction; and the contagion of military pursuits, whether it was to be desired or regretted, began to spread rapidly. The habits of a people, who had been thirty years at peace, and constantly occupied in industrious callings, could not be changed suddenly: but men are by nature warlike, and they cannot exist long in the midst of martial scenes and preparations, without catching their spirit. It was no hazardous prediction, that the enemy of a party, would soon be considered as the enemy of the whole country.

CHAPTER XIV.

War with the Creek Indians—Massacre by the Creeks at Fort Mims—Expedition under Generals Jackson and Cocke against Tallushatches—Battle of Talladega—General Cocke surprises the Indians on the Tallapoosa River—General Floyd's Expedition against the Autossee Towns—Claiborne's Expedition against the Towns of Eccanachaca—General Jackson marches to the relief of Fort Armstrong—His Critical Situation, and Retreat—Defeats an Indian Ambuscade—Indians attack General Floyd at Camp Defiance, and are repulsed—General Jackson gains the sanguinary victory of Horse-Shoe-Bend—Terminates the Creek War and dictates Peace on Severe Terms

OUR affairs to the south had assumed a serious aspect ; and when the northern armies had retired into winter quarters, the public attention was kept alive, by the interesting events which transpired in the country of the Creeks. That ill-fated people, under British influence, had at length declared open war.

In consequence of the threatening appearances to the south, and the hostilities which already prevailed among the Indians inhabiting what was then the Spanish territory, governor Mitchel of Georgia was required by the secretary of war to detach a brigade to the Ocmulgee river, for the purpose of covering the frontier settlements of that state. Governor Holmes, of the Mississippi territory, was at the same time ordered to call out a body of militia, which were to join the volunteers under General Claiborne then stationed on the Mobile. In the course of the summer of 1813, the settlers in the vicinity of that river became so much alarmed at the hostile deportment of the Creeks, that the greater part of them had abandoned their plantations, and sought refuge in the nearest fortresses. Those among the Creeks who were well disposed to the United States, being much the weaker party, had also, in some places, shut themselves up in forts, where they were already besieged by their countrymen.

The commencement of hostilities was signalized by one of the most shocking massacres that can be found in the history of our Indian wars. The settlers, under an imperfect idea of their danger, had thrown themselves into small forts or stations, at great distances from each other, on the various branches of the

Massacre by the Creeks at Fort Mims

Mobile.   Early in August it was ascertained, that the Indians
intended to make an attack upon all these stations, and destroy
them in detail.   The first place which they determined to attempt, was Fort Mims, in which the greatest number of families had been collected.   Toward the close of August, information was brought that the Indians were about to assail this
post; and in the first moments of the alarm caused by this news,
the occupants made some preparations for defence.   It seems,
however, that it was almost impossible to awake them to a sense
of the proximity of their danger.   The fort was commanded
by major Beasley, of the Mississippi territory, a brave officer
and as a private citizen highly respected, and garrisoned by
about one hundred volunteers.   By some fatality, notwithstanding the warnings he had received, the commander was not sufficiently on his guard, and suffered himself to be surprised at
noon-day of the 30th, entirely unprepared.   Scarcely had the
sentinel time to give notice of the approach of the Indians, ere
they rushed, with a dreadful yell, through the gate, which was
wide open.   The garrison was instantly under arms, and the
major flew towards the gate, with some of his men, in order to
close it, and if possible expel the enemy; but he soon after fell
mortally wounded.   After great slaughter on both sides, the gate
was at length closed; but a number of the Indians had taken
possession of a block-house, from which they were not expelled,
until after a bloody contest.   The assault was continued for an
hour, on the outside of the pickets; and the portholes were
several times carried by the assailants, and as often retaken by
those within the fort.

The Indians now for a moment withdrew, apparently disheartened by their loss; but on being harangued by their chief,
Weatherford, they returned with augmented fury to the assault.
Having procured axes, they cut down the gate and made a
breach in the pickets; and, possessing themselves of the area
of the fort, compelled the besieged to take refuge in the houses.
Here a gallant resistance was made by the inmates, until the
Indians set fire to the roofs; when the situation of these unfortunate people became altogether hopeless.   It is only by those
who have some faint idea of the nature of Indian warfare, that
the horror of their situation can be conceived.   The agonizing
shrieks of the unfortunate women and children at their unhappy
fate, might have awakened pity in the breasts of any but Indians.   Not an individual was spared by these monsters: from the
most aged person to the youngest infant, all became the victims
of their indiscriminate butchery; excepting only those who
threw themselves into the flames, to avoid a worse fate! and a

Q

few who escaped by leaping over the pickets. About two hundred and sixty persons, of all ages and sexes, thus perished, including some friendly Indians and about one hundred negroes. The panic which this dreadful massacre excited at the other posts can scarcely be described . the wretched inhabitants, fearing a similar fate, abandoned their retreats of fancied security in the middle of the night, and, in their endeavours to escape to Mobile, encountered every species of suffering. The dwellings of the settlers were burnt, and their cattle destroyed.

On the receipt of this disastrous intelligence, the Tennessee militia, under the orders of general Jackson and general Cocke, immediately marched to the country of the Creeks. On the 2d of November, general Coffee was detached, with nine hundred men, against Tallushatches, a Creek town, and reached the place about daylight on the 3d. The Indians, aware of his approach, were prepared to receive him. Within a short distance of the village they charged upon him with unexampled boldness ; and although repulsed, made a most obstinate resistance. They refused to receive quarter, and were slain almost to a man. Nearly two hundred of their warriors were killed in this affair. The women and children were taken prisoners. The loss of the Americans was five killed and forty wounded.

Late in the morning of the 7th, an express brought intelligence to general Jackson, that, about thirty miles below his camp, at a place called Fort Talladega, a considerable number of hostile Creeks were engaged in besieging some friendly Indians, who must inevitably perish unless speedily relieved. This officer, whose resolutions were executed as rapidly as they were formed, marched at twelve o'clock the same night, at the head of twelve hundred men, and arrived within six miles of the place the next evening. At midnight he again advanced, and by seven o'clock of the following morning was within a mile of the enemy. He now made the most judicious arrangements for surrounding them ; and approached, within eighty yards, almost unperceived. The battle commenced on the part of the Indians with great fury. Being repulsed on all sides, they attempted to make their escape, but found themselves enclosed ; and had not two companies of militia given way, whereby a space was left open through which a considerable number of the enemy escaped to the mountains, they would all have been taken prisoners or destroyed. In the pursuit many were sabred or shot down. In this action the American loss was fifteen killed, and eighty wounded. That of the Creeks was little short of three hundred killed, their whole force exceeding a thousand.

General Cocke, who commanded the other division of the Tennessee militia, detached general White, on the 11th, from Fort Armstrong, where he was encamped, against the hostile towns on the Tallapoosa river. After marching the whole night of the 17th, he surprised a town at daylight, containing upwards of three hundred warriors, sixty of whom he killed and the rest took prisoners. Having burnt several villages which had been deserted by the Indians, he returned on the 23d, without losing a single man.

The Georgia militia, under general Floyd, advanced into the Creek country, about the last of November. Receiving information that a considerable body of Indians were collected at the Autossee towns, of which there were two, on the Tallapoosa river, a place which they called their beloved ground, and where, according to their prophets, no white man could molest them, general Floyd placed himself at the head of nine hundred militia and four hundred friendly Creeks, and marched from his encampment on the Chattahouchee. On the evening of the 28th, he encamped within ten miles of the place, and resuming his march at one o'clock of the next morning, reached the towns about six and commenced an attack upon both at the same moment. His troops were met by the Indians with uncommon bravery; and it was only after a most obstinate resistance, that they were forced, by his musketry and bayonets, to fly into the thickets and copses in the rear of the towns. In the course of three hours from the commencement of the engagement, the enemy were completely defeated, and their villages wrapt in flames. The troops having almost exhausted their whole stock of provisions, and being sixty miles from any depot and in the heart of a country filled with hosts of hostile savages, now returned to their encampment on the Chattahouchee. In this battle eleven Americans were killed and fifty wounded; among the latter the general himself· of the enemy, it is supposed that, besides the Autossee and Tallassee kings, upwards of two hundred were killed.

In the month of December, general Claiborne conducted a detachment, from Fort Claiborne, on the east side of the Alabama river, against the towns of Eccanachaca, on the Alabama river above the mouth of the Cahawba. On the 22d, he came suddenly upon them, killed thirty of their warriors, and after destroying their villages, returned. The loss to the Americans was, one killed and seven wounded.

After the battle of Talladega, general Jackson was left with but a handful of men, in consequence of the term of service of the militia having expired. On the 14th of January 1814 he was fortunately reinforced by eight hundred volunteers from Tennessee, and soon after by several hundred friendly Indians. He was also joined by general Coffee with a number of officers, his militia having returned home. On the 17th, with the view of making a diversion in favour of general Floyd, and at the same time of relieving Fort Armstrong, which was said to be threatened, he entered the Indian country, with the determination of penetrating still farther than had yet been attempted. On the evening of the 21st, believing himself, from appearances, in the vicinity of a large body of Indians, he encamped with great precaution and kept himself in the attitude of defence. During the night, one of his spies brought information that he had seen the enemy a few miles off, and that as they were busily engaged in sending away their women and children, it was evident they had discovered the Americans, and would either escape or make an attack before morning. While the troops were in this state of readiness, they were vigorously assailed on their left flank about daylight. The enemy were resisted with firmness, and after a severe contest, fled in every direction. General Coffee having been detached with four hundred men, to destroy the enemy's camp, with directions not to attack it if strongly fortified, returned with information that it would not be prudent to attempt it without artillery. The attack already made was soon discovered to be a feint; and half an hour had scarcely elapsed, when the enemy commenced a second fierce attack on Jackson's left flank. It seems they had intended, by the first onset, to draw the Americans into a pursuit, and by that means produce confusion; a result which was completely prevented by Jackson's causing his left flank to keep its position. General Coffee, with about fifty of his officers, acting as volunteers now assailed the Indians on the left, and two hundred friendly Indians came upon them on the right; while the whole line in front, after discharging their first fire, resolutely charged, and forced the enemy to fly with precipitation. On the left flank of the Indians the contest was kept up some time longer. As soon as possible, a reinforcement of friendly Indians was sent to general Coffee, with whose aid he speedily compelled the enemy to retire, leaving fifty of their warriors on the ground. In this action general Coffee was severely wounded, and his aid, A. Donaldson, killed.

Being apprehensive of another attack, General Jackson fortified his camp for the night. The next day, fearing a want of provisions, he found it necessary to retreat, and before night reached Enotachopco creek, having passed a dangerous defile without interruption. In the morning he had occasion to cross a second defile, where he had good reason to fear an ambuscade of the enemy. Having made the most judicious arrangements for the disposition of his force in case of attack, he moved forward towards the pass. The advanced guard, with part of the flank columns and the wounded, had scarcely crossed the creek just named, when the alarm was given in the rear. Jackson immediately gave orders for his right and left columns to wheel on their pivots, and crossing the stream above and below, to assail the flanks and rear of the enemy, and thus completely enclose them. When, however, the word was given for these columns to form, and a few guns were fired, they precipitately gave way. This flight had well nigh proved fatal : for it drew along with it the greater part of the centre column, leaving not more than twenty-five men to maintain the ground against overwhelming numbers. All that could now be opposed to the enemy, were the few who remained of the rear guard, the artillery company, and captain Russel's company of spies. Their conduct however was admirable. Lieutenant Armstrong, with the utmost coolness and intrepidity, and aided by a few more, dragged a six-pounder to the top of a hill, although exposed to a heavy fire ; and having gained his position, loaded the piece with grape, and fired it with such effect, that after a few discharges, the enemy were repulsed. They were pursued for several miles by colonel Carrol, colonel Higgins, and captains Elliot and Pipkins. Captain Gordon, of the spies, had partly succeeded in turning their flank, and thus contributed greatly to restore the day. The Americans now continued their retreat without further molestation. In these different engagements, about twenty Americans were killed and seventy-five wounded ; the loss of the enemy in the last engagement was about one hundred and eighty slain.

Meanwhile general Floyd was again advancing towards the Indian territory, from the Chattahouchee river. On the 27th, of January, at Camp Defiance, he was attacked by a large body of Indians, about an hour before day. They stole upon the sentinels, and after firing on them, rushed with great impetuosity towards the main body. The action soon became general The front of both flanks was closely pressed, but the firmness of the officers and men repelled the assaults at every point. As soon as it became sufficiently light, general Floyd strengthened his right wing and formed his cavalry in the rear, and then directed a charge. The enemy gave way before the bayonet, and being pursued by the cavalry, were many of them killed. The loss of general Floyd was seven-

Q*

teen killed and one hundred and thirty-two wounded. That
of the Indians could not be ascertained; although it must have
been very considerable: thirty-seven of their warriors were left
dead on the field.

By this time, it might be supposed that the Creeks had been
satisfied with the experiment of war; but they appear to have
been infatuated to a most extraordinary degree. Under the
influence of their prophets, they were led on from one ruinous
effort to another, in hopes that the time would at last arrive
when their enemies would be delivered into their hands.

General Jackson having received considerable reinforcements
from Tennessee, and being joined by a number of friendly
Indians, set out on an expedition to the Tallapoosa river. He
proceeded from the Coosa on the 24th of March, and reached
the southern extremity of the New Youca on the 27th, at a
place called the Horse-Shoe-Bend of the Tallapoosa. Nature
furnishes few situations so eligible for defence, and here the
Creeks, by the direction of their prophets, had made their last
stand. Across the neck of the peninsula formed by the curva-
ture of the river they had erected a breast-work of the greatest
compactness and strength, from five to eight feet high, and
provided with a double row of portholes, artfully arranged. In
this place they considered themselves perfectly secure; as the
assailants could not approach without being exposed to a double and cross fire from those who lay behind the breast-works.
The area thus enclosed was little short of one hundred acres.
The warriors from the Oakfuskee, Oakshaya, and Hillabee
towns, the Fish Ponds, and the Eupauta towns, were here collected, in number exceeding a thousand.

Early in the morning of the 27th, general Jackson, having
encamped the preceding night within six miles of the Bend.
detached general Coffee, with the mounted men and nearly the
whole of the friendly Indian force, to pass the river at a ford
about three miles below the Creek encampment, and instructed
him to surround the Bend in such a manner, that none of the
savages should effect their escape by crossing the river. With
the remainder of his force, he advanced to the point of land which
led to the front of the breast-work; and at half past ten, planted
his artillery on a small eminence within eighty yards of the
nearest, and two hundred and fifty of the farthest point of the
works. A brisk cannonade was opened upon the centre; and a
severe fire directed with musketry and rifles, whenever the
Indians ventured to show themselves above or outside of their
defences. In the meantime, general Coffee, having crossed
below, had advanced towards the village. When within half a

mile of that part which stood at the extremity of the peninsula, the Indians uttered their yell. Coffee, expecting an immediate attack, drew up his men in order of battle, and in this manner continued to move forward. The friendly Indians had previously taken possession of the bank of the river, for the purpose of preventing the retreat of the enemy: but they no sooner heard the artillery of Jackson, and saw the approach of Coffee, than they rushed to the bank, while Coffee's militia, in consequence, were obliged to remain in order of battle. The former were unable to remain silent spectators : some began to fire across the stream, about one hundred yards wide, while others plunged into the river, and swimming across, brought back a number of canoes. In these the greater part embarked, and landing on the peninsula, advanced into the village, drove the enemy from their huts up to the fortifications, and continued to annoy them during the whole action. This movement of the Indians rendered it necessary that a part of Coffee's line should take their place.

General Jackson finding that his arrangements were complete, yielded at length to the earnest solicitations of his men to be led to the charge The regular troops, led by colonel Williams and major Montgomery, were in a moment in possession of the nearest part of the breast-works: the militia accompanied them with equal firmness and intrepidity. Having maintained for a few minutes a very obstinate contest, muzzle to muzzle, through the portholes, "in which many of the enemy's balls were welded to the American bayonets,"* they succeeded in gaining the opposite side of the works. The event could no longer be doubtful; the enemy, although many of them fought with that kind of bravery which desperation inspires, were routed and cut to pieces. The whole margin of the river which surrounded the peninsula was strewed with the slain. Five hundred and fifty-seven were found dead, besides those thrown into the river by their friends or drowned in attempting to fly. Not more than fifty, it was supposed, escaped. Among the slain were their great prophet Manahoe, and two other prophets of less note. About three hundred women and children were taken prisoners. Jackson's loss was, twenty-six Americans killed, and one hundred and seven wounded, eighteen Cherokees killed, and thirty-six wounded; and five friendly Creeks killed, and eleven wounded.

This most decisive victory put an end to the war with the

* General Jackson's own words.

Creeks ; and broke the spirit and power of these misguided men completely. The victory of Tallushatches, won by Coffee; of the Tallapoosa, by Cocke ; the two victories of general Floyd, on the Georgia side of the Indian territory ; those of Talladega and Enotachopco won by Jackson ; and the fatal battle of the Horse-Shoe-Bend, fought by Jackson and Coffee, may be said to have "cut up the war by the roots."

Jackson soon after scoured the country on the Coosa and Tallapoosa rivers. A party of the enemy on the latter river, on his approach, fled to Pensacola. The larger portion of the Creeks, and among them their most able and sanguinary chief Weatherford, now came forward and threw themselves on the mercy of the victors. A detachment of militia from North and South Carolina, under the command of colonel Pearson traversed the country on the Alabama, and received the submission of a great number of Creek warriors and prophets.

In the course of the summer a treaty of peace was dictated to the Creeks by general Jackson, on severe terms. They agreed to yield a large portion of their country as an indemnity for the expenses of the war ; they conceded the privilege of opening roads through their country, together with the liberty of navigating their rivers; they engaged to establish trading houses, and to endeavour to bring back the nation to its former state; they also stipulated to hold no intercourse with any British or Spanish post or garrison, and to deliver up the property they had taken from the whites and the friendly Indians. The general, on the part of the United States, undertook to guaranty their remaining territory to them, to restore all their prisoners, and, in consideration of their destitute situation, to furnish them gratuitously with the necessaries of life until they could provide for themselves.

It was truly lamentable to contemplate the ruin of tribes which were making such rapid advances to civilization. Their villages were entirely destroyed, and their herds, which had become numerous, were killed by themselves at an early part of the contest.

CHAPTER XV.

Plans of Operations against Canada proposed—General Brown marches to Sackett's Harbour—General Wilkinson retires to Plattsburg—Attacks the British at La Colle and is repulsed—Suspended from the command—Discouraging Difficulties in the Economy of the Army—Smuggling—Unsuccessful Attack by the British at Otter Creek—British Fleet enters Lake Champlain—Lake Ontario—Contest for Superiority there—Gallant Defence of Oswego—British land at Pulteneyville—Blockade of Sackett's Harbour—Engagement at Sandy Creek and Capture of the British there—Death of Colonel Forsythe—of Captain Mallory, in a Skirmish—Colonel Campbell's Expedition against Dover, Canada—Affairs to the Westward—Colonel Baubee taken Prisoner—Gallant Defence by Captain Holmes—Serious Crisis in our Affairs—Napoleon overthrown—Great Britain directs her undivided Energies against the United States—Northern Sea Coast invaded by Commodore Hardy—Attack on Saybrook and Brockway's Ferry—Engagement in Long Island Sound—Ravages at Wareham and Scituate—Attack on Booth Bay repelled—Occupation of all the Islands in Passamaquoddy Bay by the British—Gallant Defence of Stonington—Territory east of the Penobscot River claimed and occupied by the British—Destruction of the Frigate John Adams.

AFTER the failure of the campaign against the British provinces, the army remained in winter quarters, without the occurrence of any incident of much importance, until towards the latter end of February of the year 1814. General Wilkinson had submitted several plans of attack on the different British posts in his vicinity, with the view of cutting off the communication between Upper and Lower Canada, to the department of war. These, however, did not meet the approbation of the secretary, who gave orders that the American force should be withdrawn from its present position : that two thousand men should march under general Brown to Sackett's Harbour, with a suitable proportion of field artillery and battering cannon ; and that the residue should fall back on Plattsburg. The general-in-chief, in obedience to these orders, destroyed his barracks and the flotilla, and retired to the place designated. The British, apprized of his retreat, detached a large force under colonel Scott, of the One hundred and third British regiment, against French Mills, who destroyed the public stores and pillaged the property of private citizens, but, on hearing of the approach of an American force, retreated in

the most precipitate manner. His whole party suffered much
from a severe snow storm, besides losing upwards of two hundred men by desertion, who surrendered themselves to the Americans. It was about this time, that loss by desertions became
one of the serious difficulties which the enemy had to encounter.
The practice of permitting their soldiery to plunder in almost
every instance, may perhaps have arisen from the necessity of
some such indulgence as this, in order to retain them in their
service.

Towards the latter end of March, general Wilkinson determined to erect a battery at a place called Rouse's Point, where
his engineer had discovered a position from which the enemy's
fleet, then laid up at St John's, might be kept in check and
their contemplated movement on Lake Champlain impeded or
prevented. The breaking up of the ice on the lake at an earlier period of the season than usual, defeated his plan. A body
of the enemy, upwards of two thousand strong, on discovering
his design, had been collected at La Colle mill, three miles
below Rouse's Point, for the purpose of opposing him. With a
view of dislodging this party, the commander-in-chief, at the head
of about four thousand men, crossed the Canada line on the 30th
of March. After dispersing several of the enemy's skirmishing
parties, he reached La Colle Mill, a large fortified stone house
situated in the centre of an open piece of ground, and defended by a strong corps of British regulars under the command
of major Hancock. For the purpose of effecting a breach, an
eighteen-pounder was ordered up by general Wilkinson; but
owing to the nature of the ground over which it had to pass,
the transportation was found impracticable, and a twelve and a
five-and-a-half inch howitzer were therefore substituted. These
pieces, under the direction of captain M'Pherson, and lieutenants Larrabee and Sheldon, were posted at the distance of
two hundred paces from the house, and covered by the second
brigade: with part of colonel Clarke's command, under general
Smith, on the right; and the third brigade, under general Bissel,
on the left. Colonel Miller was ordered to take a position
with the Twelfth and Thirteenth regiments which would enable
him to cut off the enemy's retreat; while the reserve, composed
of a select corps of the first brigade, was placed under the
command of general Macomb. These arrangements being made,
the battery opened upon the house. The fire was promptly returned; and, owing to the unavoidable exposure of the American troops, was extremely destructive. Captain M'Pherson
was wounded at the commencement of the attack, but continued
at his post until a second shot had broken his thigh; his next

officer, Larabee, was shot through the lungs; and, lieutenant Sheldon, who kept up the fire until the end of the affair, dbehave in a manner which drew forth the warm praise of his general.

The British commander, perceiving that the Americans persisted in bombarding the house, made a desperate sortie, and several times charged upon the cannon. He was as often repulsed by the covering troops, and was at last compelled to retire into his fortress with loss. It being now found impracticable to make an impression on the unusually thick walls of this strong building, with such light pieces, notwithstanding that they were managed with great skill, the commander-in-chief called in his different parties, and fell back in good order. The loss of the Americans was upwards of one hundred and forty in killed and wounded, that of the British was not ascertained.

The unfortunate issue of this affair, together with the failure of the last campaign, brought general Wilkinson into disrepute with the public. The administration, yielding to the popular voice, thought proper to suspend him from the command, and placed the army under the charge of general Izard. General Wilkinson was afterwards tried, and honourably acquitted of all the charges alleged against him. One great fault inherent in the nature of our form of government, is a disposition to hasty and harsh decision respecting the conduct and character of public men, which no more ceases to be injustice when entertained by ten millions than if by ten individuals. Men are often ruined in public estimation, for slight causes, or for uncontrollable accidents, and they are as often elevated to the highest pinnacle of celebrity, for actions which may be better considered as the effect of chance than the test of merit.

The most discouraging difficulties presented themselves in the economy, equipment and government of the American forces, to the very last hour of the war. The severity of the climate on the borders of the St Lawrence and the lakes to which our tyros were exposed, and their want of the knowledge and experience requisite to render themselves comfortable in camp, were the causes of fatal diseases, which carried off a number greater than fell in battle; and the proportion of sick and unfit for duty was at all times very great. From the want of that system, regularity and strictness which belong to old establishments, there existed at one moment a superabundance of all the necessary munitions, and at another, as great a scarcity. There was no end to the irregular and unforeseen expenses which the government was constantly called upon to incur. Abuses the most vexatious, and which baffled every

effort to reform, were practised in all the subordinate department.   All this must be attributed to the true causes : our
settled habits of peace, and the slowness with which the
organization of military establishments must ever be effected
under a government like ours.   We had yet to learn and put
in practice, the ceaseless and ever varying minutiæ of camp
police.   We had no regular soldiers until almost the close of
the war : and what school of experience had we in which to
train and form them ?   Our subalterns, at first, were generally
men of little education of any kind, and required themselves
the instruction which they undertook to communicate.

To these unavoidable misfortunes, was to be superadded the
disgraceful conduct of many of our frontier inhabitants, who
supplied the enemy with every thing of which they stood in
want.   In spite of vigilant exertion to prevent it, a constant
intercourse was kept up across the Canada line ; and the British
were not only furnished with immense quantities of provisions
without which they could not have subsisted their armies, but
were also regularly advised of each matter of importance which
transpired on the American side.

Shortly after the affair of La Colle, the greater part of the
enemy's force was collected at St John's and Isle Aux Noix,
for the purpose of securing the entrance of the British squadron into Lake Champlain, on the breaking up of the ice.   This
movement was effected early in May.   Some time before this,
on the suggestion of general Wilkinson, commodore M'Donough
had fortified the mouth of Otter river by the erection of a battery on the cape at its entrance, so as to secure a passage to the
lake for his flotilla, which then lay at Vergennes, some miles
higher up the river, waiting for its armament.   This precaution proved of great service.   The commodore had laboured
with indefatigable industry to provide a naval force for this
lake which might cope with that of the enemy ; and the
first object of the British, when they found the navigation open,
was to attempt its destruction, before it could be prepared to
meet them.   On the 12th of May, a bomb vessel and eight
large galleys were stationed by the enemy across the river, for
the purpose of blockading the squadron, and at the same time
to intercept the naval supplies, required for completing its
armament, and which it was supposed would be sent thither by
water.   Captain Thornton of the light artillery, and lieutenant
Cassin with a number of sailors, were ordered to the defence
of the battery ; and indications being at the same time discovered of an attempt by the enemy to assail the battery in the
rear, general Davis, of the Vermont militia, called up part of

his brigade, in order to oppose the landing. At daybreak on the 14th, the enemy commenced an attack upon the works, but were so effectually resisted, that they were compelled to withdraw from their position, leaving behind them in their retreat two of their galleys. Commodore M'Donough had attempted to bring down some of the American vessels to the mouth of the river; but the British squadron had disappeared before he could attain his object. Soon afterwards their whole squadron moved down into the lake, but not without some skirmishing with a small body of militia under general Wright, as they passed Burlington.

While the naval preparations were making on Lake Champlain, the winter and spring were taken up with similar preparations for the coming contest on Lake Ontario. At Kingston, the British were building a ship of extraordinary size; for they no longer trusted, as they had done with other nations, to superior seamanship and valour. Commodore Chauncey therefore was under the necessity of building an additional vessel, for the purpose of maintaining as nearly as possible an equality of force. While these vessels were in course of construction, numerous attempts were made to destroy them, which it required all the vigilance of each party to prevent the other from carrying into effect. On the 25th of April, three of the enemy's boats, provided with the means of blowing up the vessels, succeeded in getting close into Sackett's Harbour; but they were discovered, and fired upon by lieutenant Dudley, the officer then on guard, before they could execute their purpose, and compelled to throw their powder into the lake, in order to prevent the explosion of their own boats. Foiled in this attempt, by the vigilance of the Americans, they next formed the determination to intercept the rigging, naval stores and guns, for the new ship Superior, then on their way. These had been deposited at Oswego; and thither sir James Yeo proceeded with his whole fleet, having on board a large body of troops under general Drummond, for the purpose of storming the fort and capturing so valuable a booty. The British arrived on the 5th of May, and immediately commenced a heavy bombardment of the place. The force at Fort Oswego consisted of three hundred men under the command of lieutenant-colonel Mitchell—a number too small to contend with so superior a force; and had five guns, three of which were almost useless, besides a shore battery of one twelve-pounder. The Americans no sooner perceived the enemy, than they sunk the schooner Growler, then in Oswego creek receiving the cannon; strengthened the garrison of the fort by the addition of the sailors of the Growler, under lieutenant

R

Pierce; and planted all the tents that could be procured on the village side of the creek, in order to give the appearance of a large force of militia. The shore battery was commanded by captain Boyle, seconded by lieutenant Legate. At one o'clock, fifteen barges filled with troops moved towards the shore, preceded by several gun-boats to cover the landing, while the cannonade from the larger vessels was still continued. As soon as the enemy got within range of shot, they were so warmly received by the gun on the shore, that their boats were twice repulsed, one of the largest falling into the hands of the Americans; and at last were compelled to retire to their shipping.

The British squadron now stood off, but this was evidently for the purpose of renewing the attack in such a manner as to render it effectual. On the 6th, the enemy again approached, having resolved to land under cover of their ships. They accordingly kept up a heavy fire for three hours, while their land forces, two thousand in number, under general De Watteville, succeeded in gaining the shore, after a gallant resistance by lieutenant Pierce and his seamen. Colonel Mitchell now abandoned the fort. and joining his corps to the marines and seamen, engaged the enemy's front and flanks, and did great execution. Finding further resistance useless, he fell back, formed his troops, and took up his march to the Falls of Oswego, thirteen miles distant, destroying the bridges in his rear. Hither the naval stores had already been removed, and for all the trouble and loss which they had sustained, the British procured nothing more than the cannon of the fort, a few barrels of provisions and some whiskey. These were purchased with a loss of two hundred and thirty-five men, in killed and wounded. The loss of the Americans was sixty-nine in killed, wounded and missing; among the first, a promising officer, lieutenant Blaney. On the morning of the 7th, the enemy evacuated the place.

On the 15th, a part of this force proceeded to Pulteneyville, and demanded the public stores. The inhabitants were unable to repel the invaders, and the British commodore landed a party of sailors and marines, who indulged themselves in their usual depredations; when general Swift, of the New York militia, opportunely arriving with a part of his brigade, put them to flight. The enemy did not attempt to re-land, but, along with the other vessels of the squadron, sailed for Sackett's Harbour.

The British fleet approached Sackett's Harbour on the 19th; and cast anchor in such a manner as to cut off all communication between that port and other places on the lake. The object of sir James Yeo was to prevent the Superior, which had just been launched, from receiving her armament and equipments, which he conceived must come by water; and consequently, when he heard that she had obtained them from the interior by land conveyance, he broke up the blockade, and returned to Kingston.

In the meantime, some additional cannon and ordnance stores intended for vessels of the American fleet, had arrived at Oswego. Another new ship, the Mohawk, was at this time on the stocks, and in order to prepare her for the lake early in June these supplies were indispensably necessary. Recent experience had taught the American commander to avoid the expense and delay of land carriage; and it was therefore determined, since the British fleet had disappeared, to transport them by water. To deceive the enemy, who had numerous gun-boats hovering about the different creeks, a report was circulated that the stores were to be forwarded to the Oneida Lake. Nineteen barges, then lying at Oswego Falls, were assigned for their conveyance, and were placed under the command of captain Woolsey; and major Appling was despatched by general Gaines, with a detachment to aid in their defence. On the 28th of May, captain Woolsey brought his flotilla down the creek and reached the village of Oswego by sunset. Finding the coast clear, he took advantage of the darkness of the night and put into the lake. The next day he reached Sandy Creek, and ascended it a few miles. A boat was now despatched to look out for the British on the lake, which was discovered by some of their gun-vessels and immediately chased. Major Appling and captain Woolsey determined to draw them into an ambuscade. As had been foreseen, the enemy pushed their gun-boats and cutters up the creek, while a party of them landed and ascended along the bank. The Americans now suddenly rushed upon them, and in a few moments, after one fire by which a number of them were killed and wounded, the whole party, consisting of four lieutenants of the navy, two lieutenants of marines and one hundred and thirty men, were taken prisoners, and all their boats and cutters captured. Major Appling, for this affair, was breveted, and his officers, lieutenants Smith, M'Intosh, Calhoun, M'Farland and Armstrong, and ensign Austin, were publicly thanked. The conduct of captain Woolsey and his officers was not less applauded. A party of Oneida Indians, who had joined the Americans in this affair and had been the first to reach the British after their surrender, were about to commence the mode of warfare practised by the savages in the British service at the river Raisin, Lewistown and Tuscarora; but they were compelled, greatly to their displeasure, to desist. The barges soon after arrived at Sackett's Harbour in safety.

The consequences of this affair were severely felt by the
British : they lost a number of their best seamen and officers, and
commodore Chauncey once more became master of the lake.
He accordingly sailed out, and several times presented himself
before Kingston ; but sir James did not think it prudent to stir
until his large ship of one hundred and twelve guns, then on
the stocks, should be completed. This mode of warfare was
exceedingly expensive to both parties, but especially so to the
enemy: it is ascertained that their outlay was more than twice
what was incurred by us, in consequence of the greater difficulties which attended the transportation of their supplies.

No other event of material consequence transpired in this
quarter, nor on lakes Erie or Champlain, until late in the summer.

In a skirmish on the borders of the latter, colonel Forsythe,
an active but eccentric partizan officer, lost his life.   On the
28th of June he made an incursion as far as Odelltown ; and
having attacked a party of the enemy, retreated, with the view
of drawing them into an ambuscade.   Before he had completely succeeded in this, however, he showed himself and
his men, and a severe skirmish ensued.   In this engagement
seventeen of the enemy were killed ; among the number, the
celebrated partizan officer captain Malloux, a Canadian, who
was shot by lieutenant Riley.   Colonel Forsythe was wounded
in the neck, and died a few days afterwards.   After his death,
the command of his corps devolved on major Appling.

It would be improper, also, to pass unnoticed the following
affair.   Colonel Campbell, having crossed the lake from Erie
with about five hundred men, landed at Dover, a small village
on the Canada side of Lake Erie, and proceeded to destroy the
mills together with the greater part of the private dwellings.
This expedition was undertaken by him without orders ; and as
his conduct in it was generally reprobated, a court of inquiry, at
which general Scott presided, was instituted.   The court decided, that the destruction of the distilleries and mills, as they
furnished the British troops with their necessary supplies, might
be justified by the usages of war ; but the other part of his conduct, although excused in some measure by the example of the
enemy in laying waste and pillaging the villages on the Niagara, was condemned.   The offence of colonel Campbell was
mitigated by his humane treatment of the defenceless part of
the inhabitants.

To the westward, but little of moment transpired during the
remainder of the war, as we were once more in quiet possession
of all our territory except Michilimackinac.   Early in the

spring, however, intelligence was received by colonel Butler, who commanded at Detroit, that a considerable number of regulars, Indians and militia had been collected at the river Thames. Captain Lee, with a party of mounted men, was sent to reconnoitre ; and succeeded in gaining the rear of the British forces unobserved, and making prisoners of several officers—among the rest, of colonel Baubee, who had commanded a body of Indians which took part in the British depredations on the New York frontier.

A gallant affair was soon after achieved by captain Holmes, a youth of promising talents, and brother to the governor of the Mississippi territory. With a party of about one hundred and sixty rangers and mounted men, he was despatched by colonel Butler, on the 21st of February, against some of the enemy's posts. On the 3d of March, he received intelligence, that a British force, then at a village fifteen miles distant, and which afterwards proved to be double his own, was about to descend the river Thames to attack him. Finding himself not in a situation to give battle, from the fatigue which his men had already encountered and his ignorance of the number of the enemy's party, captain Holmes fell back a few miles, and chose a position, in which he was confident of being able to maintain himself, until he could obtain the necessary information. For this purpose, he despatched a small body of rangers, which soon returned, pursued by the enemy, but without being able to learn his force. The British, perceiving the strength of captain Holmes's position, resorted to stratagem for the purpose of drawing him from it. They feigned an attack, and then retreated, taking care not to show more than sixty or seventy men. Captain Holmes pursued, but with caution ; and after proceeding about five miles, discovered their main body drawn up to receive him. Immediately returning to his former position, he disposed his troops in the most judicious manner, and firmly waited for the enemy ; having in front a deep ravine, and the approaches on the other sides being somewhat difficult and also protected by logs hastily thrown together. The attack was commenced at the same moment on every point, with savage yells and the sound of bugles ; the regulars charging up the heights from the ravine, while the other sides were rapidly assailed by militia and Indians. The former approached within twenty paces of the American line, against a very destructive fire ; but their front section being cut to pieces, those who followed severely wounded, and many of their officers cut down, they retired to the woods, which were within thirty paces ; from whence they continued their fire with great spirit. The Ameri-

R*

can regulars, being unsheltered, were ordered to kneel, that the brow of the height might assist in screening them from the enemy. On the other three sides, the attack was sustained with equal coolness, and with considerable loss to the foe. No charge being made, the Americans, behind the logs, could aim their pieces at leisure, with that deadly certainty which belongs to the backwoodsman. The British, after an hour of hard fighting, ordered a retreat. As the night was approaching, captain Holmes thought it unadvisable to pursue them: besides, his men were much fatigued, and many of them had nearly worn out their shoes on the hard frozen ground. The American loss on this occasion did not amount to more than six killed and wounded. According to the statement of the British, their loss was sixty-five in killed and wounded, besides Indians. Captain Holmes soon afterwards returned to Michigan territory; and, in consequence of his good conduct in this affair, was promoted to the rank of major.

Hitherto nothing of moment had occurred, which could have much influence on the final result of the war. On the ocean, it had been glorious for us; on the lakes and on the frontier, our arms during the last year, had retrieved our former disgraces; and on the sea coast, the enemy had discovered that it was not an easy matter to make an impression. It is true, the disastrous issue of the campaign against Canada took from us all hope of being able to make a conquest of that province, under present circumstances; but the happy termination of the Indian war to the westward, and its success in the south, afforded some consolation. An important crisis, however, had arrived in the general state of our affairs. The third year of the war found the situation of this country materially changed for the worse. The gloomiest periods of the revolution had scarcely presented a state of things more painfully discouraging. The distresses of the northern states, whose subsistence in a great measure depended upon their shipping, and of the people of the south, whose staples had almost ceased to be of any value; together with the embarrassments of the banks in the middle states; had begun, at last, to make us feel that we were at war. To a nation who had been for years in the most flourishing state, a check to the general prosperity, however it might result in ultimate good, was felt as a positive affliction. To the farming interest the effects of hostilities were rather beneficial: produce advanced greatly in price, and lands increased in value; and the wealth of the cities, no longer employed in commerce, was diverted to the interior, and soon discovered itself in the improvement of the lands, the erection of towns, and the establishment of manufactures. But the number of those whom the war distressed or ruined, was proportionally great ; and as men are louder in crying out against calamities, than forward to exult in their good fortune, the unfavourable side of the picture only was exhibited. The philosopher might say, that what was lost to the nation by one interest, was gained in another ; but this reasoning could have little weight with individual sufferers. In several of the New England states, the complaints assumed a more serious aspect ; and it was even insinuated, that they meant to secede from the union. Such an event would indeed have filled every American bosom with grief, and would have inflicted a deeper injury on our common country than a thousand wars. The collisions between the state authorities and those of the union were beginning to produce all the embarrassments which had been predicted by Patrick Henry, at the formation of the constitution ; and the supposed existence of such misunderstandings, at the period of our utmost need, could not fail to weaken the hands of the administration, and increase the disposition of England to prosecute the war. The disorders in our financial system were alarming ; and it was confidently predicted, that, from the want of funds, the administration would be compelled to yield up the reins of government, or throw the nation upon the mercy of the enemy.

An event had occurred in Europe, which could not be viewed with indifference, even on these distant shores ; and its consequences threatened us with serious danger. The ambitious emperor of France had been hurled from his throne, and the house of Bourbon restored, by the combined powers of Europe. This event was received by some of our fellow citizens with open rejoicing, as though it brought some signal good fortune to this country, or to the human race. To this country it could bring no benefit ; for it was not likely that the Bourbon king of France, although he might not so cordially hate or despise us, could, any more than Napoleon, entertain much regard for a republic, the contagion of whose example was said to have contributed much to that dreadful revolution, in which his family had so severely suffered. Indeed it is natural that a republic like ours should not be viewed with much complacency by any monarch ; for, to use the expression of Demosthenes, " we are considered as a spy upon their actions." It was a matter of indifference to us, whether the throne of France was occupied by an emperor or a king. But, as Great Britain had claimed the chief merit of effecting this wonderful operation, public rejoicings for the event wore the appearance of sympathy with the success of our enemies. The event was, in reality, greatly adverse to our

national interests. Fired by her success in the wars of the
continent, and extravagantly elated by her supposed power
and greatness, our enemy could now send her veteran troops
and her numerous fleets to chastise America, while our commissioners in Europe were allowed to remain for months unnoticed. This turn of affairs, so far from affording ground for
exultation, ought rather to have depressed the friends of liberty
and America. Great Britain was highly incensed that we had
not, with all due patience and meekness, continued to endure
her numerous and flagrant outrages, until, disengaged from her
European war, she should have leisure to cope with us on what
she called equal terms, or, in other words, be in a condition to
direct the undivided force of her immense army and navy against
us. It now behoved us to think no more of invading Canada : our
northern frontier was to be laid waste, our sea coast devastated;
and the utmost to be expected, was a successful self-defence.
In the plenitude of her arrogance, Britain talked of recolonizing
our country, and of crippling us for fifty years to come. Such
was the situation of America at this eventful period. The time
was approaching which would test the strength of our confederation, and our ability for defence, and, what was still more
interesting, the sincerity of our attachment to political institutions, which, if not venerable from time, deserved the highest
admiration for their justice and wisdom.

The northern sea coast, which had thus far experienced little
molestation from the enemy, became the object of attack early
in the spring. On the 7th of April, a body of sailors and marines, to the number of two hundred, ascending the Connecticut
river, landed at Saybrook, and spiked the cannon and destroyed the shipping they found there: thence, proceeding to
Brockway's Ferry, they did the same; and, remaining there,
amused themselves, unapprehensive of attack, for twenty-four
hours. In the meantime, a body of militia, aided by a number of
marines and sailors, under captain Jones and lieutenant Biddle,
from the neighbouring American squadron, had collected for
the purpose of cutting off their retreat; but the British, taking
advantage of a very dark night, and using muffled oars, escaped
safely to their fleet, having destroyed two hundred thousand
dollars worth of shipping.

About this time, the coasting trade was almost destroyed by
a British privateer, the Liverpool Packet, which cruised in Long
Island Sound. Commodore Lewis sailed with a detachment of
thirteen gun-boats, and succeeded in chasing her off. Proceeding to Saybrook, on his arrival there he found upwards of fifty
vessels bound eastward, but afraid to venture out. The com-

modore consented to take them under convoy, without promising
them protection against the British squadron then blockading
New London. He sailed with them on the 25th, and in the
afternoon of the same day, was compelled to throw himself
between his convoy and a British frigate, a sloop of war and
a tender, and maintain a contest until all the coasters had
safely reached New London. Having attained this object, he
determined to try what he could do with his gun-boats against
the enemy's ships Furnaces being hastily constructed, he
began to throw hot balls at the sides of the enemy's ships, and
repeatedly set them on fire, without receiving any injury himself.
The sloop soon withdrew, and the fire was now principally
directed against the frigate. One shot passed through her,
very near the magazine ; her lieutenant, and a great number of
her men, were already killed ; and her captain was on the
point of surrendering, when he observed that the gun-boats had
ceased firing. The night having closed in, and it being excessively dark, commodore Lewis had been obliged to order the
gun-boats to desist from the attack, and to wait until morning.
At daylight, he perceived that the enemy were towing away
their vessels, and instantly resolved to pursue them, but several
other frigates soon after making their appearance, he abandoned this design. This affair, together with that of Craney
Island, revived the discussion of the utility of gun-boats in the
defence of harbours and the coast. Great service had been
rendered by captain Lewis, on this as well as many other occasions, by means of them.

Formidable squadrons were maintained by the enemy before
the ports of New York, New London and Boston ; and the
whole eastern coast was exposed to their ravages. The war
was carried on here in a very different manner from that to the
south. Commodore Hardy would not permit any wanton outrages upon private property, or upon defenceless individuals.
In spite, however of his prohibition, there were particular instances on the part of the officers commanding smaller parties,
in which they gave way to their insatiable thirst for plunder.
At Wareham and Scituate, they burned all the vessels at their
moorings ; and at the former town, they set fire to an extensive cotton manufactory : but at a place called Booth Bay,
they met with a spirited resistance, and were repeatedly repulsed, in various desperate attacks. by the militia of the neighbourhood.

An invasion of a more serious nature was made in July.
On the 11th of that month, sir Thomas Hardy, with a strong
force, made a descent on Moose Island, in Passamaquoddy

Bay, and after taking possession of Eastport, situated on that
island, declared all the islands and towns in the bay to ap-
pertain to his Britannic majesty, and required the inhabitants
to appear within seven days and take the oath of allegiance.
About two-thirds of the inhabitants submitted, in the expectation of enjoying the privileges of subjects: nevertheless, in the
month of August, the council of the province of New Bruns-
wick declared, that notwithstanding the oath of allegiance
which they had taken, they should be considered as a conquered
people, and placed under military government.   Eastport was
soon after strongly fortified, and remained in the possession of
the British until the conclusion of the war; but they found extreme difficulty in subsisting their troops, and desertions were
so frequent that the officers were often compelled to perform
the duties of sentinels.

On the 9th of August, Commodore Hardy sailed with a part of
his squadron, for the purpose of attacking Stonington.   The appearance of this force before the town excited much alarm, which
was not diminished when the inhabitants received a message from
the commodore, directing them to remove the women and children, as he had received orders to reduce the place to ashes.
Although with very trifling means of defence, the citizens determined to make an attempt to save their property; having first
complied with the terms of the commodore's note.   The handful
of militia of the place repaired to a small battery erected on the
shore, and to a breast-work thrown up for musketry; and at the
same time despatched an express to obtain assistance from general
Cushing, commanding at New London.   In the evening, five
barges and a large launch, filled with men, approached the shore,
under cover of a heavy fire from the enemy's ships.   The
Americans, reserving their fire until the enemy were within
short grape distance, opened two eighteen-pounders on the invaders, and soon compelled them to retire out of the reach of
the battery.   The British next endeavoured to land at the east
side of the town, which they supposed defenceless; but a part
of the militia being detached thither with a six-pounder, they
were again repulsed.   The enemy now retired to their ships,
determined to renew the attack in the morning; and in the
meantime kept up a bombardment until midnight.   The next
morning, at dawn, one of the enemy's vessels approached within
pistol shot of the battery, and the barges advanced in still greater
numbers than the day before: these were again gallantly repulsed, and the vessel was driven from her anchorage.   The
squadron then renewed the bombardment of the town, but without effect; and on the 12th, the commodore thought proper to

retire. The inhabitants, after this gallant defence, which, considering the means with which it was effected and the great disparity of force opposed to them, deserves much praise, once more occupied their dwellings in security.

It was not long after this, that the British claimed all that part of the territory of Maine between the river Penobscot, and Passamaquoddy Bay. On the 1st of September, the governor of Nova Scotia, and admiral Griffith, entered the Penobscot, and seized the town of Castine, which the garrison had previously evacuated. A proclamation was then issued, declaring that possession of that portion of Maine which lies east of the Penobscot was formally taken in the name of his Britannic majesty. The country, which contained about thirty thousand inhabitants, was then gradually occupied, and was retained until the termination of the war.

A few days before the occupation of Castine, the frigate John Adams, captain Morris, entered the Penobscot river, after a successful cruise, and having run upon the rocks near that port, was obliged to be hove down at Hampden, thirty-five miles up the river, for the purpose of being repaired. On the 3d of September, several of the British vessels, and ten barges, manned by about one thousand men, ascended from Castine for the purpose of capturing the frigate. Captain Morris, apprized of their approach, erected several batteries on eminences near his vessel, and armed the militia. Finding, however, that there was no possibility of successfully resisting the enemy, he ordered the greater part of his crew to retreat under lieutenant Wadsworth, while he himself and a few men remained, to blow up the ship. This they effected ; and then plunged into the river, and reached a place of safety by swimming. The British, disappointed in this undertaking, retired to Castine.

CHAPTER XVI.

Naval Events—The Plantagenet Seventy-Four declines a Contest with Commo
dore Rodgers—Captain Stewart chases a British Frigate of equal force—Cruise of
Commodore Porter in the Essex—He captures twelve armed British Whale Ships—
Arrives at the Island of Nooaheevah—Takes possession in the name of the American
Government—His Difficulties with the Savages there—He burns the Typee Villages—
British Abuse—Commodore Porter arrives at Valparaiso—Is attacked by the Phœbe
and Cherub—His Desperate Resistance—Capture of the Essex and Essex Junior—
The Peacock captures the British Brig Epervier—The Wasp captures the Reindeer—
The Wasp sinks the Avon—Mysterious Loss of the Wasp—Cruise of the President,
the Peacock and the Hornet—The President captured by a British Squadron—The
Constitution engages and captures the Cyane and the Levant—The Hornet, Captain
Biddle, captures the Penguin—Exploits of Privateers—Capture of the American Priva
teer Armstrong, after a dreadful Carnage of the Enemy.

THE naval incidents of eighteen hundred and fourteen, were
as grateful to the feelings of the nation as those of the two previous years.

An occurrence took place in the beginning of it, which afforded
much mortification to the enemy. In the month of February,
commodore Rodgers, on his return from a cruise in the President, found himself off Sandy Hook, in the neighbourhood of
three large British ships of war, the nearest of which was the
Plantagenet, a seventy-four. Believing that an engagement
with one, or all of them, was unavoidable, he immediately cleared
for action, determining not to surrender his ship without selling
it as dearly as he could. But notwithstanding he fired a gun to
windward as a proof of his willingness to engage, the British
vessels did not think proper to approach, and he reached New
York safely. Captain Lloyd, of the Plantagenet, after returning to England, accounted for his conduct, by alleging a mutiny
in his ship ; and several of his sailors were executed on the
charge.

In the month of April, captain Stewart was on his return in
the Constitution from a cruise, when he was chased by two
British frigates and a brig, but escaped by superior seamanship
into Marblehead. Some time before, after capturing the public schooner Pictou, he fell in with the British frigate La Pique,

captain Maitland, which fled on the approach of the Constitution, and finally escaped during the night, after a long chase. Captain Maitland, on his arrival in England, was complimented by the board of admiralty, for thus obeying their instructions, in not fighting an American frigate. The enemy had become equally shy of the gun-boat flotilla. Commodore Lewis repeatedly beat off the British vessels near Sandy Hook, and facilitated the return of the American ships. The brig Regent, laden with a very valuable cargo, was chased by the Belvidera, when commodore Lewis, throwing himself with eleven of his gun-boats between them, the frigate moved off without returning the shot of the gun-boats.

That brave and adventurous seaman, commodore Porter, of the Essex, terminated this year his glorious cruise in the Pacific. From Lima, in the neighbourhood of which he had chastised the pirates of the ship Nereyda, he proceeded to the Gallipagos, where he cruised from April until October 1813; and in the course of that time captured twelve armed British whale ships, carrying in all one hundred and seven guns, and three hundred and two men. Several of these he fitted out as American cruisers and store ships; and one of them, the Atlantic, which he called the Essex Junior, he equipped with twenty guns and sixty men, and assigned it to lieutenant Downes, his first officer. Those prizes which were to be laid up were convoyed by this latter officer to Valparaiso. On his return, he brought intelligence to commodore Porter, that a British squadron, consisting of one frigate and two sloops of war, and a store ship of twenty guns, had sailed in quest of the Essex. The commodore, having been almost a year at sea, with little intermission, found it absolutely necessary that his ship should undergo considerable repairs. With this view, he steered to the island of Noonheevah, of which he took possession in the name of the American government; calling it Madison's Island, in honour of the president. Here he found a fine bay, and a situation in every other respect suitable to his wishes. The inhabitants at first were apparently friendly; but it was not long before he perceived that his situation would be unsafe, in consequence of a war which prevailed between the inhabitants of a neighbouring village, and those by whom he had been received. The latter insisted upon his joining them in their wars, and threatened to drive him away if he did not. Compelled by a regard to his own safety, the commodore sent a party of sailors with the natives, who, by their assistance, defeated their enemies. At his instance, a peace was brought about between them: in return for which, the natives erected

8

a village for his accommodation, and freely traded with him
for provisions; and for some time the greatest harmony prevailed.

His security was again menaced by the hostile conduct of
the Typees, one of the most warlike tribes on the island, who
were continually urging the friendly savages to destroy the
strangers. Finding his situation growing every day more
critical, and being very unwilling to engage in a war with them;
the commodore sent them presents, and requested that they
would remain quiet and be at peace. This had no other effect
than to increase their insolence to the Americans, whom they
represented as cowardly, or they would not have condescended
to beg for peace. He now discovered that his safety depended
entirely upon making these people feel his strength; as it was
impossible for him to leave the island until his vessel could be
repaired, and while the greater part of his effects were actually
on shore. He therefore set off against them at the head of
thirty-five men, determined to give them battle, and, by showing
the efficacy of his weapons, to compel them to a pacific course.
The necessity for this step was great, as those tribes which had
hitherto been friendly were on the point of breaking out into
hostilities. But the force with which he marched, was insufficient to make any impression on his savage enemies. Their
country being exceedingly mountainous, and abounding in thick
ets, it was easy for them to escape. The commodore was,
therefore, compelled to return from this expedition without
achieving his object. To prevent the friendly savages from
rising, he found it necessary to inform them, that he would
proceed the next day with a much larger body of men. He
now, with the greater part of his crew, marched across the
mountains, notwithstanding the extreme difficulties of the route,
and penetrated into the valleys of the natives. Being unable
to come at them, as they again took refuge in their inaccessible
fastnesses, he burnt nine of their villages, and then retreated.
The Typees now gladly accepted terms of peace; and all the
tribes on the island vied with each other in friendship towards
the whites, as long as the commodore remained.

The destruction of the Typee villages furnished the British
writers with occasion for the most scandalous abuse of commodore Porter and the American people. The burning by an
American officer, in self defence and for the sake of peace, of a
few wigwams covered with palm leaves, erected merely for shelter
from the heats or rains of the torrid zone, was to be viewed
with horror; while the conduct of the British government in
India, in America, and throughout the world, without any motive

but that of a base rapacity, was to be passed over unnoticed
There is one part of commodore Porter's conduct which could not
be approved; and that was the taking possession of the island in
the name of the American government. This, although it gave
satisfaction to the natives, who regarded it as an expression of
friendship, was following the evil example of European states,
which have usually considered themselves entitled, by the right
of prior discovery, to territories inhabited only by uncivilized
men. Had the Typee war ensued in consequence of this act,
it could have found no justification

The Essex being completely repaired and supplied with
provisions for four months, the commodore sailed for Valparaiso on the 12th of December, accompanied by lieutenant
Downing with the Essex Junior, and arrived there on the 12th
of January 1814. He left behind him three of his prizes,
secured under a fort which he had erected, in the charge of
lieutenant Gamble, of the marines, with orders to proceed to
Valparaiso after a certain time.

It was not long after the arrival of commodore Porter at Valparaiso, when commodore Hillyar appeared there in the Phœbe
frigate, accompanied by the Cherub sloop of war. These vessels had been equipped for the purpose of meeting the Essex;
and carried flags bearing the motto, "God and our country,
British sailors' best rights : *traitors offend them.*" This was
in allusion to Porter's celebrated motto, "Free trade and sailors'
rights." He now hoisted at his mizzen, "God, our country,
and liberty: tyrants offend them."

The British vessels soon after stood out, and cruised off the
port about six weeks, rigorously blockading the Essex. Their
united force amounted to eighty-one guns, and five hundred
men; while that of the Essex and Essex Junior was only
sixty-six guns, and three hundred and twenty men. Commodore Porter, being prevented by this great disparity of power
from engaging, made repeated attempts to draw the Phœbe
singly into action, as well by manœuvring as by sending formal
challenges; but commodore Hillyar carefully avoided it. The
American commander, hearing that an additional British force
was on its way, and having discovered that his vessel could
outsail those of the British, determined to put to sea, and, by
diverting the pursuit to himself, to enable the Essex Junior
to escape to a place of rendezvous previously appointed.

On the 28th of March, the wind blowing fresh from the southward, the Essex parted her starboard cable, and dragged her
larboard anchor to sea. Not a moment was lost in getting sail
on the ship. In endeavouring to pass to the windward of the

enemy, a squall struck the American vessel, just as she was doubling the point forming the western side of the harbour, which carried away her main topmast. Both British ships immediately gave chase. Being unable to escape in his crippled state, the commodore endeavoured to put back into the harbour; but finding this impracticable, he ran into a small bay, about three quarters of a mile to the eastward of the harbour, and anchored within pistol shot of the shore, where, from a supposition that the enemy would continue to respect the neutrality of the port, he thought himself secure. He soon found, however, by the manner in which they approached, that he was mistaken. With all possible despatch, therefore, he prepared his ship for action, and endeavoured to get a spring on his cable: he had not accomplished this when the enemy commenced the attack, at fifty-four minutes past three P. M. At first, the Phœbe placed herself on his stern, and the Cherub on his larboard bow; but the latter, finding herself exposed to a hot fire, soon changed her position, and with her consort kept up a raking fire under his stern. The Americans, being unable to bring their broadside to bear on the enemy, were obliged to rely for defence against this tremendous attack, on three long twelve-pounders, which they ran out of the stern ports. These were worked with such bravery and skill, and so much injury to the enemy, as in half an hour to compel them to haul off and re-pair. It was evident that commodore Hillyar meant to risk nothing from the daring courage of the Americans; all his manœuvres were deliberate and wary: his antagonist was in his power, and his only concern was to succeed with as little loss to himself as possible. The situation of the Essex was now most deplorable · already many of the gallant crew were killed and wounded; and the crippled state of their ship rendered it impracticable for them to bring her guns to bear upon the enemy. Still they were not disheartened: aroused to desperation, they expressed their defiance to the enemy, and their determination to hold out to the last.

The enemy having repaired his damages, now placed himself, with both ships, on the starboard quarter of the Essex, where none of her guns could be brought to bear; and the commodore saw no hope of injuring him but by getting under way, and becoming the assailant   The flying-jib was the only sail he had left: causing this to be hoisted, and cutting his cable, he ran down on both ships, with the intention of laying the Phœbe on board. For a short time he was enabled to close with the enemy. Although the decks of the Essex were strewed with dead, and her cockpit was filled with the wounded; although she had been several times on fire, and was, in fact, a perfect wreck ; a feeble hope now arose that she might yet be saved, in consequence of the Cherub being so much crippled as to be compelled to haul off.   She did not return to close action again; but she kept up her fire at a distance, with her long guns.   The Essex was unable. however, to take advantage of the circumstance; as the Phœbe edged off, and also kept up, at a distance, a destructive fire. Commodore Porter, finding that the enemy had it in his power to choose his distance, at last gave up all hope of again coming to close quarters, and attempted to run his vessel on shore. The wind at that moment favoured the design; but it suddenly changed, turning her head upon the Phœbe, and exposing her to a raking fire   The ship was totally unmanageable; but as she drifted with her head to the enemy, commodore Porter again encouraged the hope of being able to board.   At this moment lieutenant-commandant Downes, of the Essex Junior, came on board. to receive orders, in the expectation that his commander would soon be a prisoner.   His services could be of no avail in the present deplorable state of the Essex: and finding, from the enemy's putting up his helm, that the last attempt at boarding would not succeed, he directed Downes to repair to his ship, to be prepared for defending her in case of attack, and, if necessary, of destroying her.

The slaughter on board the Essex now became horrible, the enemy continuing to rake her, while she was unable to bring a single gun to bear.   Still her commander refused to yield while a ray of hope appeared.   Every expedient that a fertile and inventive genius could suggest was resorted to, in the forlorn chance, that he might be able, by some lucky circumstance, to escape from the grasp of the foe.   A hawser was bent to the sheet anchor, and the anchor cut from the bows to bring the ship's head round.   This succeeded ; and the broadside of the Essex was again brought to bear.   As the enemy was much crippled and unable to hold his own, it was hoped that he might drift out of gun-shot, before he discovered that the Essex had anchored : but alas' this last expedient failed ; the hawser parted, and with it went the last lingering hope of the Essex.   At this moment her situation was awful beyond description.   She was on fire both before and aft; the flames were bursting up each hatchway ; a quantity of powder had exploded below ; and word was given that the fire was near her magazine. Thus surrounded by horrors, with no probability of maintaining his ship, the commodore directed his attention to saving as many of his gallant companions as he could ; and as the distance to the shore did not exceed three quarters of a mile, he hoped that

s*

many of them would make their escape before the ship blew up. The boats had been destroyed by the enemy's shot: he therefore ordered such as could swim to jump overboard and endeavour to gain the land. Some reached it, some were taken by the enemy, and some perished in the attempt; but the greater part of his generous crew resolved to stay by the ship, and share the fate of their commander.

They now laboured to extinguish the flames, and succeeded. After this, they again repaired to their guns, but their strength had become so much exhausted, that an effort at further resistance was vain. Commodore Porter then summoned a consultation of the officers; but was surprised to find only one acting lieutenant, Stephen Decatur M'Knight, remaining. The accounts from every part of the ship were deplorable indeed: she was in imminent danger of sinking, and so crowded with the wounded, that the cockpit, the steerage, the wardroom and the birth deck could hold no more. In the meantime the enemy, at a secure distance, continued his fire; and the water having become smooth, he struck the hull of the Essex at every shot. At last, despairing of saving his ship, the commodore was compelled, at twenty minutes past six P. M., to give the painful orders to strike the colours. The enemy, not seeing probably that this had taken place, continued to fire for ten minutes after; and Porter, under a belief that they intended to give no quarter, was about to direct the colours to be again hoisted, when the firing ceased. The loss on board the Essex was fifty-eight killed, thirty-nine wounded severely, twenty-seven slightly, and thirty-one missing. The loss of the British was five killed, and ten wounded. Their vessels were both much cut up in their hulls and rigging; and the Phœbe could scarcely be kept afloat until she anchored in the port of Valparaiso next morning.

Commodore Porter was permitted, on his parol, to return to the United States in the Essex Junior, which was converted into a cartel for the purpose. On arriving off the port of New York, he was brought to and detained by the Saturn razee; and, to the disgrace of the British arms, compelled to give up his parol, and declared a prisoner of war. The Essex Junior was ordered to remain under the lee of the Saturn. Commodore Porter now determined to attempt his escape, though thirty miles from shore. Manning a boat with a sufficient crew, he put off; and notwithstanding that he was pursued from the Saturn, he arrived safely in New York. His countrymen received him with open arms; and the most unbounded demonstrations of joy prevailed wherever he appeared.   Certainly his services to his country justly claimed its gratitude and esteem.

Perhaps a more dreadful example of determined, unconquerable courage than the unsuccessful defence of the Essex was never exhibited: to an American, no *victory* could afford more grateful and proud recollections.   It was pleasing to see the spontaneous expression of human feeling in favour of the weak, when contending against superior force.   Thousands of the inhabitants of Valparaiso covered the neighbouring heights, as spectators of the conflict   Touched with the forlorn situation of the Essex, and filled with admiration at the unflagging spirit and persevering bravery of her commander and crew, a generous anxiety animated the multitude for their fate.   Bursts of delight arose when, by any vicissitude of battle or prompt expedient, a change seemed to be taking place in their favour; and the eager spectators were seen to wring their hands and to utter groans of sympathy, when the transient hope was defeated.

During the third year of the war, every naval combat, without a single exception, where there was any thing like equality of force, terminated in favour of the Americans.   The sloop of war Peacock, captain Warrington, launched in October 1813, performed a cruise during the winter, and on her return, was chased into St Mary's.   She soon after put to sea again, and on the 29th of April discovered the British brig of war Epervier, captain Wales, with several vessels under convoy which immediately made sail on her approach.   An engagement between the two vessels of war followed soon afterwards.   At the first broadside, the foreyard of the Peacock was totally disabled by two round shot in the starboard quarter.   By this, she was deprived of the use of her fore and foretop sails, and was obliged to keep aloof during the remainder of the action, which lasted forty-two minutes.   In this time, she received considerable damage in her rigging, but her hull was not at all injured. The Epervier struck with five feet water in her hold, her topmast over the side, her main boom shot away, her foremast cut nearly in two, her fore rigging and stays shot away, and her hull pierced by forty-five shot, twenty of which were within a foot of her water line.   Of her crew eleven were killed, and her first lieutenant and fourteen men wounded.   She was immediately taken possession of by lieutenant Nicholson, first officer of the Peacock, who, with lieutenant Voorhees of the same ship, had been already distinguished in another naval action.   The sum of one hundred and eighteen thousand dollars, in specie, was found in her, and transferred to the Peacock.

Captain Warrington immediately set sail, with his prize, for
one of the southern ports. The day following, the captain discovered two frigates in chase. At the suggestion of lieutenant
Nicholson, he took all the prisoners on board the Peacock; and
leaving only sixteen men on board the Epervier, directed her
to seek the nearest port. By skilful seamanship the captain
succeeded in escaping from the enemy's ships, and reaching
Savannah. Here he found his prize; lieutenant Nicholson
having brought her in, after beating off a launch well manned
and armed, which had been despatched from the frigates to
overtake him.

Captain Blakely, of the new sloop of war the Wasp, sailed
from Portsmouth on the 1st of May. After seizing seven merchantmen, on the 6th of July, while in chase of two other vessels,
he fell in with the British brig of war Reindeer, captain Manners,
and immediately altered his course, and hauled by the wind, in
chase of her. At fifteen minutes past one P. M., he prepared
for action; but it was two hours later, in consequence of their
manœuvring and the endeavours of the Reindeer to escape, ere
he approached sufficiently near to engage. Several guns were
fired from the Wasp before her antagonist could bring her guns
to bear; and the helm of the latter was therefore put a-lee. At
half past three, captain Blakely commenced the action with his
after carronades on the starboard side. Shortly afterwards, the
larboard bow of the Reindeer being in contact with the Wasp,
captain Manners gave orders to board. The attempt was gallantly repulsed by the crew of the Wasp, and the enemy several
times beaten off. At forty-four minutes past three, orders were
given to board in turn. Throwing themselves with prompti-
tude upon the deck of the enemy's ship, the boarders succeeded
in the execution of their orders; and at forty-five minutes past
three, her flag came down. She was almost cut to pieces,
and half her crew were killed or wounded. The loss of the
Wasp was five killed and twenty-one wounded: among the
latter, midshipmen Langdon and Toscan; both of whom expired
some days after. The Reindeer having been found altogether
unmanageable, was blown up; and captain Blakely steered for
L'Orient, to provide for the wounded of both crews.

After leaving L'Orient, and capturing two valuable British
merchantmen, captain Blakely fell in with a fleet of ten sail,
under convoy of the Armada seventy-four, and a bomb ship.
He stood for them, and succeeded in cutting out of the squadron a brig laden with brass and iron cannon, and military stores,
from Gibraltar. After taking out the prisoners and setting her
on fire, he endeavoured to cut out another, but was chased off by

the seventy-four. In the evening, at half past six, he descried two vessels, one on his starboard and one on his larboard bow, and hauled for that which was farthest to windward. At seven, she was discovered to be a brig of war, making signals with flags which could not be distinguished owing to the darkness, and at twenty-nine minutes past nine she was under the lee bow of the Wasp. An action soon after commenced, which lasted until ten o'clock, when captain Blakely, finding his antagonist to have ceased firing, paused and asked if he had surrendered. No answer being returned, he commenced firing again, and the enemy returned broadside for broad-side for twelve minutes. Perceiving that his two last broadsides were not returned, he hailed again, and was informed that she was sinking, and that her colours were struck. Before the boats of the Wasp could be lowered, a second brig of war was discovered: the crew were instantly sent to their quarters, and preparations made for another engagement, when two other brigs appeared. He now made sail, and endeavoured to draw the brig first discovered after him, but without effect. The name of the prize was subsequently ascertained to have been the Avon, captain Arbuthnot; of the same force as the Reindeer. She sunk immediately after the last man had been taken out of her into one of the vessels which had come in sight. She had eight killed, and thirty-one wounded, including her captain and several other officers.

The Wasp soon repaired the damages received in this engagement, and continued her cruise. On the 21st of September, she captured, off the Madeiras, her thirteenth prize, the British brig Atalanta, of eight guns, and the only one which she sent into port. The return of this vessel, after her brilliant cruise, was for a long time fondly, but unavailingly, looked for by our country. There is little doubt that the brave commander and his gallant crew found a common grave in the waves of the ocean: they will always live in the gratitude and recollection of their country.

The blockade of commodore Decatur's squadron at New London having been maintained until after the season had passed in which there existed any prospect of escape, the ships of which it was composed were ordered up the river and dismantled, while the commodore, with his crew, was transferred to the frigate President, then at New York. A cruise was projected for a squadron to consist of the President, the sloops of war Peacock and Hornet, and the Tom Bowline store ship, under the command of commodore Decatur. As the enemy still blockaded New York, the commodore thought it safer for

the President to venture out singly ; and after ordering the other
vessels to follow, and appointing a place of rendezvous, he sailed.
In consequence of the negligence of the pilot, the President
struck upon the bar, and remained there thumping for two hours,
by which her ballast was deranged and her trim for sailing
entirely lost. The course of the wind preventing his return
into port, he put to sea, trusting to the excellence of the vessel. At daylight he fell in with a British squadron, consisting of the Endymion, Tenedos and Pomona frigates, and
the Majestic razee. In spite of his exertions they gained upon
him; and the foremost, the Endymion, getting close under his
quarters, commenced firing. The commodore determined to
bear up and engage her, with the intention of carrying her
by boarding, and afterwards escaping in her and abandoning
his own ship. In this he was prevented by the manœuvring
of the enemy. The engagement was protracted for two hours,
and ended in reducing the Endymion almost to a wreck, and
killing or wounding a large proportion of her crew. The President was also considerably damaged, and lost twenty-five men in
killed and wounded : among the former, lieutenants Babbit and
Hamilton, and acting lieutenant Howell; among the latter, midshipman Dale, who afterwards died, and the commodore himself.
The squadron was now fast approaching, and the gallant commodore, unwilling to sacrifice the lives of his men in a useless
contest, on receiving the fire of the nearest frigate, surrendered.
He was taken on board the Endymion, for the purpose of acting
the miserable farce of surrendering his sword to the officer of a
frigate which would have fallen into his hands, but for the approach of an overwhelming force. The President was sent to
England; and in order to satisfy the good people there that
she was a seventy-four in disguise, she was lightened, and laid
in dock alongside of an old seventy-four, which had been diminished to appearance by being deeply laden.

Not the least among the exploits of our naval heroes, was
the capture of two of the enemy's ships of war by the Constitution, captain Stewart. Having sailed from Boston, on the
17th of December 1814, on a cruise, he discovered, on the 20th
of February 1815, two ships; one of which bore up for the
Constitution, but soon after changed her course to join her
consort. The Constitution gave chase to both, and at six P. M.
ranged ahead of the sternmost, brought her on the quarter and
her consort on the bow, and opened a broadside. The fire was
immediately returned; and exchanges of broadsides continued
until both ships were enveloped in smoke. When it cleared
away, the Constitution finding herself abreast of the head-

most ship, captain Stewart ordered both sides to be manned, backed topsails, and dropped into his first position. The ship on the bow backed sails also. The Constitution's broadsides were then fired from the larboard battery; and in a few moments the ship on the bow, perceiving her error in getting sternboard, filled away with the intention of tacking athwart the bows of the Constitution. Meanwhile the ship on the stern fell off entirely unmanageable. The Constitution now pursued the former, and coming within a hundred yards, gave her several raking broadsides, and so crippled her that no further apprehensions were entertained of her being able to escape. The captain then returned to the latter, from which a gun was fired to leeward, to signify that she had surrendered ; and took possession, by lieutenant Hoffman, of the frigate Cyane, captain Gordon Falkon, of thirty-four carronade guns. Captain Stewart now steered in pursuit of the other vessel ; and after a short resistance, in which she suffered considerably, she struck, with five feet water in her hold. She proved to be the sloop of war Levant, captain Douglass, of eighteen thirty-two-pound carronades. The loss on board the two ships amounted to about eighty in killed and wounded : of the crew of the Constitution there were only four killed and eleven wounded ; and the ship received but a very trifling injury. On the 10th of March, captain Stewart entered the harbour of Praya, in the island of St Jago, with his prizes ; and on the 11th, a British squadron of two ships, of sixty guns each, and a frigate, appeared off the entrance of the harbour. Captain Stewart, having no faith in his security, although in a neutral port, made sail with one of his prizes, the Cyane, and though closely pursued, had the good fortune to escape with it into the United States. The Levant was recaptured in the Portuguese harbour, in contempt of the neutrality of the port and of the laws of nations.

The Peacock, Hornet and Tom Bowline left New York a few days after the President, not knowing of her capture. On the 23d of January 1815, the Hornet, captain Biddle, parted company, and directed her course to Tristan d'Acunha, the place of rendezvous. On the 23d of March she descried the British brig Penguin, captain Dickenson, of eighteen guns and a twelve-pound carronade, to the southward and eastward of that island. Captain Biddle hove to, while the Penguin bore down. At forty minutes past one P. M., the British vessel commenced the engagement. The firing was hotly kept up for fifteen minutes, the Penguin gradually nearing the Hornet, with the intention of boarding. Her captain was killed by a grape shot before he saw his orders executed ; and her lieutenant, on whom the command of the Penguin then devolved, bore her up, and running her bowsprit between the main and mizzen rigging of the Hornet, directed his crew to board. His men, however, perceiving the boarders of the Hornet not only ready to receive them, but waiting for orders to spring on the Penguin's deck, refused to follow him. At this moment the heavy swell of the sea lifted the Hornet ahead, and the enemy's bowsprit carried away her mizzen shrouds and spanker boom; while the Penguin hung upon the Hornet's quarter deck, with the loss of her foremast and bowsprit. Her commander then cried out that he surrendered. Captain Biddle had ordered his men to cease firing, when a man in the enemy's shrouds was discovered taking aim at him, by an officer of the Hornet, who called to him to avoid the fire. Scarcely had he changed his position, when a musket ball struck him in the neck, and wounded him severely. Two marines immediately levelled their pieces at the wretch, and killed him before he brought his gun from his shoulder. The Penguin had by that time got clear of the Hornet, and the latter wore round to give the enemy a broadside, when they a second time cried out that they had surrendered. It was with the greatest difficulty that captain Biddle could restrain his crew from discharging the broadside, so exasperated were they at the conduct of the enemy. In twenty-two minutes after the commencement of the action, the Penguin was taken possession of by lieutenant Mayo, of the Hornet. She was so much injured, that captain Biddle determined on taking out her crew, and scuttling her. He afterwards sent off his prisoners to St Salvador by the Tom Bowline, by which vessel, and the Peacock, he had been joined on the 25th of the month. The enemy lost fourteen in killed, and had twenty-eight wounded: the Hornet one killed, and eleven wounded, among the latter, her lieutenant, Conner, dangerously.

Captain Biddle was compelled to part from the Peacock by the appearance of a British ship of the line, and, after being closely chased for several days, effected his escape into St Salvador, by throwing all his guns but one, and every heavy article, overboard. The news of peace soon after arrived there. The capture of the Cyane, the Levant and the Penguin took place before the expiration of the time specified by the second article of the treaty.

The exploits of the privateers continued to rival those of our national vessels. In one instance the enemy was compelled to pay dearly for his disregard of the sanctuary of a neutral port. The privateer Armstrong lay at anchor in the harbour of Fayal, when a British squadron, consisting of the Carnation, the Plantagenet and the Rota, hove in sight. Captain Reid, of the privateer, discovering by the light of the moon that the enemy had put out their boats and were preparing to attack him, cleared for action, and moved near the shore. Four boats filled with men were seen approaching. On being hailed and making no answer, a fire was opened upon them from the ship, which soon compelled them to haul off. Captain Reid now prepared for a more formidable attack; and anchored the privateer a cable's length from the shore, and within pistol shot of the castle. The next day the enemy sent a fleet of boats, supported by the Carnation, which stood before the harbour, to prevent the escape of the privateer. At midnight the boats approached a second time, to the number of twelve or fourteen, and manned by several hundred men. They were suffered to come alongside of the privateer, when they were assailed with such tremendous fury, that in forty minutes scarcely a man of them was left alive. During these attacks the shores were lined with the inhabitants, who, from the brightness of the moon, had a full view of the scene. The governor, with the first people of the place, stood by and saw the whole affair. After the second attack, the governor sent a note to the commander of the Plantagenet, captain Lloyd, requesting him to desist: to which the captain replied, that he was determined to have the privateer at the risk of knocking down the town. The American consul having communicated this information to captain Reid, he ordered his crew to save their effects, and carry the dead and wounded on shore as fast as possible. At daylight the Carnation stood close to the Armstrong, and commenced a heavy fire; but being considerably cut up by the privateer, she hauled off to repair. On her re-appearance, captain Reid, thinking it useless to protract the contest, scuttled his vessel and escaped to land. The British loss amounted to the astonishing number of one hundred and twenty killed, and one hundred and thirty wounded: that of the Americans was only two killed, and seven wounded. Several houses in the town were destroyed, and some of the inhabitants hurt.

T

CHAPTER XVII.

FROM reviewing the events of the war on the ocean, we return to the war on the northern frontier. Not to be without a
plan of campaign, although experience had already shown how
small a portion of plans formed in the cabinet, and depending
upon so many contingencies not susceptible of calculation,
could be carried into execution, the following was adopted.
Colonel Croghan, with the assistance of commodore Sinclair,
was to proceed against the British on the upper lakes, with a
view of recovering the American posts of Michilimackinac and
St Joseph. An army, under general Brown, now raised to the
rank of major-general, was to cross the Niagara and take possession of Burlington Heights; and afterwards, in conjunction with
commodore Chauncey, to attack the British posts on the peninsula. General Izard, commanding the Northern Army, was to
push a number of armed -boats into the St Lawrence, so as to
command the Rapids, and cut off the communication between
Montreal and Kingston. Batteries were also to be thrown up for
the purpose of protecting the American fleet on Lake Champlain, and to prevent that of the British from entering it. The

greater part of these arrangements were controlled by unforeseen circumstances.

The spring passed away before general Brown was in a situation to attempt any thing against the British posts on the opposite side of the river; even Fort Niagara, on this side, still remained in their hands. He had, however, been assiduously occupied, with his gallant officers general Scott and general Ripley, in collecting and disciplining a force in the neighbourhood of Black Rock and Buffalo. By the beginning of July, this consisted of two brigades of regulars, the first commanded by brigadier-general Scott, and the second by brigadier-general Ripley; and a brigade of volunteers, with a few Indians, under generals Porter and Swift. In the meantime, the force of the enemy, under lieutenant-general Drummond, had been greatly increased, by the addition of a number of veteran regiments, which, since the pacification of Europe, Great Britain had been enabled to send to Canada.

The first step to be taken, with a view to any future operations against Canada, and to recover the possession of Fort Niagara, was the capture of Fort Erie; for if the Americans were possessed of this post, it was supposed that the enemy would evacuate the American side of the frontier. and besides, that this garrison could be carried with more ease than the other, from the circumstance of an attack being less expected. Fort Erie was at that time commanded by captain Buck, with about one hundred and seventy men. The two brigades of regulars, in obedience to general Brown's orders, embarked on the morning of the 3d of July. General Scott, with the first, and a detachment of artillery under major Hindman, crossed to the Canada shore, about a mile below Fort Erie, and general Ripley, with the second brigade, at about the same distance above; while a party of Indians, who had also crossed over, got into the woods in the rear of the fort. The garrison, being taken by surprise, and surrounded before the movements of the assailants were discovered, was compelled to surrender after firing a few shot. Immediate possession was taken of the fort, and the prisoners were marched into the interior of New York.

General Brown next resolved to proceed immediately and attack major-general Riall, who, with a division of British regulars, occupied an intrenched camp at Chippewa; arrangements having first been made for the defence of the fort, and or protecting the rear of the army.

On the morning of the 4th, general Scott advanced with his brigade and captain Towson's artillery; and was followed in the course of the day by general Ripley, and the field and

park artillery under major Hindman, together with general
Porter's volunteers. The army was then drawn up in regular
order on the right bank of Street's creek, within two miles of
the British camp. In approaching to this post, the first brigade had encountered the advance corps of the enemy, which
retreated, after destroying the bridge over the creek. Captain
Crooker, who had been directed to flank them on the left, had
in the meantime crossed the stream at a point some distance
above the bridge, and had come up with the enemy while the
American brigade was still on the right bank of the creek. The
British now turned upon and surrounded him ; but he defended
himself in so gallant a manner, that he was enabled to keep
them off, until captains Hull and Harrison, and lieutenant Randolph, with a small party of men who had been hastily thrown
across the stream, came to his relief.

The army remained in this position until the next day,
when, early in the morning, the British commenced attacks
upon the picket guards surrounding it. One of these, commanded by captain Treat, was suddenly fired upon by a party
concealed in some high grass ; one man fell, and the rear broke
and retreated. The exertions of the captain to rally them were
mistaken for cowardice, and he was stripped of his command.
Being resolved to do away the imputation, he requested to engage in the approaching battle as a volunteer, and was accordingly directed to lead a platoon of the same company which
he had just commanded into action. He was afterwards tried
and honourably acquitted. These assaults continued throughout the greater part of the day. General Riall, perceiving that
an engagement was unavoidable, now resolved to strike the
first blow ; he therefore issued from his encampment with his
whole force, and, crossing the Chippewa creek, soon appeared
with the main body on the left bank of Street's creek. He had
previously sent a considerable body of troops into a wood on
the left of the American camp, for the purpose of turning their
flank. The movement in the wood was discovered early
enough to frustrate it; and general Porter, with the volunteers
and Indians, after a sharp conflict, compelled the enemy's right
to retire. While in pursuit of it on the Chippewa road, he came
suddenly in contact with the main body of the British. The
volunteers were now severely pressed by troops greatly superior in numbers and discipline. General Brown, perceiving
this, ordered Scott's brigade and Towson's artillery to advance,
and draw the enemy into action on the plains of Chippewa.
This was effected immediately on crossing the bridge.

The first battalion, under major Leavenworth, took a position on the right; and the second was led to its station by colonel Campbell, who, on being wounded shortly afterwards, was succeeded by major M'Neill. Major Jesup, a gallant young officer, who commanded the third battalion, which was formed on the left, resting in a wood, was ordered to turn the right flank of the British, then steadily advancing upon the American line. Whilst warmly engaged in this service, he was compelled to detach captain Ketchum, to attack some troops coming up to the assistance of the body with which the third battalion was engaged. The major, having cleared his front, moved to the relief of his captain, who had maintained an unequal contest against superior numbers. He had not accomplished this until after a severe struggle: being closely pressed in front and flank, and his men falling in numbers around him, he had deliberately given orders to advance, under a dreadful fire; until, gaining a position of more security, he compelled the enemy to retire, and came up in time to co-operate with captain Ketchum's detachment. The admirable coolness and intrepidity of his corps were worthy of veterans, and proved the great progress the Americans had made in discipline. The battalion on the American right, under major Leavenworth, was not only engaged with the British infantry, but often exposed to the fire of their batteries. One of its officers, captain Harrison, had his leg shot off by a cannon ball; but so doubtful did he consider the contest, that he would not suffer a man to be taken from his duty to bear him from the field, and supported the torture of his wound until the action ceased. After the lapse of an hour from the time the action became general, captain Towson having completely silenced the enemy's most powerful battery, now turned upon their infantry at that moment advancing to a charge. The fire from Towson's artillery, which poured upon them; the oblique discharges of a part of M'Neill's battalion, which was so posted as to assail both in front and flank; the steadiness of the two battalions; and the apparent issue of the contest on his right flank with major Jesup, compelled general Riall to retire, until he reached the sloping ground which led to Chippewa. From this point the British fled in confusion to their intrenchments, which were too strong to be assailed.

In this engagement general Ripley's brigade was not concerned. He had proposed to the commander-in-chief, at the commencement of the action, to take a position to the left of the first brigade, and passing it, to turn the enemy's right, and prevent his retreat to Chippewa. At that time general Brown

T*

declined his proposal ; but afterwards, when the British began to retire, he directed him to put his plan in execution. The precipitation of their movements however frustrated it.

The result of this first regular pitched battle furnished convincing proof, that nothing but discipline was wanting to give to our soldiers on land the same excellence which our seamen had discovered on the ocean. The battle was fought with great judgment and coolness on both sides, and its result, considering the numbers engaged, was exceedingly sanguinary. The loss of the Americans in killed, wounded and missing, amounted to three hundred and thirty-eight. Among the wounded were, colonel Campbell ; captains King, of the Twenty-third, Read, of the Twenty-fifth, Harrison, of the Forty-second ; lieutenants Palmer and Brimhall, of the Ninth, Barron, of the Eleventh, and De Wit and Patchim, of the Twenty-fifth. The total loss of the British, according to the report of general Drummond, was five hundred and five, of whom forty-six were missing, and the remainder either killed or wounded. Among the wounded were, seven captains, seventeen lieutenants, captain Holland aid to general Riall, lieutenant-colonel the marquis of Tweeddale and lieutenants-colonel Gordon and Dickson. Few occurrences during the war afforded a more lively gratification to the people. The most honourable testimonials of approbation were bestowed upon the principal officers concerned : the brevet rank of lieutenant-colonel was conferred upon majors Jesup, Leavenworth and M'Neill, and of major on captains Towson, Crooker and Harrison. Several other officers were named as having distinguished themselves, among these, major Wood of the engineers, captain Harris of the dragoons, and lieutenant M'Donald, acquitted themselves with much credit.

The defeat of Riall having been communicated to lieutenant general Drummond, he sent a regiment to reinforce him, and enable him to repel any attack upon his works. General Brown meanwhile remained at his encampment, determined to dislodge the British. As the most effectual mode, he detached general Ripley, on the 8th of the month. to a point three miles above the enemy's camp, to open a road to the Chippewa river, and to construct a bridge over it for the passage of the troops. This order was executed with so much secrecy, that the bridge was nearly completed before it was discovered by the enemy. General Riall now ordered his artillery to advance and prevent the Americans from completing their works ; but the cannon of general Ripley compelled the British to retire. Fearing an attack on his right flank and in front, general Riall soon after abandoned his works, which were occupied by

general Brown that evening; and fell back on Queenstown.   On
the following day he retired to Ten Mile creek.

The American army, moving forward, encamped at Queenstown.   General Swift, at his own request, was now detached
with one hundred and twenty men, to reconnoiter the enemy's
works at Fort George.   On his arrival in the neighbourhood, he
surprised an outpost, and took prisoners a corporal and his guard.
One of these, after having asked and received quarter, suddenly
raised his piece, and wounded Swift mortally.   The general
instantly killed the assassin; and on the approach of a party of
the enemy brought up by the firing of the soldier, he continued,
regardless of his wound, to fight at the head of his detachment
until the enemy was repulsed.   This gallant officer died soon
after he was brought to camp, and was interred with all the
honours the army could bestow.   He had been a distinguished
soldier of the revolution; and his loss was sincerely regretted.

The question as to the step next to be taken—whether to
follow up the enemy rapidly and annihilate his force, or first
to attack Forts Niagara and George—was submitted by general
Brown to a council of war.   The latter was resolved upon.
Preparatory to this, general Ripley and general Porter were
ordered to reconnoiter the forts—the one along the Niagara,
the other by the way of St David's, for the purpose of ascer-
taining their respective situations and obtaining other information necessary for the attack.   This service they successfully
performed, although much exposed to the fire of the garrison of
Fort George, and assailed by skirmishing parties sent out from
thence.   The plan, however, was abandoned, in consequence, as
was alleged by general Brown, of the failure of the fleet to
co-operate with him, commodore Chauncey being at this time
extremely ill.   The general therefore, withdrawing from the advanced position to which he had moved on the Niagara and Lake
Ontario, prepared to pursue the British army to Burlington
Heights; and, with a view to this, on the 24th he fell back to
the junction of the Chippewa with the Niagara.

Lieutenant-general Drummond, mortified that his veteran
troops should have been beaten by what he considered raw
Americans, was anxious for an opportunity of retrieving his
credit.   He had collected every regiment from Burlington and
York, and the lake being free, had been able to transport troops
from Fort George, Kingston and even Prescott.   General Riall
took post at Queenstown, immediately after it was abandoned
by the Americans in their retreat to Chippewa; thence he threw
a strong detachment across the Niagara to Lewistown, to
threaten the town of Schlosser, which contained the supplies of

general Brown, and also his sick and wounded ; and at the same time despatched a party in advance of him on the Niagara road. With the view of drawing off the enemy from his attempt on the village across the river, general Brown, having no means of transporting troops to its defence, directed general Scott to move towards Queenstown with his brigade. seven hundred strong, together with Towson's artillery and one troop of dragoons and mounted men. At four o'clock in the afternoon of the 25th, general Scott led his brigade from the camp, and after proceeding along the Niagara about two miles and a half from the Chippewa, and within a short distance of the cataracts, discovered general Riall on an eminence near Lundy's Lane, a position of great strength, where he had planted a battery of nine pieces of artillery, two of which were brass twenty-four pounders. On reaching a narrow strip of woods which intervened between the Americans and the British line, captains Harris and Pentland, whose companies formed a part of the advance, and were first fired on, gallantly engaged the enemy. The latter now retreated for the purpose of drawing the American column to the post at Lundy's Lane. General Scott resolutely pressed forward, after despatching major Jones to the commander-in-chief with intelligence that he had come up with the enemy. He had no sooner cleared the wood, and formed in line on a plain finely adapted to military manœuvres, than a tremendous cannonade commenced from the enemy's battery, situated on their right, which was returned by captain Towson, whose artillery were posted opposite, and on the left of the American line, but without being able to bring his pieces to bear on the eminence. The action was continued for an hour, against a force three times that of the American brigade. The Eleventh and Twenty-second regiments having expended their ammunition, colonel Brady and lieutenant-colonel M'Neill being both severely wounded, and nearly all the other officers either killed or wounded, they were withdrawn from action. Lieutenant Crawford, lieutenant Sawyer, and a few other officers of those regiments, attached themselves to the Ninth, in such stations as were assigned them. This regiment, under its gallant leader lieutenant-colonel Leavenworth, was now obliged to maintain the whole brunt of the action. Orders had been given him to advance and charge on the height, and with the Eleventh and Twenty-second regiments to break the enemy's line, but, on information being communicated to general Scott of the shattered condition of the latter, the order was countermanded. Colonel Jesup, at the commencement of the action, had been detached, with the Twenty-fifth regiment, to attack the left of the enemy's line.

The British now pressed forward on the Ninth regiment, which with wonderful firmness withstood the attack of their overwhelming numbers. Being reduced at length to not more than one half, and being compelled at every moment to resist fresh lines of the British, colonel Leavenworth despatched a messenger to general Scott, to communicate its condition. The general rode up in person, roused the flagging spirits of the brave men with the pleasing intelligence that reinforcements were expected every moment, and besought them to hold their ground. Lieutenant Riddle, already well known as a reconnoitering officer, was the first to come to their assistance, having been drawn to the place by the sound of the cannon, while on a scouring expedition in the neighbouring country. The same circumstance advised general Brown of the commencement of the action, and induced him to proceed rapidly to the scene after giving orders to general Ripley to follow with the second brigade. He was already on his way when he met major Jones, and, influenced by his communication, he despatched him to bring up general Porter's volunteers, together with the artillery.

The situation of Scott's brigade was every moment becoming more critical. Misled by the obstinacy of their resistance, general Riall overrated their force, and despatched a messenger to general Drummond, at Fort George, for reinforcements, notwithstanding that the number engaged on his side, thus far, had been more than double that of the Americans. During the period that both armies were waiting for reinforcements, a voluntary cessation from combat ensued; and for a time no sound broke upon the stillness of the night, but the groans of the wounded, mingling with the distant thunder of the cataract of Niagara. The silence was once more interrupted, and the engagement renewed with augmented vigour, on the arrival of general Ripley's brigade, major Hindman's artillery, and general Porter's volunteers, and at the same time of lieutenant-general Drummond with reinforcements to the British. The artillery were united to Towson's detachment, and soon came into action; Porter's brigade was displayed on the left, and Ripley's formed on the skirts of the wood to the right, of Scott's brigade. General Drummond took the command in person of the front line of the enemy with his fresh troops.

In the meantime, colonel Jesup, who, as before mentioned, had been ordered, at the commencement of the action, to take post on the right, had succeeded during the engagement, after a gallant contest, in turning the left flank of the enemy. Taking advantage of the darkness of the night, and the carelessness of the enemy in omitting to place a proper guard across a road on his left, he

threw his regiment in the rear of their reserve ; and surprising
one detachment after another, made prisoners of so many of
their officers and men, that his progress was greatly impeded by it. The laws of war would have justified him in
putting them to death; " but the laurel, in his opinion, was
most glorious when entwined by the hand of mercy," and he
generously spared them. One of his officers, captain Ketchum,
who had already distinguished himself at the battle of Chippewa, had the good fortune to make prisoner of general Riall,
who, on the arrival of general Drummond, had been assigned
to the command of the reserve, and also of captain Loring,
the aid of general Drummond. The latter was a most fortunate
circumstance, as it prevented the concentration of the British
forces contemplated by that officer, before the Americans were
prepared for his reception. After hastily disposing of his prisoners, colonel Jesup felt his way through the darkness to the
place where the hottest fire was kept up on the brigade to which
he belonged ; and drawing up his regiment behind a fence, on
one side of the Queenstown road, but in the rear of a party of
British infantry, posted on the opposite side of the same road,
he surprised them by a fire so destructive, that they instantly
broke and fled. " The major," said general Brown, " showed
himself to his own army in a blaze of fire." He received the
applause of the general, and was ordered to form on the right
of the second brigade.

General Ripley, seeing the impracticability of operating upon
the enemy from the place at which he had been ordered to post
his brigade, or of advancing from it in line through a thick
wood, in the impenetrable darkness of the night, determined,
with that rapid decision which characterizes the real commander,
to adopt the only measure by which he saw a hope of saving
the first brigade from destruction, or of ultimately achieving the
victory ; and which. when made known to the commander-in-
chief, was instantly sanctioned. The eminence occupied by the
enemy's artillery was the key to their position. Addressing
himself to colonel Miller, the same who had distinguished himself at Magagua, he inquired whether he could storm the battery
at the head of the Twenty-first regiment, while he would himself
support him with the younger regiment, the Twenty-third. To
this the wary, but intrepid veteran replied, in unaffected phrase,
I WILL TRY, SIR ; words, which were afterwards worn on the
buttons of his regiment; and immediately prepared for the
arduous effort, by placing himself directly in front of the hill.
The Twenty-third was formed in close column, by its commander, major M'Farland ; and the First regiment, under co-

lonel Nicholas, which had that day arrived from a long and
fatiguing march, was left to keep the infantry in check. The
two regiments moved on to one of the most perilous charges
ever attempted ; the whole of the artillery, supported by the
fire of a powerful line of infantry, pouring upon them as they
advanced. The Twenty-first moved on steadily to its purpose :
the Twenty-third faltered on receiving the deadly fire of the
enemy, but was soon rallied by the personal exertions of general Ripley. When within a hundred yards of the summit,
they received another dreadful discharge, by which major
M'Farland was killed, and the command of his regiment devolved on major Brooks. To the amazement of the British,
the intrepid Miller firmly advanced, until within a few paces
of their cannon, when he impetuously charged upon the artillerists, and after a short but desperate resistance, carried the whole
battery, and formed his line in its rear, upon the ground previously occupied by the British infantry. In carrying the
largest pieces, the Twenty-first suffered severely : lieutenant
Cilley, after an unexampled effort, fell wounded by the side
of the piece which he took ; and there were few of the officers
of this regiment who were not either killed or wounded. By
the united efforts of these two regiments, and the bringing into
line of the First, the fate of this bold assault was determined :
the British infantry were in a short time driven down the eminence, out of the reach of musquetry, and their own cannon turned
upon them. This admirable effort completely changed the
nature of the battle : every subsequent movement was directed to
this point, as upon the ability to maintain it the result of the conflict entirely depended. Major Hindman was now ordered to
bring up his corps, including captain Towson's detachment,
and post himself, with his own and the captured cannon, to
the right of Ripley's brigade, and between it and the Twenty-
fifth, Jesup's, regiment, while the volunteers of general Porter
retained their position on the left of Scott's brigade.

Stung with rage and mortification at this most extraordinary
and successful exploit of the Americans, general Drummond, the
British commander, now considered it absolutely essential to the
credit of the British army, and to avoid insupportable disgrace,
that the cannon and the eminence on which they were captured
should be retaken. Having been greatly reinforced, he advanced
upon Ripley, with a heavy and extended line, outflanking him
on both extremes. The Americans stood silently awaiting his
approach, which could only be discovered by the sound attending it, reserving their fire, in obedience to orders, until it could
be effective and deadly. The whole division of the British now

marched at a brisk step, until within twenty paces of the summit of
the height, when it poured in a rapid fire, and prepared to rush
forward with the bayonet. The American line being directed by
the fire of the enemy, returned it with deadly effect. The enemy
were thereby thrown into momentary confusion; but being rallied,
returned furiously to the attack. A most tremendous conflict
ensued; which for twenty minutes continued with violence indescribable. The British line was at last compelled to yield, and
to retire down the hill. In this struggle general Porter's volunteers emulated the conduct of the regulars. The gallant
major Wood, of the Pennsylvania corps, and colonel Dobbin,
of the New York, gave examples of unshaken intrepidity.

It was not supposed, however, that this would be the last
effort of the British general; general Ripley therefore had the
wounded transported to the rear, and instantly restored his line
to order. General Scott's shattered brigade having been consolidated into one battalion, had during this period been held
in reserve behind the second brigade, under colonel Leavenworth; colonel Brady having been compelled, by the severity
of his wound, to resign the command. It was now ordered to
move to Lundy's Lane, and to form with its right towards the
Niagara road, and its left in the rear of the artillery.

After the lapse of half an hour, general Drummond was
heard again advancing to the assault with renovated vigour.
The direction at first given by general Ripley was again
observed. The fire of the Americans was dreadful; and the
artillery of major Hindman, which were served with great skill
and coolness, would have taken away all heart from the British
for this perilous enterprise, had not an example of bravery
been set them by the Americans. After the first discharge,
the British general threw himself with his entire weight upon
the centre of the American line. He was firmly received by
the gallant Twenty-first regiment, a few platoons only faltering,
which were soon restored by general Ripley. Finding that
no impression could be made, the whole British line again recoiled, and fell back to the bottom of the hill. During this
second contest, two gallant charges were led by general Scott
in person, the first upon the enemy's left, and the second on
his right flank, with his consolidated battalion; but having to
oppose double lines of infantry, his attempts, which would
have been decisive had they proved successful, were unavailing. Although he had most fortunately escaped unhurt thus
far, subsequently, in passing to the right, he received two severe
wounds: he did not quit the field, however, until he had directed

colonel Leavenworth to unite his battalion with the Twenty-fifth regiment, under the command of colonel Jesup.

Disheartened by these repeated defeats, the British were on the point of yielding the contest, when they received fresh reinforcements from Fort George, which revived their spirits, and induced them to make another and still more desperate struggle. After taking an hour to refresh themselves and recover from their fatigue, they advanced with a still more extended line, and with confident hopes of being able to overpower the Americans. Our countrymen, who had stood to their arms during all this time, were worn down with fatigue, and almost fainting with thirst, which there was no water at hand to quench. From the long interval which had elapsed since the second repulse, they had begun to cherish hopes that the enemy had abandoned a further attempt ; but in this they were disappointed. On the approach of the British for the third time, their courageous spirit returned, and they resolved never to yield the glorious trophies of their victory, until they could contend no longer. The British delivered their fire at the same distance as on the preceding onsets. But although it was returned with the same deadly effect, they did not fall back with the same precipitation as before ; they steadily advanced, and repeated their discharge A conflict, obstinate and dreadful beyond description, ensued. The Twenty-first, under its brave leader, firmly withstood the shock ; and although the right and left repeatedly fell back, they were as often rallied by the personal exertions of the general, and colonels Miller, Nicholas and Jesup. At length the two contending lines were on the very summit of the hill, where the contest was waged with terrific violence at the point of the bayonet. Such was the obstinacy of the conflict, that many battalions, on both sides, were forced back, and the opposing parties became mingled with each other. Nothing could exceed the desperation of the battle at the point where the cannon were stationed. The enemy having forced themselves into the very midst of major Hindman's artillery, he was compelled to engage them across the carriages and guns, and at last to spike two of his pieces. General Ripley, having brought back the broken sections to their positions and restored the line, now pressed upon the enemy's flanks and compelled them to give way. The centre soon following the example, and the attack upon the artillery being at this moment repulsed, the whole British line fled a third time ; and no exertions of their officers could restrain them, until they had placed themselves out of reach of the musquetry and artillery. The British now consented to relin-

U

quish their cannon, and retired beyond the borders of the field, leaving their dead and wounded.

General Brown had received two severe wounds at the commencement of the last charge, and was compelled to retire to the camp at the Chippewa, leaving the command to general Ripley. The latter officer had made repeated efforts to obtain the means of removing the captured artillery ; but the horses having been killed, and no drag ropes being at hand, they were still on the place where they had been captured, when orders were received from general Brown, to collect the wounded and return to camp immediately. The British cannon were therefore left behind, the smaller pieces having first been rolled down the hill. The whole of the troops reached the camp in good order about midnight, after an unmolested march.

It is much to be regretted that these trophies of victory could not have been secured ; as the circumstance of their recovery by the British gave them occasion, surprising as it may seem, to claim the victory. To high praise they certainly were entitled ; but to the merit of " a complete defeat of the Americans," they had no claim, and the assertion was an outrage to truth. A compliment for such a victory ought to infuse the blush of shame into the cheek of any honourable soldier who had a share in the contest so named.

The British force engaged, of whom twelve hundred were militia and five hundred Indians, was little short of five thousand men ; being nearly a third greater than that of the Americans. The loss on either side was proportioned to the nature of this dreadful and sanguinary battle. its aggregate, in both armies, amounted to one thousand seven hundred and twenty-nine ; and the killed and wounded alone to near one thousand four hundred. In the records of the most bloody battles we seldom meet with so great a number of officers killed and wounded. On the side of the British, one assistant adjutant-general, one captain, three subalterns, and seventy-nine non-commissioned officers and privates, were killed ; lieutenant-general Drummond, three lieutenant-colonels, two majors, eight captains, twenty-two subalterns, and five hundred and twenty-two non-commissioned officers and privates were wounded : one major general (Riall, who was also wounded), one aid-de-camp—captain Loring, five other captains, nine subalterns, and two hundred and twenty non-commissioned officers and privates, were prisoners or missing : making in all eight hundred and seventy-eight men. The American loss was, one major, five captains, five subalterns, and one hundred and fifty-nine non-commissioned officers and privates, killed ; major-general Brown, brigadier-generals Scott and Porter, two aids-de-camp, one brigade major, one colonel, four lieutenant-colonels. one major, seven captains, thirty-seven subalterns, and five hundred and fifteen non-commissioned officers and privates, wounded; and one brigade major, one captain, six subalterns, and one hundred and two non-commissioned officers and privates, prisoners or missing: making a grand total of eight hundred and fifty-one. Thus there was a difference of twenty-seven only, between the respective losses of the contending parties.

The commander-in-chief ordered general Ripley to refresh the troops on their arrival at the camp, and in the morning to proceed to the battle ground, and engage the enemy if circumstances permitted. On reconnoitering the enemy, he found them drawn up in advance of their position of the preceding day on the eminence, and presenting a formidable appearance. It would have been madness to renew the combat with a force which, on examination, amounted to only fifteen hundred men fit for duty; and he therefore properly declined it. His conduct was hastily censured by general Brown, in his despatches to the government. General Ripley, in consequence, had for a long period to contend with the obloquy of public opinion; and it was not until some time subsequently that the full extent of his merit was known. It is now generally admitted, that much of the praise of this brilliant victory is due to the skill and valour of this officer.

General Ripley, finding himself unable to make a stand against the superior force of the British, retreated to Fort Erie, and anticipating their approach, immediately set about extending its defences. The enemy, notwithstanding their pretended victory, did not think proper to follow up the Americans, until they had been reinforced by general De Watteville, with one thousand men. Their whole force, now amounting to upwards of five thousand men, appeared, on the 3d of August, before a fortification which a few days previously had been considered untenable, and commenced the erection of regular intrenchments. The besieged, at the same time, laboured incessantly to complete their arrangements for defence. The position which the American army had taken, for the purpose of maintaining itself against so great a superiority, possessed few natural advantages; and the work called Fort Erie was little more than a small unfinished redoubt. Situated about one hundred yards from the lake shore at its nearest angle, and on a plain of about fifteen feet elevation, this fort could be considered as nothing more than the strongest point of a fortified camp. A line of works was yet to be constructed in front, and

on the right and left to the lake ; the rear on the shore being
left open.   The fort itself probably did not occupy more than
a sixth of the space occupied by the line of defences ; and the
remainder could not be otherwise than hastily constructed.
Indeed, notwithstanding the slow and cautious approaches of
the British, much remained unfinished at the last moment.

On the same day that the enemy appeared before Fort Erie,
a detachment, under colonel Tucker, crossed the Niagara, for
the purpose of attacking Buffalo and recapturing general Riall.
This party, although subsequently increased by reinforcements to twelve hundred men, was repulsed by major Morgan
with but two hundred and forty men.   In this affair captain
Hamilton and lieutenants Wadsworth and M'Intosh were killed.

The defences of Fort Erie were sufficiently completed, by
the 7th, to keep at bay an enemy who had learned to respect
our arms.   From this day, until the 14th, there was an almost
incessant cannonade between the batteries of the besiegers and
the besieged.   In the frequent skirmishes which took place,
the Americans were generally victorious ; in one of them, however, they lost major Morgan, a brave officer, who had distinguished himself as above mentioned, and whose death was
sincerely lamented.   General Gaines had arrived shortly after
the commencement of the siege, and before any regular firing
had been entered upon   Being the senior officer, he assumed
the chief direction, and general Ripley returned to the command of his brigade.

On the night of the 14th, general Ripley perceived a bustle
in the British camp ; and conceiving that an assault was about
to be made, he despatched a messenger to apprize general
Gaines of his convictions, who, however, had already formed
a similar opinion.   Dispositions, in which the troops enthusi-
astically participated, were now rapidly made to receive the
expected assailants.

General Drummond had made arrangements to assail the
American fortifications on the right, centre and left at the same
instant ; and general Gaines, not knowing where the enemy
would make his attack, was prepared to meet him at all points.
The fort and bastions were placed under the command of captain Williams, of the artillery ; and a battery on the margin of
the lake was assigned to captain Douglass of the engineers.
A blockhouse, near the salient bastion of the fort, was occupied
by major Trimble with a detachment of infantry.   Captains
Biddle and Fanning, supported by general Porter's volunteers
and the riflemen, commanded the batteries in front.   The
whole of the artillery throughout the garrison were directed by

major Hindman. The first brigade, lately commanded by general Scott, now under lieutenant-colonel Aspinwall, was posted on the right; and general Ripley's, the second, brigade, supported Towson's battery at the southwestern extremity of the works, and the line of the works on the left. A few hours before the commencement of the assault, one of the enemy's shells exploded a small magazine within the American works, which was succeeded by a loud shout from the besiegers. The shout was returned by the Americans; and captain Williams, amid the smoke of the explosion, immediately discharged all his heavy guns.

At half past two in the morning, the darkness being excessive, the approach of the enemy's right column, one thousand three hundred strong, under lieutenant-colonel Fischer, was distinctly heard on the left of the garrison. The second brigade, and the artillery of Towson's battery were ready to receive them. Advancing steadily and quickly, the British assailed the battery with scaling ladders, and the line towards the lake with the bayonet. They were permitted to approach close up to the works, when a tremendous fire was opened upon them, and their column fell back in confusion. Colonel Fischer, rallying his men, again advanced furiously to the attack; but was a second time compelled to retire, with still greater loss. The possession of Towson's battery being considered essential to the general plan of assault, he next essayed to pass round the abattis by wading breast deep in the lake; but in this attempt he was unsuccessful, and nearly two hundred of his men were either killed or drowned. Without seeking to learn the result of the attack on other points, he now ordered a retreat to the British encampment.

The enemy's central and left columns having waited until colonel Fischer was completely engaged, colonel Scott, who commanded the left column, approached on the right along the lake; while lieutenant-colonel Drummond, with the central column, at the same moment advanced to the assault of the fort proper. Colonel Scott was checked by captain Douglass's battery, captains Boughton and Harding's New York and Pennsylvania volunteers on its right, the Ninth infantry under captain Foster on its left, and a six-pounder stationed there under the direction of colonel M'Ree. Their fire was so well directed, that the approaching column made a momentary pause at the distance of fifty yards, and then recoiled. Notwithstanding the rapid and heavy fire from captain Williams's artillery, the column of colonel Drummond, composed of eight hundred select troops, firmly advanced to the attack of the fort.

u

Suddenly applying his scaling ladders, he mounted the parapet, his officers calling out to the line extending to the lake on their left to cease firing. This artifice succeeded so well, that Douglass's battery and the infantry, supposing the order to have been given within the garrison, suspended their fire, and suffered colonel Scott, who had rallied his men, to approach their line. When the deception was discovered, it availed nothing, for the column, on its second charge, was resisted with so much effect, as to be compelled again to retreat, with the loss of its commander and a third of its numbers. The central column was, in the meanwhile, with great difficulty thrown back, although the troops within the fort were quickly reinforced from general Ripley's brigade, and general Porter's volunteers. Repeated assaults were made by colonel Drummond. Each time they were repulsed by colonel Hindman's artillery, and the infantry under major Trimble ; and now that colonel Scott's column had withdrawn from the action, lieutenant Douglass was engaged in giving such a direction to the guns of the battery, as to cut off the communication between colonel Drummond, and the reserve which was to be brought up to his support under lieutenant-colonel Tucker.

Colonel Drummond, although three times repulsed, was unwilling to renounce his undertaking. Availing himself of the darkness of the morning, which was increased by the smoke, he stole silently along the ditch, and suddenly applying his ladders, once more rapidly gained the parapet, crying out to his men to charge vigorously, and *give the Yankees no quarter!* This order was faithfully executed ; and the most furious strife now ensued that had been witnessed during the assault. All the efforts of major Hindman and the corps supporting him could not dislodge the enemy from the bastion, though they prevented him from approaching further. Captain Williams was mortally wounded ; lieutenants Watmough and M'Donough, severely. The latter, no longer able to fight, called for quarter. This was refused by colonel Drummond, who repeated his instructions to his troops to deny it in every instance. The declining and almost exhausted strength and spirits of the lieutenant being restored and roused by the barbarity of this order, he seized a handspike, and, with the desperation of madness, defended himself against the assailants, until he was shot by colonel Drummond himself. The latter survived this act only a few minutes : he received a ball in his breast, which terminated his existence. Brutal courage merits nothing but abhorrence, it is only when tempered with mercy, that valour is a virtue. The enemy still maintained their position, notwithstanding the death of their leader, and repulsed every attempt to dislodge them until daylight : they had, in the meantime, suffered excessively. The contest along the whole line of defences, with this exception, having ceased, considerable reinforcements were ordered up. The enemy now began to recoil ; and in a few moments many of them were thrown over the bastion. The reserve coming up to their support, the cannon of the Douglass battery enfiladed the column as it approached, and the artillery of lieutenant Fanning played upon it with great effect ; while a gun under the charge of captain Biddle was served with uncommon vivacity. A part of the reserve, to the number of from three to four hundred men, was nevertheless about to rush upon the parapet to the assistance of the recoiling soldiers, when a tremendous explosion took place under the platform of the bastion, which carried away the bastion and all who were on it. The reserve now fell back ; and the contest, in a short time, terminated in the entire defeat of the enemy, and their return to their encampment.

The British left on the field two hundred and twenty-two killed, among them fourteen officers of distinction ; one hundred and seventy-four wounded; and one hundred and eighty-six prisoners . making a total of five hundred and eighty-two. The official statement of general Drummond makes it in all nine hundred and five, of which fifty-seven were killed. The American loss amounted to seventeen killed, fifty-six wounded, and one lieutenant (Fontain, thrown out while defending the bastion) and ten privates prisoners : in all, eighty-four men. It was not until all hopes of carrying the fort were at an end, that the British deigned to make prisoners of a few wounded men who fell into their power.

The explosion of the bastion furnished the British with an excuse for their defeat ; and they represented its consequences as much more serious than they really were. It is certain, however, that the assault had already failed at every other point; and the small body of men in possession of the outer bastion could not by possibility have subdued the whole garrison. Nor was the number killed by the explosion so great as they stated : the slaughter of the enemy took place during the assault, which, at the time when the occurrence took place, had lasted upwards of an hour.

The enemy now remained quiet in his intrenchments until he received a reinforcement of two regiments. When they arrived, he renewed his assault on the fort from enlarged batteries, continuing it, with little intermission, to the latter end of August. On the 28th, general Gaines being severely wounded by the bursting of a shell, which compelled him to retire to Buffalo, the command again devolved on general Ripley.

The situation of the army in Fort Erie had begun to excite considerable uneasiness ; but the operations of sir George Prevost, about this time, in the vicinity of Champlain and Plattsburg, rendered it for a period very uncertain whether any relief could be sent by general Izard. It afterwards appeared, that orders to that effect had been given to this officer by the secretary of war ; but he was prevented, by a variety of causes, from moving as rapidly as could have been desired. The garrison, however, was strengthened by the daily arrival of militia and volunteers : and general Brown, having sufficiently recovered from his wounds, had returned to the command on the 2d of September. The siege was still maintained with vigour by the British, who had abandoned the idea of carrying the place otherwise than by regular approaches, although their force had been considerably augmented since their last defeat. The Americans laboured with unrelaxing assiduity, to complete their fortifications. Frequent skirmishes occurred, and a cannonade on either side was kept up ; but nothing of importance took place until the 17th of September. General Brown, observing that the enemy had just completed a battery, which would open a most destructive fire the next day, planned a sortie, which has been considered a military chef d'œuvre, and which was carried into execution on the day just mentioned. The British force consisted of three brigades, of one thousand five hundred men each . one of them was stationed at the works in front of Fort Erie ; the other two occupied a camp two miles in the rear. The design of general Brown was to " storm the batteries, destroy the cannon, and roughly handle the brigade on duty, before those in reserve could be brought up." A road had previously been opened by lieutenants Riddle and Frazer, in a circuitous course, through the woods, within pistol shot of the right flank of the line of hostile batteries, and with such secrecy as to have escaped the notice of the enemy. At two o'clock P. M. the troops were drawn up in readiness to make the sortie. The division on the American left, commanded by general Porter, was composed of riflemen and Indians under colonel Gibson, and two columns, the right commanded by colonel Wood, the left by general Davis of the New York militia; and was to proceed through the woods by the road which had been opened. The right division of the troops, under general Miller, was stationed in a ravine between the fort and the enemy's works, under general Miller, with orders not to advance until general Porter should have engaged their right flank.

The troops of general Porter advanced with so much celerity and caution, that their attack upon the enemy's flank gave the first intimation of their approach. A severe conflict ensued, in which those gallant officers, colonel Gibson and colonel Wood, fell at the head of their columns. Their respective commands now devolved on lieutenant-colonel M'Donald and major Brooks. In thirty minutes, possession was taken of the two batteries in this quarter, and also of a blockhouse in the rear, and its garrison. Three twenty-four-pounders were rendered useless, and their magazine blown up by lieutenant Riddle, who narrowly escaped the effects of the explosion. At this moment the troops under general Miller came up. Aided by colonel Gibson's column, they pierced the British intrenchments, and, after a sharp conflict, carried a battery and a blockhouse. In this assault brigadier-general Davis fell at the head of his volunteers. These batteries and the two blockhouses being in the possession of the Americans, general Miller's division directed its course toward the battery erected at the extremity of the enemy's left flank. At this moment they were joined by the reserve under general Ripley. The resistance here was much bolder and more obstinate. The works being exceedingly intricate, from the studied complexity of the successive lines of intrenchments, a constant use of the bayonet was the only mode of assailing them. The enemy had also, by this time, received considerable reinforcements from their encampment in the rear. General Miller continued to advance, notwithstanding the absence of those valuable officers, colonel Aspinwall and major Trimble, the former severely, the latter dangerously wounded. The Twenty-first regiment, under lieutenant-colonel Upham, belonging to the reserve, and part of the Seventeenth, uniting with the corps of general Miller, charged rapidly upon the battery, which was instantly abandoned by the British infantry and artillery. General Ripley, being the senior officer, now ordered a line to be formed for the protection of the detachments engaged in destroying the batteries, and was engaged in making arrangements for following up, on the rear of general Drummond, a success which had so far transcended expectation, when he received a wound in the neck, and falling by the side of major Brooks, was immediately transported to the fort. The objects of the sortie having been completely effected, general Miller called in his detachments, and retired in good order, with the prisoners and many trophies of this signal exploit. Thus, in a few hours, the labour of the enemy for forty-seven days, was destroyed; and, in addition to the loss of their cannon, upwards of a thousand of their men were placed hors de combat, of whom three hundred and eighty-five were taken prisoners. The American loss amounted to eighty-three killed, two hundred and sixteen wounded, and a like number missing. Besides those already mentioned, several other officers of great merit were killed in this affair: captains Armistead of the rifle corps, Hall of the Eleventh infantry, Bradford of the Twenty-first, and Buel of the volunteers; ensign O'Fling, of the Twenty-third infantry, a gallant officer; and lieutenants Brown, Belknap, and Blakesley, of the volunteers. On the third day after the British had achieved this splendid victory ! for as such it was claimed by them, they broke up their encampment, and marched to Fort George.

Soon after this affair, general Izard arrived with reinforcements from Plattsburg, and being the senior officer, succeeded to the command ; while general Brown was ordered to Sackett's Harbour. By this accession of force, and the completion of the defences, all apprehensions of any further attempt against Fort Erie were removed. About the latter end of July, the secretary at war, hearing that the British were sending strong reinforcements from Montreal to Kingston, had intimated to general Izard, the propriety of proceeding from Plattsburg to Sackett's Harbour with the principal part of his forces, for the purpose of threatening Prescott and Kingston, and at the same time of aiding general Brown in the prosecution of his part of the campaign. In pursuance of this intimation, the general moved to Sackett's Harbour, with nearly all his effective force, amounting to four thousand men, arriving there on the 17th of September. The events which had in the meantime occurred, and which have been already detailed, had given a new face to the campaign. Shortly before the arrival of the general at Sackett's Harbour, he had received a letter from general Brown, giving information of his critical position, and calling for speedy relief. It was not before the 20th, that general Izard was enabled to embark his troops on lake Ontario, and the 12th of October had arrived before he actually reached Fort Erie. It will be seen, in a subsequent chapter, that the post which he left was, soon after his departure, placed in a situation as critical as that which he had come to relieve. These were the unavoidable results of prosecuting the war with a handful of men, along a frontier of such immense extent, in the expectation that small corps, at distances of four or five hundred miles apart, could march to the relief of each other, or act on concerted plans, subject to innumerable contingencies. Fortunately, before the arrival of general Izard, the success of the sortie planned by general Brown, had compelled the enemy to raise the siege. The approach of general Izard, in all probability, had furnished some inducement to the adoption of this step by the enemy.

A sufficient garrison, under lieutenant-colonel Hindman, being left for the protection of Fort Erie, the army moved towards the Chippewa, to operate offensively against the enemy ; but nothing of moment occurred for some time, in consequence of the shyness of the latter.

Before the close of the campaign, a gallant affair was achieved by general Bissel, of the second brigade of the first division. On the 18th of October, he was detached with nine hundred men, to the neighbourhood of Cook's mills, at Lyon's creek, a branch of the Chippewa, for the purpose of destroying the enemy's stores in that quarter. After driving in a picket guard and capturing its officers, he threw across the creek two light companies under captain Dorman and lieutenant Horrel, and a rifle company under captain Irvine, and then encamped. The next morning the detachment was assailed by the marquis of Tweeddale with twelve hundred men. The companies on the other side of the creek received the enemy's first fire, and sustained the attack until general Bissel had formed his men and brought them to their support. Colonel Pinkney, with the Fifth regiment, was ordered to turn the enemy's right flank and cut off a piece of artillery which they had brought into action, while major Barnard advanced in front with instructions to make a free use of the bayonet. These orders were rapidly carried into execution. The whole line of the enemy began to recoil ; and the American reserve, composed of the Fifteenth regiment under major Grindage, and the Sixteenth under colonel Pearce, was no sooner discovered advancing, than the marquis fell back in disorder to his intrenchments at the mouth of the river, leaving his killed and wounded behind. After pursuing him for a small distance, general Bissel, in compliance with his orders, proceeded to destroy the stores at the Mills ; and then retreated, with a loss of sixty-seven killed, wounded and missing.

Immediately after the repulse of the marquis of Tweeddale, the weather growing cold and the season for military operations drawing to a close, it was determined to destroy Fort Erie, and evacuate Upper Canada. This was accordingly effected ; and the troops were transported to the American side.

and distributed in winter quarters at Buffalo, Black Rock and Batavia.

Thus terminated the third invasion of Canada, if it could properly be so called ; for it was not generally expected that any thing further would be accomplished, than keeping in check the forces of the enemy and regaining what we had lost on our own side. At the opening of the campaign, general Brown indulged a hope of being able, in conjunction with commodore Chauncey, to subdue the British forces in the neighbourhood of Lake Ontario and to possess himself of Kingston ; but towards the beginning of autumn, so material a change had occurred in our situation, in consequence of the great augmentation of the British force on the Canada frontier, and the invasions of our territory on the sea coast, that all idea of making an impression on Canada, with the means then on foot, was abandoned. It was asserted by the friends of the administration, that the best mode of protecting the Atlantic coast, was to threaten Canada, and thus compel Great Britain to concentrate the greater part of her force in that quarter. While the British regulars, it has since been ascertained, exceeded twenty thousand, nearly all veterans ; those of the Americans scarcely reached ten thousand—the whole of which force, distributed in the different Atlantic cities, could not have afforded much dependence for defence from the troops which would have been sent against them, had Great Britain been relieved from the defence of Canada. It is very questionable whether the permanent acquisition of that province would materially have benefited us. Many of its inhabitants were persons who fled from this country during our contest for independence , and it was not likely that they would willingly consent that it should be incorporated into our republic.

The most important results, however, followed the campaign on the Niagara. The character of American troops when under proper discipline, was thereby developed ; and was productive of as much honour to the United States, as of surprise to the enemy. The experience gained in the two first years of the war was scarcely sufficient to form good officers ; but during the residue of the period, the army was composed of better materials, the aversion for enlistment was gradually subsiding, and commissions were sought by young men of education and talents. Another year would have produced an army, which Great Britain might have regarded with some uneasiness. That spirit, which bestows superiority to man in every station, was beginning to discover its resistless power ; and the closing scenes of this campaign placed the army on a level with the navy.   What is that spirit?   It is the spirit of freedom ; it is that which gives conscious dignity and worth to the soldier and the citizen.   It is that which gave victories to Greece, and gained triumphs for Rome, and which has carried the power of Britain round the globe.   It was already proved to the world, that we could conquer on land as well as at sea. The battles of Niagara and Chippewa, both, were won by a combination of military skill and personal courage ; and the defence of Fort Erie, and the sortie from thence, had they been achieved by the arms of Great Britain, would have ranked among the most distinguished acts of valour.

In the course of the summer, several expeditions were undertaken to the westward.   An attempt was made by major Croghan, with the co-operation of the fleet of Lake Erie under commodore Sinclair, to regain possession of the fort and island of Michilimackinac.   On the 4th of August, the gallant young officer effected a landing on the island, but soon found that the enemy was in such strength as to render the capture of the place hopeless : he therefore, after a severe conflict, returned to the shipping, with the loss of about sixty in killed and wounded ; among the former, major Holmes, a valuable officer, and of the latter captain Desha of Kentucky.   The expedition was not altogether useless : Fort St Joseph's, and the British establishment at Sault St Mary's were destroyed.   On leaving the island, commodore Sinclair stationed two of his schooners, the Scorpion and Tigress, near St Joseph's, to cut off the supplies of the British garrison at Michilimackinac.   These were unfortunately surprised by a very superior force of the enemy, and carried by boarding, after great slaughter.

On the 22d of October, general M'Arthur, with about seven hundred men, marched from Detroit into the enemy's country, and, after dispersing all their detachments in the neighbourhood of the river Thames, destroying their stores, and taking one hundred and fifty prisoners, arrived, without loss, at Detroit on the 17th of the following month.   A severe injury was thus inflicted upon the British, and their project of attacking Detroit rendered impracticable.

v

CHAPTER XVIII.

War on the Sea Coast—Engagements between the Enemy and Barney's Flotilla in Chesapeake Bay—Plunderings of the British—Washington and Baltimore threatened —Preparations for Defence—General Winder appointed to command the Troops to be assembled—Impracticability of collecting a sufficient Force—Arrival of Reinforcements to the British—Landing of the British Army under General Ross—Advance of the British on Washington—American Army takes post at Bladensburg—Battle of Bladensburg—Defeat of the Americans—Washington abandoned to the Enemy— British burn the Public Buildings—Retreat of the British to their Shipping—Plunder of Alexandria—Repulse of the British at Moors Fields, and Death of Sir Peter Parker— Resignation of the Secretary of War—Trial and Acquittal of General Winder— Letter of Admiral Cochrane to the American Secretary of State—His Reply—Reflections.

THE shifting scenes of this war, carried on over a surface so extensive, and with objects so various, once more bring us back to the Atlantic sea coast. With the return of spring, the British renewed their practice of petty plundering and barbarous devastation on the waters of Chesapeake Bay, and to an extent still greater than they had carried it the year before. A flotilla, for the defence of the inlets and smaller rivers of the bay, consisting of a cutter, two gun-boats and nine barges, was placed under the command of that gallant veteran, commodore Barney. On the 1st of June 1814, he gave chase to two of the enemy's schooners, one of which carried eighteen guns, but on the appearance of a large ship, which despatched a number of barges to cut him off, the commodore ordered his flotilla, by signal, to sail up the Patuxent. Here he engaged the enemy's schooners and barges, and succeeded in beating them off and inflicting considerable injury on them. In a few days, the enemy, having been reinforced, followed the flotilla into St Leonard's creek, and made another attempt on it, but were again compelled to retire, and pursued to their ships. On the 10th, the enemy made a still more formidable attack upon the flotilla, with the two schooners and with twenty barges. After a smart action, the barges were driven for shelter to the eighteen-gun schooner, which was then so roughly handled at long shot, that her crew ran her aground and abandoned her. These attempts were frequently repeated until the 26th, when the commodore, having received a reinforcement of artillerists and marines, moved against the enemy's squadron, two of the vessels of which were frigates, and, after an action of two hours, drove them from their anchorage. The commodore, finding the blockade of the St Leonard's raised, sailed out, and ascended the Patuxent.

After this, the enemy were constantly engaged in making inroads on the defenceless and unprotected settlements and villages along the bay and its various inlets. The towns of Benedict and Lower Marlborough, on the Patuxent, were plundered of considerable quantities of tobacco, merchandize and cattle. In the detail of these operations given by themselves, it appears to have been their uniform practice, to destroy the shipping, carry away the tobacco and other articles which they found in quantities, and induce the negroes to join them. A great number of individuals in easy, and even affluent circumstances were reduced to poverty. Several gallant attempts were made by general Taylor, and general Hungerford, in one of which the former was wounded and unhorsed and narrowly escaped capture, to repress their incursions into Virginia; but, generally, the militia, being hastily assembled, were found inefficient. At Kinsale, St Mary's, and various other places, admiral Cockburn obtained considerable booty in tobacco, negroes and household furniture.

Towards the close of June, apprehensions began to be entertained, that the enemy had in view some more serious object of attack—either Baltimore, or Washington. Much alarm had been felt in these places the previous year; but after it had subsided, an opinion, probably well founded, was indulged, that a land force, greatly more considerable than was then at the command of the British, would be required to make any serious impression upon either of these places, or even upon Annapolis or Norfolk. This was particularly proved in the attack upon the latter; and it was justly thought, that the enemy then received a lesson which would render him cautious of attacking the larger towns. But sudden and unforeseen occurrences in Europe had entirely changed the face of things: Great Britain was now able to supply what she was not possessed of the year before, a powerful land force. Our government received certain intelligence from Messrs Gallatin and Bayard, that our enemy was about to send powerful reinforcements to America. From the English prints it appeared that England was extravagantly elated by the great events which had transpired on the continent of Europe, took to herself the whole merit of being the conqueror of Napoleon, and in reality believed herself the mistress of the world. She was well acquainted with our situation : she knew that our regular troops on the Canada frontier could not be withdrawn from thence, at a moment when she was preparing a powerful army to penetrate our northern states ; and that it was impossible for us, in the short space of time which had elapsed since the overthrow of Bonaparte and the consequent release of her land troops from occupation, to embody a considerable and efficient force. The American cities, although tolerably well fortified against any approach by water, were all exposed to attack by land. A few thousand regulars scattered along a coast of fifteen hundred miles, and inexperienced militia drawn together on the spur of the occasion, were all the force we had to oppose to the veteran soldiers of our enemy. There is no doubt that militia constitute the best materials for armies, because, individually, each man is influenced by higher motives than those which generally actuate the enlisted soldier ; but, in order to be efficient, to use the words of a great friend of this species of force, " they must be on a right foot ;" they must be encamped, disciplined, harmonised, accustomed to see danger, and taught to obey and confide in their officers. This is not the work of a day. In the open field, where active and practised evolutions are necessary, the novelty of the duty, as well as the want of mutual reliance, renders it impossible for this description of force to encounter, with effect, an army of veterans, used to dangers, and so regularly compacted by discipline as to act as it were with one mind.

The attention of the president of the United States being seriously awakened to the approaching danger, by the news that reinforcements were to be sent to the British fleet then in Chesapeake Bay, he called a council of the heads of the departments, and suggested the propriety of collecting all the regulars within reach, of forming a camp of at least three thousand men at some point between the Patuxent and the Eastern Branch of the Potomac, and of embodying ten thousand militia at Washington These ideas appeared to meet the approbation of all ; and there is little doubt, that could they have been carried into execution, both the cities of Baltimore and Washington might safely have bid defiance to the British arms. Steps were immediately taken in furtherance of these views. Requisitions were made on the District of Columbia, for her whole quota of militia, amounting to two thousand men ; on Maryland for the same, six thousand men ; on Pennsylvania for five thousand men ; and on Virginia for two thousand men : making

JAMES MADISON.

in the whole fifteen thousand men ; of which ten thousand, it
was thought, would not fail to take the field.   It was ascertained, that about a thousand regulars could be depended on ;
besides a squadron of horse then in Pennsylvania, some additional regulars which were ordered from North Carolina, and
commodore Barney's men, in case it should be found necessary
to abandon his flotilla.   This, on paper, was a formidable army :
but, with the exception of the regulars, the soldiers of which
it was to be composed were at their respective homes—many
of them at a considerable distance ; and the work of collecting,
embodying. arming and disciplining them, operations requiring
time and subject to delays, was yet to be performed.

A new military district, composed of Maryland, the District
of Columbia and part of Virginia, was formed ; and on the 5th
of July the command of it was given to general Winder, an
officer who had been taken prisoner by the British at the battle
of Stony Creek, and who had recently been exchanged.   The
duties assigned to him were among the most important entrusted
to any one during the war, and were of an exceedingly arduous and difficult nature.   The army, with which he was to
defend the important cities of Baltimore and Washington, existed
only in prospect; and whether it could be brought into the field
or not, depended upon events beyond his control.   In justice
to himself, it is to be regretted, that, in these circumstances,
he had not declined the command ; but the desire of distinction
and a sincere wish to serve his country overcoming every personal consideration, he diligently employed himself, from the
moment of his appointment, in visiting every part of the country and examining its different fortifications—itself a work of
considerable labour and time, and in assiduously collecting his
force.   In this latter undertaking, unexpected difficulties occurred.   The governor of Maryland, after issuing draughts for
three thousand men, found that scarcely as many hundred could
be collected.   With the governor of Pennsylvania, matters were
still worse : he informed the secretary at war, that in consequence of the deranged state of the militia law, the executive
had at that moment no power to enforce a draught ; but that
he would appeal to the patriotism of the people, in the hope
that the legal objection would not be made.   Seven thousand
men were thus at once out of the question, and of the remaining eight thousand men, not more than one-third could be
relied on.   At the beginning of August, the general had but a
thousand regulars, actually collected ; and about four thousand
militia, of which only the smaller part were collected,   On
the failure of the draught in the state of Maryland, the force
v*

then embodied at Annapolis was, by the consent of the governor, taken as part of the state requisition. A brigade of Maryland militia, under general Stansbury, was also placed at the disposal of general Winder ; but the inhabitants of Baltimore, near which city it was collected, recollecting their own exposed situation, could not part with it without reluctance.

This is a candid statement of the causes which produced the subsequent disaster; for in the circumstances the event could scarcely have happened otherwise than as it did, without the occurrence of one of those extraordinary turns of fortune, of which we can form no calculation. It would be wrong to charge the blame, which was justly due, exclusively to the agents in the affair. A portion must be assumed by the nation, and by our political institutions.

The expected reinforcements to the British fleet, twenty-one sail of the line, under admiral Cochrane, arrived in Chesapeake Bay on the 16th of August, and were soon joined by a fleet in great force under admiral Malcolm. Accompanying these were several thousand land troops, under one of Wellington's most active officers, general Ross. An expedition was destined against Baltimore or Washington, but until the last moment it was uncertain against which in particular. The enemy divided his force into three parts. One division was sent up the Potomac, under captain Gordon, for the purpose of bombarding Fort Warburton, and opening the way to the city of Washington; and another, under sir Peter Parker, was despatched to threaten Baltimore. The main body, whose proceedings we are now to relate, ascended the Patuxent, apparently with the intention of destroying commodore Barney's flotilla, which had taken refuge at the head of that river, but with the real intention, as it was soon discovered, of attacking Washington. In prosecution of this plan, the expedition proceeded to Benedict, the head of frigate navigation. This place, on the west bank of the Patuxent, was reached on the 19th of August; and on the next day the debarkation of the land forces under general Ross, to the number of six thousand, was completed. On the 21st, pursuing the course of the river, the troops moved to Nottingham, and on the 22d arrived at Upper Marlborough; a flotilla, consisting of launches and barges, under the command of admiral Cockburn, ascending the river and keeping pace with them. The day following, the flotilla of commodore Barney, in obedience to orders to that effect, was blown up by men left for the purpose ; the commodore having already joined general Winder with his seamen and marines.

General Winder at this time, when the enemy were within

twenty miles of the capital, was at the head of only three thousand men, fifteen hundred of whom were militia entirely untried. The Baltimore militia, those from Annapolis, and the Virginia detachment, had not yet arrived. His camp was at the Woodyard, twelve miles from Washington. It was still doubtful whether the British intended an attack upon Fort Warburton, which could offer but little resistance to their land forces, although it could be formidable to their ships, or intended to march directly on Washington. The first was certainly the safer course of action, and as the enemy did not take it, it must be inferred that they were well acquainted with the incapacity of the city at this moment to resist an attack. On the afternoon of the 22d, the British army again set out, and after skirmishing with the Americans, halted for the night, five miles in advance of Upper Marlborough. General Winder now retreated to a place called the Old Fields, which covered Bladensburg, the bridges on the Eastern Branch of the Potomac, and Fort Warburton. Colonel Monroe, the secretary of state, and subsequently president of the United States, had been with him for several days, assisting him with his counsel, and actively engaged in reconnoitering the enemy; and he was now joined by the president and heads of departments, who remained until the next evening. The anxious and painful situation of the general rendered him desirous of benefiting by the counsel of the first officers of the nation; and their uneasiness, in the urgency of the moment, induced them to hazard their opinions, perhaps too freely, on matters purely executive. Where prompt decision is necessary, the suggestions and expedients of too many minds do more harm than good. On the 23d, colonel Scott and major Peter were detached with some field pieces, and the companies of captains Davidson and Stull, to skirmish with the enemy; who however continued to advance, and took a position, on the evening of the same day, within three miles of Old Fields. Apprehensive of a night attack, which would deprive him of his great superiority in cannon, general Winder retired to the city, intending to select a position between it and Bladensburg, where he might oppose the enemy with his whole force.

On the preceding evening, general Stansbury had arrived with his brigade at Bladensburg, after a very fatiguing march, and immediately despatched his aid, major Woodyear, with the intelligence to general Winder. On the evening following, he was joined by colonel Sterrett's, the Fifth Baltimore, regiment, five hundred strong, and a rifle battalion under major Pinkney, late attorney-general of the United States. General Stansbury's command amounted to two thousand men. About twelve o'clock at night, the secretary of state arrived at the general's quarters, and communicating the circumstance of the enemy's advance on general Winder, advised him to fall in the enemy's rear immediately; but the general objected, on the score of having been ordered to this post, and besides, that his men were so much harassed and fatigued by their march (a considerable portion having only just arrived), that it would be impracticable. During the night several false alarms were given, by which the troops were prevented from taking the repose they so much required, after fatigues to which the greater part of them were unaccustomed. On the receipt of the intelligence of general Winder's retreat, general Stansbury, on consultation with his officers, determined to move towards the city. Before day he crossed the bridge over the Eastern Branch of the Potomac, and after securing his rear, halted for a few hours. Early in the morning he again moved forward, with the view of taking possession of some ground for defence, when orders were received from general Winder to give battle to the enemy at Bladensburg; he therefore retraced his steps, and between ten and eleven o'clock halted his troops in an orchard field, to the left of the road from Washington to that place. The enemy were then within three miles of him, and in full march.

The best arrangements the time would permit were made. About five hundred yards from the bridge, the artillery from Baltimore, consisting of six six-pounders, under the command of captains Myers and Magruder, were posted behind a kind of breastwork; and major Pinkney's riflemen were placed in ambush to the right and left, so as to annoy the enemy when attempting to cross the stream, and at the same time, in conjunction with captain Doughty's company, to support the artillery. The Fifth Baltimore regiment was drawn up about fifty yards in the rear; and afterwards, perhaps injudiciously, removed much further. The other parts of the brigade were also so disposed, as to support the artillery, and annoy the enemy in his approach. Shortly after this disposition was made, lieutenant-colonel Beall arrived with about five hundred men from Annapolis, and was posted higher up in a wood on the right of the road. General Winder having, by this time, brought up his main body, had formed it in the rear of Stansbury's brigade, and in a line with Beall's detachment, and the heavy artillery under commodore Barney posted to the right on an eminence near the road. This line had scarcely been formed, when the engagement commenced. The president, with the heads of the departments, who had until now been present, with·drew ; as he conceived it proper to leave the direction of the combat to the military men.

About twelve o'clock of the 24th, a column of the enemy made its appearance on the hill which overhangs the stream, and moved down towards the bridge, throwing rockets, and apparently determined to force the passage. He now made an attempt to throw a strong body of infantry across the stream, but a few well directed shot from the artillery compelled him to shelter himself behind some houses. After a considerable pause, a large column of the British rapidly advanced in the face of the battery, which, although managed by officers of acknowledged skill and courage, was unable to repress them ; and they continued to push forward, until they formed a considerable body on the Washington road. These troops had not advanced far. when the company under captain Doughty, having discharged their pieces, fled, in spite of the efforts of their commander and of major Pinkney to rally them. The major's corps began its fire too soon, but did some execution. The British now were every moment drawing nearer the artillery, which could no longer be brought to bear upon them In the absence of troops to support them, it became unavoidably necessary for the artillerists to retire. which they did, followed by major Pinkney's riflemen, and leaving one gun behind them. The whole fell back upon the Fifth regiment, the nearest rallying point. A volunteer company of artillery now opened a cross fire upon the enemy, who were advancing through the orchard, but not with much effect. Colonel Sterrett was next directed to advance; but he was almost immediately halted in consequence of the other two regiments of Stansbury's brigade having been thrown into confusion by rockets and begun to give way. In a few minutes they took to flight. Sterrett's regiment evinced a disposition to make a gallant resistance ; but the enemy having by this time outflanked it, a retreat was ordered. This unfortunately was effected in confusion and disorder, the unavoidable consequence of the retreat of militia. Thus the first line was completely routed. The Baltimore artillery had, before this, taken a position higher up on the hill. On the right, colonel Beall, commanding the Annapolis militia, had thrown forward a small detachment under colonel Kramer, which, after maintaining its ground some time with considerable injury to the enemy, retired upon the main body. On the retreat of this detachment, the enemy advanced along the turnpike road, and coming in front of commodore Barney's artillery, were exposed to the fire of an eighteen-pounder, by which their

progress was checked; and in several subsequent attempts to
pass the battery, they were repulsed with great loss. In consequence of this, they attempted to flank the commodore's
right, by passing through an open field ; but this was frustrated
by captain Miller of the marines, with three twelve-pounders,
and the men of the flotilla acting as infantry. After being thus
kept in check for half an hour, the enemy succeeded in outflanking the right of the battery , and pressed upon the militia
of Annapolis, who fled, after giving an ineffectual fire. The
command of commodore Barney was now left to maintain the
contest alone : but the enemy no longer appeared in front ; he
continued to outflank, pushing forward a few scattering sharp-
shooters, by which the commodore was wounded and his horse
killed under him. His corps was by this time outflanked on
both sides; two of his principal officers were killed, and two
others wounded ; and, in the confusion, the ammunition wagons
had been driven off. His men therefore retreated, leaving
their pieces in the hands of the enemy   The commodore himself, after retiring a short distance, fell, exhausted by loss of
blood, to the ground. Being taken prisoner by the enemy, he
was treated with that courtesy which his gallantry merited,
and received the immediate attendance of their surgeons.

The Georgetown and City militia, and the regulars, still remained firm, having been stationed in the rear of the second
line, in positions the most convenient for annoying the enemy
and supporting the other corps. These being in danger every
moment of being outflanked, orders were sent to them to
retreat towards the city. After retiring a few hundred paces
as directed, they were joined by a regiment of Virginia militia,
which had arrived the evening before, but had not been ready
until now to take the field   General Winder still entertained
hopes of being able to rally his troops, and of fighting the
enemy between this place and Washington. He had ordered
the Baltimore artillery to move on towards the city ; and expected to find that Stansbury's command had fallen down the
road to that place. With the view of making another struggle to
save the capital, he rode forward for the purpose of selecting
a position ; but he soon found that, instead of proceeding towards
Washington, they had scattered in every direction. It afterwards appeared, that the greater part had fled towards Montgomery Courthouse. The City and Georgetown militia were
thus compelled to retire, without having had the slightest opportunity of defending their homes and their firesides. On
his arrival at the city, general Winder was met by the secretary at war and the secretary of state ; and after a consulta-

tion, it was agreed, that, with the small remains of the army, it was in vain to think of making a stand there. It was therefore proposed to rally the troops on the Heights of Georgetown. The general soon found, however, that but few of the militia could be collected. Some had strayed off in search of food or refreshment, having suffered much during the day ; and those who remained were exhausted by the privations and fatigues which they had experienced. The next day he proceeded, with such as he could collect, to Montgomery.

Thus did we experience the mortification (for it was more a matter of feeling than of actual injury) of having our capital entered by a hostile army. It was a feat of desperate temerity on the part of an enemy who was compelled to retire as rapidly as he had approached ; and had no effect upon the contest, other than to exasperate the people of this country of both political parties, and to dispose them to unite in carrying on the war. To use the common language, it was the name of the thing which caused the wound, for there was nothing wonderful in a large body of veteran soldiers stealing a march upon an unfortified town, and defeating an equal number of raw militia. The greater part of our troops had arrived on the spot so short a time before the battle, that they were not permitted to take any repose from their fatigue; the different corps and their officers were unknown to each other, and to the commander ; and the arrangements for meeting a powerful regular force were made at the very moment of battle. That we should have been defeated under such circumstances, is not to be wondered at, and furnishes no inference unfavourable to militia, or to the officers who commanded. The British troops would probably have met with the same success, had they moved at that moment against any of the larger cities which were no better prepared than Washington. The censure passed upon general Winder, who had already been unfortunate, but always meritorious, was undeserved ; as the task which he undertook was exceedingly arduous. To make success the criterion of merit in all cases, would be highly unjust ; it would be to imitate the tyrants of Turkey, who make their generals pay for misfortunes, by the forfeit of their lives.

The loss of the British in the battle of Bladensburg was little short of a thousand men killed, wounded or missing : that of the Americans, between thirty and forty killed, from fifty to sixty wounded, and about one hundred and twenty taken prisoners. By the issue of this battle, general Ross obtained possession of the bridge over the Eastern Branch of the Potomac. After halting his army for a short time for refreshments, he moved on to Washington, where he arrived about eight o'clock the same evening. Having stationed his main body at the distance of a mile and a half, he entered the city at the head of about seven hundred men, without meeting any opposition.

In the American metropolis, or rather its site, the British found about nine hundred houses, scattered in groups over a surface of three miles; and two splendid buildings, the Capitol, as yet unfinished, and the President's House, among the finest specimens of architecture in the new world. Orders, issued by admiral Cockburn and general Ross, for the conflagration of these noble edifices, were immediately executed. The great bridge across the Potomac was also wantonly burnt; together with an elegant hotel, and several other private dwellings. This barbarous destruction is detailed in the official letter of the British general, in a manner of perfect indifference! The blaze produced by the conflagration was seen even in Baltimore. All that was combustible about the Capitol and the President's House, including therein all the furniture and articles of taste or value and the valuable libraries of the senate and house of representatives, was reduced to ashes; and the walls of these stately buildings, blackened with smoke and in melancholy ruin, remained, for a time, the monuments of British barbarity. All the public buildings, with the exception of the patent office, shared the same fate. The public stores, vessels and buildings at the navy yard had been destroyed by order of government, to prevent them from falling into the enemy's hands. What remained was destroyed by the enemy, who took particular pains to mutilate the beautiful monument erected in honour of the naval heroes who fell at Tripoli. The plundering of private houses was not carried on to the extent that might have been expected, probably from the shortness of the time during which the British remained. On the evening of the following day, the 25th of August, they retreated from Washington.

It being now conjectured that the enemy meant to proceed immediately to Baltimore, the inhabitants of that place were thrown into the greatest consternation, a feeling which the arrival of the city militia from the field of battle was not likely to allay. Notwithstanding this disheartening panic, the citizens, rejecting all thoughts of capitulation, prepared themselves under generals Smith and Stricker to oppose the enemy; and in all probability, they would have made that desperate resistance which renders inexperienced troops, when fighting for their families and their homes, superior even to veterans. These measures proved to be unnecessary however. General Ross returned

over the same road by which he had advanced. He did not
reach Benedict until the evening of the 27th; and in such
straggling confusion was this movement effected, that his troops
wore the appearance of a vanquished rather than a victorious
army.

The squadron under captain Gordon, that division of the
enemy's fleet which ascended the Potomac, and consisting of
eight sail, passed Fort Warburton two days after the retreat of
the British from Washington. The fort had been abandoned
and blown up by captain Dyson, the commandant, in a most
extraordinary manner; probably under the influence of the
dreadful panic which generally prevailed. His orders had
been to abandon it only in case of an attack by land forces;
but on a mere rumour, and without waiting the enemy's approach, he thought proper to take this measure. On the 29th,
the squadron reached Alexandria, and the inhabitants of that
place, being completely in the power of the enemy, offered
terms for the preservation of the town from conflagration and
pillage. The insatiable avarice of the latter imposed the
hardest conditions : all the merchandise then in the town, as
well as all which had been removed thence since the 19th, was
required to be put on board the shipping at the wharf, at the expense of the inhabitants, and, together with the shipping, including those vessels which had been sunk on the approach of the
enemy, and the public and private naval and ordnance stores, to
be delivered up to the enemy. These terms, somewhat modified,
were complied with ; and captain Gordon moved down the river
with a fleet of prize vessels and a rich booty. In the meantime, preparations had been hastily made, by the naval heroes
captains Porter and Perry, to throw difficulties in the way of
his descent. The first, at the battery of the White House,
was assisted by general Hungerford's brigade of Virginia
militia, and captain Humphreys's rifle company ; and at the
battery at Indian Head, captain Perry was supported by the
brigade of general Stewart, and the volunteer companies of
major Peter and captain Burch. From the 3d until the 6th
of September, the British vessels were greatly annoyed in
passing these batteries. Frequent attempts to destroy them
were also made by commodore Rodgers, by means of small
fire-vessels , but, owing to a change of wind, they proved ineffectual. These respective forces were afterwards concentrated under commodore Rodgers, at Alexandria ; which place
he determined to defend, should the enemy, who was not yet
out of sight of the nearest battery, think proper to return.

Sir Peter Parker, who ascended the Chesapeake, was not
W

so fortunate as the other officers. He landed at night in the neighbourhood of Moors Fields, with the view of surprising a party of militia, encamped there under the command of colonel Reid. In this he was disappointed, for the militia, having heard the approach of the barges, were prepared to receive him. Sir Peter, having landed, moved forward at the head of about two hundred and fifty men, and, on approaching within seventy yards of the Americans, was received with a heavy fire. He endeavoured to press forward on the centre of the line ; but being foiled in this, he threw himself on the flank, where also he was repulsed. Colonel Reid, being informed that the ammunition was nearly expended, ordered his men to retire a small distance until they could procure a supply. In the meantime, the British, having suffered severe loss, thought proper to retire ; carrying with them the wounded. Among the latter was sir Peter Parker, who died shortly afterwards, greatly lamented by his countrymen and much respected by us.

The capture of Washington, as we have stated, excited the most painful sensations throughout the United States ; and the indignation of the people, at first levelled against the whole administration, was soon concentrated on the secretary of war and general Winder. Against the former, the cry was every where so loud, that the president, from motives of prudence, intimated to him the propriety of suspending his functions for a time. This his pride would not permit him to do ; and he therefore resigned. It appears, from the official letter of general Ross, since published, that he had not conceived the idea of attacking Washington, until within sixteen miles of it, and after he had received information of its defenceless state ; and that the destruction of commodore Barney's flotilla had been his real and sole object, It was. notwithstanding, an act of unparalleled rashness, and from which no commensurate advantage was to be gained. So great was the improbability of such an attempt, that the secretary at war, it is said, could not be persuaded, until the last moment, that it was seriously intended. General Winder demanded an examination of his conduct, and a court, of which general Scott was president, acquitted him honourably.

The character of Great Britain ought not soon to recover from the reproach of her numerous violations of the laws of civilized warfare on our coast. The conflagration of Washington and the plunder of Alexandria, not to mention the despicable bucaniering practised on the defenceless inhabitants, are without a parallel in modern times. Napoleon, whom the British denominated the modern Attila, entered the capitals of the principal nations of Europe, but was never disgraced by such wanton and unjustifiable destruction. These acts, grossly barbarous as they were, assumed still a deeper infamy from the manner in which they were justified. A letter from admiral Cochrane to our secretary of state, dated the day previous to debarkation, though not delivered until after the burning of the Capitol, stated, that having been called upon by the governor-general of the Canadas, to aid him in carrying into effect measures of retaliation against the inhabitants of the United States, for the wanton ravages committed by the American forces in Upper Canada, it became imperiously his duty, in conformity with the governor-general's application, to issue, to the naval force under his command, an order to destroy and lay waste such towns and districts upon the coast as might be found assailable! The American secretary of state, in reply, stated that in no instance had the United States authorised a deviation from the known usages of war. That in the few cases in which there had been a charge of such acts, the government had formally disavowed them, and had subjected the perpetrators to punishment. That amongst those few, the charge of burning the parliament house at York in Upper Canada was now for the first time brought forward ; that one of the most respectable civil functionaries at that place had addressed a letter of thanks to general Dearborne, for the good conduct of our troops ; and moreover, that when sir George Prevost, six months afterwards, professedly proceeded to measures of retaliation, the affair of burning the brick house was not mentioned. But what in the meantime were the affairs of the river Raisin, the devastations on the shores of Lake Champlain, the conflagrations and plunderings on the sea coast—were these in retaliation for burning the parliament house? But we were told, that there was, besides, the burning of a few sheds and huts at Long Point and St David's. These acts were followed up by instant retaliation ; and those who committed them, although able to plead the uniform practice of the enemy in excuse, were dismissed the service. Were the conflagrations in the Chesapeake, during the summer, in retaliation for these acts ? or were they in prospective retaliation for the burning of Newark, which happened at the close of the same year ? What was the avowed object of the British governor in burning four or five villages, putting a garrison to the sword, and laying waste the Niagara frontier ? It was to retaliate the burning of Newark, an act the American government had promptly disavowed. And why did the governor of Canada, after this, declare to the world, that he was doubly satisfied, first with the disavowal of our

government, and next with this ample measure of retaliation ?
How then could the conflagration of the noble buildings at
Washington be in retaliation for the burning a brick house
hired for the temporary occupation of the provincial legislature,
or for the burning of Newark, of a few outposts, and of the
cabins or huts of hostile savages ! Such pretexts are too flimsy
and absurd to impose upon the most ignorant. A lamentable
barbarity marked the conduct of the British in the war throughout ; while the United States sincerely desired to avoid whatever might stand in the way of the most friendly relations, on
the restoration of peace. At the very opening of the war, the
British officers permitted the savage Indians to fight by their
sides, and neglected to prevent them from perpetrating cruelties
whose bare recital causes the hair to stand on end. When the
British admirals first visited our sea coast—at a time when no
complaints had been made against us, they plundered and burnt
the villages on the shores of Chesapeake Bay ; they robbed the
defenceless planters of their stock, of their negroes, of their
furniture, and at Hampton transcended even the abominations
of the river Raisin. On the borders of Canada, the same course
of burning or plundering was pursued ; and when, under the
influence of feelings produced by these outrages, an American
officer burnt a village without authority, gladly was this seized
as the pretext for the first avowed retaliation—and the whole
frontier was laid waste. What was the conduct of the British
to American prisoners, and to those who were dragged from
their ships to be enslaved ; and what was the treatment of British
subjects prisoners with us ? What pretext of retaliation could
cover the violation of neutral ports, for the purpose of capturing our vessels ? What pretext warranted the barbarous orders
of their officers, to refuse quarter to men opposed to them in
honourable battle ? The letter of admiral Cochrane scarcely
deserved the notice of the secretary of state ; but the refutation
was certainly most ample. It is impossible to suppose that such
conduct was not as severely reprobated by the great mass of the
English people, as it was by us. The minority in the British
parliament pronounced it to be disgraceful to their country.

It has been the opinion of some, that our government was
reprehensible for not resorting, at an early period, to retaliatory measures ; but there is no American at this day, who
does not reflect with pleasure, that in no instance did our
government sanction them. It is difficult, however, to refrain
from instituting a comparison between the devastating order of
admiral Cochrane ; and the order of general Brown, issued
about the same time, on his entering Canada. " Upon enter-

ing Canada," said he, " the laws of war will govern : men found in arms, or otherwise engaged in the service of the enemy, will be treated as enemies ; those behaving peaceably, and following their private occupations, will be treated as friends. Private property will in all cases be held sacred ; public property, wherever found, will be seized and disposed of by the commanding general. Any who shall be found violating this order will be punished with death."

CHAPTER XIX.

Sensations produced by the Capture of Washington in Europe and in England— Effect of this Event in the United States—Preparations for the Defence of Baltimore —Admiral Cochrane appears at the mouth of the Patapsco—Debarkation of the British Troops at North Point—General Stricker marches from Baltimore to meet them— Battle of North Point—Death of General Ross—Retreat of the American Army—Brit- ish Army appears before Baltimore—Bombardment of Fort M'Henry—Attack on Baltimore abandoned—British fleet retires to the West Indies—Affairs on the Northern Frontier—Invasion of the State of New York by the British under Sir George Prevost —Progress of the British impeded by General Macomb—British Army occupies Platts- burg opposite the American Works—Gallant Enterprise of Captain M'Glassin—Brit- ish and American Fleets on Lake Champlain—Battle of Lake Champlain—Defeat of the British Squadron, and Capture of its principal Vessels—Retreat of the British Army from the American Territory.

THE capture of Washington was, at first, exulted in by the British ministry, as a most signal exploit ; but it was viewed in a very different light on the continent of Europe, and by the British nation at large. To say nothing of the prosecution of hostilities with augmented rigour during the negotiation of a treaty for peace, the acts of wanton barbarity which accompa- nied them aroused general indignation. In the British parlia- ment, so great a sensation was excited, that the perpetrators were fain to shelter themselves from odium by the basest falsehoods, and the ministry stated that instructions had been sent to the coast of America to desist from further inflictions of vengeance.

But if the effect was powerful abroad, it was overwhelming throughout the United States. Party spirit instantly vanished, and with it the dissensions which had almost paralysed our efforts. But one voice was heard ; a glorious union was

w*

brought about; and a nation of freemen was seen to rise in its strength. Those who had at first opposed the war on the ground of its impolicy, or who had condemned the invasion of Canada, now viewed Great Britain only as a powerful nation about to precipitate her armies on the country, with the avowed intention of desolating its fairest portions. The dissensions of political parties had terminated with the political death of Napoleon; and who could now say, that Britain was actuated by other than the mere thirst for revenge, or the less honourable thirst for plunder? The war now came home to the interests and feelings of every man. The scenes of preparation were the most animated that could be conceived. The whole country was in motion; every town was a camp; and the peaceful avocations of the citizens, which the war until now had scarcely interrupted, were laid aside. All the principal cities instituted their committees of defence; and the whole of the population, to the sound of martial music, moved in bands to the daily occupation of labouring at the erection of intrenchments and fortifications.

The New England states, at first so averse to the war, now exhibited their characteristic activity and energy, and gave satisfactory proof that nothing was further from their intentions, than secession from the confederation. The governor of Vermont, who the year before had made an attempt to recall the militia of the state from the service of the United States, and on which occasion the militia nobly refused to obey him, now made ample atonement by promptly calling them forth. The American ladies, always conspicuous for patriotic conduct in times of difficulty and danger, never appeared so lovely in their zeal for their country.

The next object of attack, it was rightly conjectured, would be Baltimore, and the cities of Philadelphia and New York awaited the result with as much anxiety as if their fate depended upon its successful issue. After the first moments of despondency occasioned by the capture of Washington had subsided in Baltimore, and it was discovered that the place would not be assailed immediately, the inhabitants set about making preparations for defence. A ditch was opened, and a breastwork thrown up by the inhabitants, on the high ground to the northeast of the city (to construct which all classes of the people united), so as completely to protect the town in the only quarter in which it was accessible by land forces. In the course of a few days, a considerable number of militia arrived from Pennsylvania, Virginia and the interior of Maryland; and the spirits of the inhabitants were greatly animated by the presence

of the naval veteran commodore Rodgers, who, with his marines, took possession of the heavy batteries on the hill above
mentioned. A brigade of Virginia volunteers, and the regular
troops were assigned to general Winder; and the City brigade
was commanded by general Stricker: the whole under the chief
direction of major-general Smith. Of these, the two latter were
distinguished revolutionary officers. The approach to the city
by water was defended by Fort M'Henry, and garrisoned by
about one thousand men, volunteers and regulars, under major
Armistead. Two batteries upon the Patapsco, to the right of
Fort M'Henry, to prevent the enemy from landing during the
night in the rear of the town, were manned, the one by lieutenant Newcombe of the Guerriere, with a detachment of
sailors; the other, by lieutenant Webster, with men from
Barney's flotilla. The former was called Fort Covington, the
latter, the City Battery. To the defence of Fort M'Henry,
and to the repulse of the British from the lines, the inhabitants
looked for safety.

Independently of the pretexts which had already led to the
scenes at Washington and Alexandria, the city of Baltimore
was a selected object of the vengeance of the enemy, in consequence of her active and patriotic exertions during the war. No
one could imagine to himself a just picture of the state of anxious
feeling in which fifty thousand people awaited the issue of the
event which should determine the safety or destruction of their
city. Even in case of successful resistance, the most painful
incertitude would, for a time, hang over the fate of those who
had risked their lives in its defence. These latter were not
strangers or mercenaries, but friends, brothers, sons, parents
and husbands; for every one who could wield a musket, even
old men and boys, was found in the ranks. The committee
of safety, composed of those advanced in life and of the most
influential citizens, (among whom was colonel Howard, a hero
of the revolution) took a large share in the preparations to meet
the approaching danger.

The British army having re-embarked on board the fleet in
the Patuxent, admiral Cochrane moved down the river and
proceeded up the Chesapeake; and, on the morning of the 11th
of September, appeared at the mouth of the Patapsco, about
fourteen miles from the city of Baltimore, with a fleet of ships
of war and transports amounting to fifty sail. On the next day,
the land forces, to the number of at least six thousand men,
debarked at North Point, and, under the command of general
. Ross, took up their march for the city. General Stricker, who
had claimed for the City brigade under his command the ho-

nour of being the first to meet the invader, was detached by
general Smith, in anticipation of the landing of the British
troops.   On the 11th, general Stricker proceeded on the road
to North Point, at the head of three thousand two hundred
effective men : consisting of the Fifth regiment, under lieutenant-colonel Steriett, five hundred and fifty strong; six hundred
and twenty of the Sixth, under lieutenant-colonel M'Donald ;
five hundred of the Twenty-seventh, under lieutenant-colonel
Long ; five hundred and fifty of the Thirty-ninth, under lieutenant-colonel Fowler ; seven hundred of the Fifty-first, under
lieutenant-colonel Amey ; one hundred and fifty riflemen, under
captain Dyer , one hundred and fifty cavalry, under lieutenant-
colonel Biays ; and the Union Artillery, of seventy-five men
and six four-pounders, under captain Montgomery, attorney-
general of the state.   A corps of light riflemen and musketry,
taken from general Stansbury's brigade, and the Pennsylvania
volunteers, were detached, under major Randall, to the mouth
of Bear Creek, with orders to co-operate with general Stricker,
and to check any landing which the enemy might effect in that
quarter.

At six o'clock P. M. general Stricker reached a meeting-
house, near the head of Bear Creek, seven miles from the city.
Here the brigade halted, with the exception of the cavalry,
who moved forward to Gorsuch's farm three miles, and the
riflemen, who took post near a blacksmith's shop two miles,
in advance of the encampment.   The following morning, the
12th, at seven o'clock, information was received from the
videttes, that the enemy were debarking troops under cover of
their gun-vessels, which lay off the bluff of North Point, within
the mouth of the Patapsco river.   The baggage was immediately sent back under a strong guard ; and general Stricker
ordered forward the Fifth and Twenty-seventh regiments, and
the artillery, to the head of Long Log Lane, posting the Fifth
with its right on the head of a branch of Bear Creek and its
left on the main road, the Twenty-seventh on the opposite side
of the road in a line with and to the left of the Fifth, and the
artillery at the head of the lane, in the interval between the
two regiments.   The Thirty-ninth regiment was drawn up three
hundred yards in the rear of the Twenty-seventh, and the Fifty-
first at the same distance in the rear of the Fifth.   The Sixth
regiment was kept as a reserve within sight, half a mile in the
rear of the second line.   Thus judiciously posted, the general
determined to wait an attack, having first given orders, that the
two regiments composing the front line, if compelled to fall

back, should retire through the Fifty-first and Thirty-ninth, and form on the right of the Sixth posted in reserve.

General Stricker now learned, from the cavalry, who according to orders had retreated, that the British were moving rapidly up the road; but at the moment when he expected their approach to be announced and impeded by the riflemen stationed in the low thick pine and firs in advance, greatly to his chagrin, he discovered that they were falling back upon the main position, under a groundless apprehension that the enemy had landed on Back river to cut them off. This part of the general's plan having been frustrated, he placed the riflemen on the right of his front line, and by this means better secured that flank. The videttes soon after bringing information that a party of the enemy were carousing in a careless manner at Gorsuch's farm, several of the officers offered their services to dislodge them. Captains Levering and Howard's companies, from the Fifth regiment, about one hundred and fifty in number, under major Heath; captain Aisquith's and a few other riflemen, in all about seventy, and a small piece of artillery and some cavalry, under lieutenant Stiles, were sent forward to chastise the insolence of the enemy's advance, and to evince a wish on the part of the American army to engage. The detachment had scarcely proceeded half a mile, when it suddenly came in contact with the main body of the enemy. In the skirmish which ensued, major Heath's horse was shot under him, and several of the Americans were killed and wounded; while the enemy lost their commander-in-chief, major general Ross This officer, who had imprudently advanced too far, for the purpose of reconnoitering, was killed by one of the company of captain Howard. After the death of general Ross, the command devolved on colonel Brooke, who continued to advance notwithstanding this occurrence. The American detachment now fell back; and general Stricker, perceiving the companies of Howard and Levering to be too much fatigued to share in the approaching conflict, ordered them to attach themselves to the reserve. At half past two o'clock, the enemy commenced throwing rockets, which did no injury; and immediately captain Montgomery's artillery opened a fire upon them, which they returned by a six-pounder and a howitzer directed upon the left and centre. The fire was brisk for some minutes, when general Stricker, with a view of bringing the enemy within canister distance, ordered it to cease on the American side. Perceiving that the efforts of the British were chiefly directed against the left flank, he now ordered up the Thirty-ninth regiment into line with and on the left of the Twenty-seventh. Two pieces of artillery were also detached to the left of the Thirty-ninth; and in order more completely to protect this flank, colonel Amey was ordered to form his regiment, the Fifty-first, at right angles with the line, with his right resting near the left of the Thirty-ninth. This movement was badly executed, and created some confusion in that quarter, which however was soon rectified.

The enemy's right column now advanced upon the Twenty-seventh and Thirty-ninth regiments. Unfortunately, at this juncture, the Fifty-first regiment, in a sudden panic, after delivering one volley at random, broke and retreated in confusion, occasioning the same disorder in the second battalion of the Thirty-ninth. The fire on the enemy by this time became general from right to left; and the artillery poured an incessant and destructive stream upon the enemy's left column. The latter endeavoured to shelter itself behind a loghouse, which soon after burst into a blaze; captain Sadtler of the Fifth regiment, who had previously occupied it, having taken the precaution to fire it, before he and his yagers abandoned it. About ten minutes past three, the British line came on with a rapid discharge of musketry, which was well returned by the Fifth and the Twenty-seventh regiments, and the first battalion of the Thirty-ninth regiment. The fire was incessant from this time until about twenty-five minutes before four o'clock, during which period general Stricker gallantly contended against four times his numbers. Finding, however, that the unequal contest could be maintained no longer, and that the enemy were about to outflank him, he was compelled to retire upon his reserve, a movement which he effected in good order. At the point occupied by this regiment he formed his brigade, and falling back, took post half a mile in advance of the intrenchments for the defence of the city. Here he was joined by general Winder, who had been stationed on the west side of the city, but was now ordered, with general Douglass's Virginia brigade and captain Bird's United States dragoons, to take post on the left of general Stricker. The enemy encamped for the night on the ground where the battle had been fought, without attempting a pursuit.

The conduct of the Baltimore brigade, with the exception of the Fifty-first regiment and the second battalion of the Thirty-ninth, who were seized with the panic to which raw troops are so much subject, deserved the highest praise: veterans could not have done more. Their loss, in killed and wounded, amounted to one hundred and sixty-three, among whom were some of the most respectable citizens of Baltimore. Adjutant James

Lowry Donaldson, of the Twenty-seventh regiment, an eminent lawyer, was killed in the hottest of the fight; majors Heath and Moore, and a number of other officers, were wounded. The loss of the British was nearly double that of the Americans, according to their own acknowledgement, and probably was much greater in reality. In their official statements they computed the American force at six thousand, a great proportion regulars, and the loss at one thousand; data from which we may infer their opinion of the manner in which they were received.

Among those who distinguished themselves in the battle of North Point, lieutenant colonel Sterrett; majors Heath and Barry of the Fifth regiment; captain Spangler of the York (Pennsylvania) volunteers; adjutant Cheston, who was slightly wounded; lieutenant-colonel Long of the Twenty-seventh regiment, which "was unsurpassed in bravery, resolution and enthusiasm;" lieutenant-colonel Fowler and major Steiger of the Thirtyninth regiment, and the volunteer companies attached to it; captain Quantril from Hagerstown, and captain Metzgar from Hanover, Pennsylvania, the former of whom was wounded; captain Montgomery; brigade-majors Calhoun and Fraily; and major George P. Stevenson, aid to general Stricker, were highly complimented in general orders. Majors Moore and Robinson, of the Twenty-seventh regiment, were also conspicuously active throughout the engagement.

The result of this affair, together with the death of the British general, served to cheer the spirits of the militia, and inspire confidence. The brigades of generals Stansbury and Foreman; the seamen and marines under commodore Rodgers; the Pennsylvania volunteers, under colonels Cobean and Findlay; the Baltimore artillery under colonel Harris; and the marine artillery under captain Stiles, manned the trenches and battery, and in this situation spent the night under arms. The enemy made his appearance early the next day to the east of the intrenchments, at the distance of two miles, whence he had a full view of the position of the Americans. During the morning, by his manœuvres to the right, he seemed to show an intention of coming down by the Harford and York roads; to baffle which design generals Winder and Stricker adapted their movements. At noon the British concentrated their force in front of the American line, approached within a mile of the intrenchments, and made arrangements for an attack that evening. General Smith, therefore, immediately drew generals Winder and Stricker nearer to the right of the enemy, and ordered them to fall upon his flank or rear, in case he should make the attempt.

In the meantime, the naval attack had already commenced. The fleet, after landing the troops, as before mentioned, proceeded to bombard Fort M'Henry, which commands the entrance of the harbour. On the 13th, about sunrise, the British had brought sixteen ships within two miles and a half of the fort. Major Armistead arranged his force in the following manner : the regular artillerists under captain Evans, and the volunteer artillerists under captain Nicholson, manned the bastions in the star fort; captains Bunbury, Addison, Rodman, Berry and lieutenant-commandant Pennington's commands were, stationed on the lower works ; and the infantry under lieutenant-colonel Stewart and major Lane were in the outer ditch, to meet the enemy, should he make an attempt to land. The assault commenced from five bomb vessels, which had anchored at the distance of two miles. Thence, finding themselves within striking distance, and at the same time out of reach of the guns of the fort, they maintained an incessant bombardment. The situation of the garrison was painfully inactive and highly perilous ; and yet every man stood to his post without shrinking. One of the twenty-four pounders, on the south west bastion, under captain Nicholson, was dismounted, killing his second lieutenant and wounding several of his men. The enemy now approaching somewhat nearer, a tremendous fire was instantly opened from the fort, which compelled him precipitately to return to his former position. The bombardment was kept up during the whole day and night. The city, assailed on both sides, awaited the result in wakeful silence : when suddenly, about midnight, a tremendous cannonade was heard in the direction of the besieged fort ; and the affrighted population believed that all was over. Their fears, however, were happily soon quieted. Some barges of the enemy, having passed Fort M'Henry unobserved, had made an unsuccessful attempt to land a body of troops ; and after suffering immense loss from the guns of the City Battery and Fort Covington, had hastily retired. At seven o'clock next morning, the 14th, the bombardment of the fort terminated, after upwards of fifteen hundred shells had been thrown, a large portion of which burst over the fort, scattering their fragments amongst its defenders and materially injuring several of the buildings. The personal damage sustained was, nevertheless, inconsiderable. Only four were killed, and twenty-four wounded : among the former, lieutenant Clagget and sergeant Clemm, of captain Nicholson's volunteers, greatly lamented by their fellow-citizens for their personal bravery and high private standing; and of the latter, lieutenant Russel, a gentleman of the Baltimore bar, of Pennington's company, who nobly persisted in continuing at his post during the whole bombardment.

In the course of the night of the 13th, admiral Cochrane had held a conference with colonel Brooke, the commander of the land forces, at which it was mutually agreed to relinquish the enterprise as impracticable. The retreat of the army commenced immediately, and was highly favoured by the extreme darkness and the continued rain; while the uninterrupted continuance of the bombardment of Fort M'Henry served to divert the attention of the Americans. In the meantime, along the American lines ten thousand men waited the approach of day with much anxiety; and there is every reason to believe, that they would have repelled the enemy with great loss, had he made an attack. When day dawned, however, it was discovered that he had disappeared. General Winder, with the Virginia brigade, captain Bird's dragoons, major Randal's light corps and all the cavalry, was immediately detached in pursuit of him: but so exhausted were the troops with continued watching, having been under arms during three days and nights, exposed the greater part of the time to very inclement weather, that it was found impossible to do any thing more than pick up a few stragglers. Besides, the time which had elapsed since the commencement of the retreat of the enemy, had given them an opportunity of protecting their embarkation in such a manner as effectually to secure their rear. The troops were taken on board in the evening of the same day; and on the morning of the following day, the 15th, the British fleet descended the bay.

The intelligence of this happy event was received in the neighbouring cities with demonstrations of rapturous joy. But a moment before, the popular dismay appeared to have reached its acme, and the most gloomy anticipations were indulged; for all the larger towns, equally with Baltimore, were threatened with devastation. The feelings of the inhabitants of the city itself, can with difficulty be conceived. Measures were taken to celebrate the occurrence, and to reward those who held distinguished commands. To such as fell in the sacred cause of the defence of their families and homes, a monument, to be erected in the centre of the city, was decreed. Admiral Cochrane, after the failure of this attempt on Baltimore, retired with all his fleet and the land forces to the West Indies, with the view of awaiting the arrival of reinforcements from England; and not only abandoned the idea for the

x

present of attacking any other of our cities or larger towns, but also withdrew all the parties which had been engaged in marauding expeditions into the country along the coast.

Meanwhile events, resulting in successes of the most brilliant character, had transpired on the northern frontier. While admiral Cochrane was threatening the sea coast with devastation, at the request, as he stated, of sir George Prevost; this officer, who was invading the United States in another quarter, held very different language. While he could direct the British forces to the south to lay waste and destroy (if he really ever gave such directions), he was a great stickler for generous and honourable warfare on the borders of Canada, and was careful to issue orders of the most conciliatory kind. On entering the state of New York, in honeyed language " he makes known to its peaceable and unoffending inhabitants, that they have no cause of alarm, from this invasion of their country, for the safety of themselves and families, or for the security of their property. He explicitly assures them, that as long as they continue to demean themselves peaceably, they shall be protected in the quiet possession of their homes, and permitted freely to pursue their various occupations. It is against the government of the United States, by whom this unjust and unprovoked war has been declared, and against those who support it, either openly or secretly, that the arms of his majesty are directed. The quiet and unoffending inhabitants, not found in arms, or otherwise aiding in hostilities, shall meet with kind usage and generous treatment; and all just complaints against any of his majesty's subjects, offering violence to them, to their families or to their possessions, shall be immediately redressed." There is nothing said of retaliation, nor the slightest hint that hostilities had not been conducted, on the part of the Americans, according to the usages of war. With these fair words, sir George led his army on Plattsburg, in the state of New York, about the beginning of September, while the British fleet, under captain Downie, proceeded up Lake Champlain on his left.

Preparations of the most extensive description had been made for this invasion. Transports with troops had been continually arriving at Quebec from England, during the months of July and August; so that, at the time when sir George Prevost entered the American territory, his army was fourteen thousand strong, among whom were large bodies of veterans who had distinguished themselves under Wellington. This force consisted of three brigades and a corps of reserve, each commanded by a major-general of experience; a squadron of light dragoons;

and an immense train of artillery. The expedition had in view
an object more important than that of a mere inroad. The
defeat and destruction of the American army, then lying in the
neighbourhood of Plattsburg; the subjugation of the country as
far as Crown Point and Ticonderoga, for the purpose of securing
a strong position in which to winter; and ultimately, in co-operation with an army which was to invade New York or Connecticut from the sea, the separation of the New England states
from the union by the line of the river Hudson, were the
results at which sir George Prevost, under the express directions of the British Prince Regent, was ordered to aim.

After general Izard had marched for the Niagara, the force
left at Plattsburg under general Macomb did not exceed fifteen
hundred regulars, and consisted chiefly of invalids and new recruits; and of these there was but one battalion properly organized. The fortifications were slight, and the stores and ordnance in great disorder. The British took possession of the
village of Champlain on the 3d of September; and, from the
proclamations and the impressments of wagons and teams in
this vicinity, it was soon discovered that the immediate object
of attack was Plattsburg. Not a minute was lost in placing the
works in a state of defence. In order to create emulation and
zeal among the officers and men, they were divided into detachments, and stationed in the several forts; and the general
declared, in orders, that each detachment was the garrison of
its own work, and bound to defend it to the last extremity. At
the same time, he called on general Mooers, of the New York
militia, and with him adopted measures for calling them out
en masse. With the exception of a few men and some boys,
who formed themselves into a company, received rifles and
were exceedingly useful, the inhabitants of Plattsburg, with their
families and effects, fled from the town.

General Mooers, having collected about seven hundred
militia, advanced, on the 4th of the month, seven miles on the
Beekmantown road, to watch the motions of the enemy and
skirmish with them as they approached, and at the same time
to obstruct the road by breaking down the bridges and felling
trees. Captain Sprowl, with two hundred men of the Thirteenth regiment, who was posted at Dead Creek bridge, on
the lake, or more eastern, road, also with similar objects, was
ordered to fortify himself with two field pieces sent with him
for the purpose, and to receive further instructions from lieutenant-colonel Appling. In advance of this position, the latter
officer, with one hundred riflemen, was reconnoitering the
movements of the enemy. At daylight on the 6th, the enemy

were seen advancing, by these roads, in two columns ; the
column on the Beekmantown road approaching more rapidly
than the other.   General Mooers's militia skirmished a little
with its advance parties, but, with the exception of a few brave
men, soon broke, and fled in the greatest disorder.   A detachment of two hundred and fifty regulars, under major Wool,
which had marched to their support, could not succeed in re-
storing them to confidence.

General Macomb, finding that the enemy's object, in making
so much more rapid a march on the western than the lake road,
was to cut off the detachments of captain Sprowl and colonel
Appling, despatched orders to the latter officer to withdraw the
troops, make a junction with major Wool, and then attack the
enemy's right flank.   While in compliance with this order,
colonel Appling fell in with the head of a column of the enemy
sent to cut him off ; and had they made this movement an
instant earlier, he must inevitably have been taken prisoner.
As he retreated, he poured a destructive fire on them from
his riflemen, and continued to annoy them until he formed a
junction with major Wool.   The column of the enemy on the
lake road, notwithstanding that considerable execution had
been done by captain Sprowl's two field pieces, and although
impeded in its advance by the fallen trees and the destruction
of the bridge over Dead Creek, as well as harassed by a galling fire from some gun-boats and galleys anchored in the creek,
still continued to press forward.

The village of Plattsburg stands on the north side of the small
river Saranac, near its entrance into Lake Champlain ; and the
American works were situated on the southern side, directly
opposite.   The town being no longer tenable, owing to its
occupation by the enemy, the parties of Appling, Wool and
Sprowl, which had contested the advance of their opponents
step by step, retreated within the American works in good
order, keeping up a brisk fire until they got under cover.   General Macomb now directed the passage over the bridge on the
Saranac to be destroyed.   This order was not executed without
some difficulty, as the enemy had thrown their light troops into
the houses near the bridge, and annoyed the Americans with
their small shot from the windows and balconies.   They were
at length dislodged by a discharge of hot shot which set the
buildings on fire.   Throughout the day attempts were made
by the British to obtain possession of the several bridges over
the river ; but they were unsuccessful in every instance.   As
soon as the whole of the American troops had gained the southern bank of the river, the planks of the bridges had been taken

up, and placed in the form of breastworks; and behind these the men charged with the defence of the passages firmly resisted the advances of the enemy.

The enemy, now masters of the village, instead of attempting to storm the American works on the opposite side of the river, which their vast superiority of force might have enabled them to do, contented themselves with erecting batteries and throwing up breastworks, and with frequent attempts to carry the bridges and cross at the fords. In the meanwhile, the main body of the British army arrived; and general Macomb was reinforced by a considerable body of New York militia, and of volunteers from the mountains of Vermont. There was now scarcely any intermission to the skirmishes which took place between detachments of the enemy, and the American militia and volunteers; while the former were getting up a train of battering cannon, and the American regulars were labouring incessantly in strengthening and extending their works. During this time a handsome affair was achieved by captain M'Glassin, who, crossing the river in the night, assailed a guard of British regulars of more than three times his numbers, stationed at a masked battery which had been for some days preparing, and which, when completed, would have given incalculable annoyance, drove them from their post, and demolished the battery. He returned to the American camp with the loss of only three men missing. For this gallant action he received the public thanks of his general, and the brevet rank of major from the president of the United States.

On the morning of the 11th of September, the fifth day of the siege, the motives which induced the British general to delay his assault upon the American works became apparent. Relying on his ability to carry them, however they might be strengthened and fortified, he had awaited the arrival of the British fleet, in the belief that, with its co-operation, he could make an easy conquest not only of the American army, but also of their fleet on Lake Champlain, then lying at anchor in Cumberland Bay, in front of the town of Plattsburg. On that day the British fleet, consisting of the frigate Confiance, carrying thirty-nine guns, twenty-seven of which were twenty-four pounders; the brig Linnet, of sixteen guns; the sloops Chub and Finch, each carrying eleven guns; and thirteen galleys, five of which carried two guns, and the remainder one gun, each, was seen coming round Cumberland Head. The American fleet, under commodore M'Donough, comprised the Saratoga, carrying twenty-six guns, eight of which were long twenty-four pounders; the Eagle, of twenty guns; the Ticonderoga,

x*

of seventeen ; the Preble, seven ; and ten galleys, six carrying two guns, and the remainder one gun. Besides the advantage which the enemy possessed in being able to choose their position, their force was much superior. The number of guns in the British fleet amounted to ninety-five, and of men, to upwards of a thousand ; while the Americans had only eighty-six guns, and eight hundred and twenty men. One of the American vessels had been built with almost incredible despatch : eighteen days before, the trees of which it was constructed were actually growing on the shores of the lake.

The American vessels were moored in line, with five gunboats or galleys on each flank. At nine o'clock, A. M., immediately on getting round Cumberland Head, captain Downie, the British commander, anchored in line abreast of the American squadron, and at about three hundred yards distance. The Confiance, captain Downie's own vessel, was opposed to the Saratoga, M'Donough's vessel ; the Linnet to the Eagle , the British galleys and one of their sloops, to the Ticonderoga, the Preble and the left division of the American galleys ; their other sloop was opposed to the galleys on the right.

In this situation the whole force on both sides became engaged ; and at the same moment, as if the firing of the first gun from the Confiance had been the signal, the contest commenced between general Macomb and sir George Prevost. One of the British sloops was soon thrown out of the engagement by running on a reef of rocks whence she could not be extricated, while several of their galleys were so roughly handled as to be compelled to pull out of the way. But the fate of this interesting battle, in which the two competitors for naval superiority were for the second time matched in squadron, depended chiefly on the result of the engagement between the two largest ships. The American commodore had now maintained the unequal contest for two hours ; and notwithstanding the greater weight of the enemy's battery seemed to incline the scale of victory in his favour, he suffered prodigiously. The chances against the Saratoga were accidentally increased by the commander of the Eagle, who, being unable to bring his guns to bear as he wished, cut his cable, and, anchoring between the Ticonderoga and Saratoga, exposed the latter vessel to a galling fire from the enemy's brig the Linnet. The guns on the starboard side of the Saratoga were, by this time, either dismounted or entirely unmanageable, and the situation of the enemy was little better : to each the fortune of the day depended upon the execution of one of the most difficult of naval manoeuvres, that of winding the vessel round, and bringing a new broadside to bear. The

Confiance essayed it in vain, but the efforts of the Saratoga were successful: a stern anchor being put on and the bower cable cut, the ship winded round. A fresh broadside was now brought to bear on the enemy's frigate; which, shortly after its delivery, surrendered. No sooner had the Confiance surrendered, than the Saratoga's broadside was sprung to bear upon the Linnet, which struck its flag fifteen minutes afterwards. One sloop had struck to the Eagle some time before; and the Ticonderoga caused the surrender of the remaining sloop. Three of the galleys were sunk, the ten others escaped. By the time this desperate contest was over, there was scarcely a mast in either squadron capable of bearing a sail, and the greater part of the vessels were in a sinking state. There were fifty-five round shot in the hull of the Saratoga, and in the Confiance one hundred and five. The Saratoga was twice set on fire by hot shot. Of the crew of the Confiance, fifty were killed, and sixty wounded; among the former was captain Downie. On board the Saratoga, there were twenty-eight killed, of whom lieutenant Gamble was one, and twenty-nine wounded. Lieutenant Stansbury, of the Ticonderoga, son of general Stansbury of Maryland, lost his life; and lieutenant Smith, acting lieutenant Spencer and midshipman Baldwin were among the wounded. The total loss in the American squadron amounted to fifty-two killed, and fifty-eight wounded. The enemy had eighty-four killed, and one hundred and ten wounded. The action lasted two hours and twenty minutes.

This engagement, so deeply interesting and on the result of which so much was at stake, took place in sight of the hostile armies. But they were by no means quiet spectators of the scene: a tremendous cannonade was kept up during the whole time, and the air was filled with bombs, rockets and hot balls. Three desperate efforts were made by the British to cross the river and storm the American works, in which they were as often repulsed with considerable loss. Their ardour, however, naturally abated, after witnessing the painful sight, so little expected, of the capture of nearly their whole fleet. Although the firing was kept up until dark, the plans of sir George Prevost were completely frustrated. Now that the Americans had the command of Lake Champlain, the possession of their works on the land could not serve him in any further design; and in the meantime, he was exposed to danger which increased with the hourly augmentation of the American force. He determined therefore to raise the siege. Under cover of the night, he sent off all the baggage and artillery for which he could obtain means of transportation; and precipitately followed with all his forces, leaving behind him the sick and wounded. At daybreak of the 12th, when this movement was discovered, he was pursued by the Americans. They captured some stragglers, and covered the escape of a great number of deserters; but were prevented by bad weather from continuing the pursuit beyond Chazy, a distance of fourteen miles from Plattsburg. The loss of the British in killed, wounded and missing was about fifteen hundred men: of the Americans, thirty-seven killed, sixty-two wounded and twenty missing. Vast quantities of provisions, ammunition and implements of war, which the enemy had not time to take with them or destroy, fell into the hands of the Americans, in the course of the day; and the amount was greatly increased by what were afterwards found hidden in marshes, or buried in the ground. Promotions of all who distinguished themselves on this glorious day immediately took place: at the head of the list were general Macomb and commodore M'Donough.

Those of the British army and navy who fell, were interred with the honours of war. The humane attention of the Americans to the wounded, and their generous politeness to the prisoners, were acknowledged in grateful terms by captain Pryng, the successor of captain Downie, in his official despatch to the British admiralty.

Thus was this portentous invasion most happily repelled; another of our inland seas made glorious in all coming time; and the " star-spangled banner" waved in triumph over the waters of Champlain, as over those of Erie and Ontario. The lakes, those noble features of our great continent, are now viewed with an interest which is associated with, and heightened by, the recollections of victories won from powerful enemies, in the assertion of our rights.

CHAPTER XX.

Unanimity of Sentiment in Congress—Negotiations with Great Britain—British
Sine Qua Non—Hartford Convention—Mr Biddle's Report in the Legislature of Penn-
sylvania—Removal of the Seat of Government from Washington agitated—Mr Dallas
appointed Secretary of the Treasury—Improvement in our Finances—Affairs to the
Southward—Attack on Fort Bowyer most gallantly repulsed—Inroad into Florida, and
Capture of Pensacola, by General Jackson—Invasion of Louisiana meditated by the
British—Preparations for Resistance—Arrival of General Jackson at New Orleans—
His Presence inspires Confidence—British Fleet arrives off the Coast—Capture of the
American Gun-Boats—Martial Law declared by General Jackson—British Forces land
within seven Miles of New Orleans—Battle of the 23d of December—Results of the
Battle—General Jackson encamps, and fortifies himself—Affairs of the 28th of December, and of the 1st of January 1815—Position of the American Troops—British prepare
to storm the American Works on both sides of the Mississippi—Memorable Battle of
the 8th of January—Death of General Packenham—Defeat and Terrible Carnage of
the British on the Left Bank of the River—Americans driven from their Intrenchments
on the Right Bank—Louisiana evacuated by the British—Unsuccessful Bombardment
of Fort St Philip by the British—Depredations of Admiral Cockburn along the Southern
Coast—Peace with Great Britain—Terms of the Treaty—Conclusion.

THE national legislature convened, near the close of the year
1814, with feelings very different from those which had existed
in that body for many years previous.   Party spirit, it is true, still
glowed beneath its ashes; but whatever variety of sentiment
might prevail with respect to the past, and as to the men in power,
there was but little as to the course to be pursued in future.   The
accusation of being subject to French influence could no longer
be brought against the administration; the war had now become
a war of defence; and the recent conduct of the British government rendered it impossible for any one to say that she was not
wantonly pursuing hostilities.
  The whole country felt the neglect with which Great Britain
had treated our ministers in Europe.   Suffering them at first
to remain for months unnoticed, and afterwards shifting the
place of negotiation, she had endeavoured, with a duplicity un-
becoming a great nation, to prolong, for half a year, a treaty
which might have been accomplished in a day.   But when the
first occurrence which took place on the meeting of the British
and American commissioners was made known, it produced

a burst of indignation from all parties, both on the floor of congress and throughout the union. It was now thought that all hopes of peace were at an end, and the people began to prepare their minds for a long and bloody war. In the instructions which they had received, our commissioners were authorized to pass the subject of impressment in silence for the present. By the pacification of Europe, the motives which had induced Great Britain to resort to impressment, no longer existed—the practice had ceased with its alleged necessity. The subject of blockade, by the fall of Napoleon, was also at an end; and could not be permitted to stand in the way of negotiations for peace. In fact there was nothing in controversy between the two nations : and a war which had grown out of the war in Europe, and the injuries inflicted upon us by the English and French belligerents, came naturally to a conclusion when peace was restored to Europe.

Perhaps our government was censurable for manifesting this great anxiety for peace ; perhaps we ought never to have yielded, until some provision had been made by the enemy to prevent the future recurrence of the detestable abuses inseparable from the practice of impressing her seamen from our vessels. But the nation at this moment required peace ; we had suffered much from our inexperience during this first war ; and a few years of repose would enable us to vindicate our rights with greater hope of success. It was reasonable to conclude that Great Britain, by this time, felt that she had paid dearly for the impressment of Americans and the confiscation of their property, and that hereafter she would be cautious of seizing the persons, or interfering with the commerce of our citizens. Besides, a war is seldom so successful as to enable the victor to wring from his enemy an acknowledgement of his wrong : it is by the resistance made, and the injury inflicted, that its object is attained. The sincere wish of the American government for peace was not met in a corresponding spirit by the British commissioners. The latter proposed at once, as a *sine qua non*, the surrender of an immense portion of the American territory, and a total relinquishment of the lake shores. These new and unwarrantable pretensions excited universal astonishment. Could it be supposed that the English commissioners would descend to the trifling artifice of prolonging the negotiation by proposing terms from which they meant to recede? Could they, consistently with the dignity of their nation, recede from them? If seriously made, such proposals argued either a surprising ignorance of the situation of the United States, or a disposition to insult our government in the grossest manner.

A subject which was brought before the legislature of Pennsylvania furnished a strong proof of the general disposition to unite in the cause of the country. The leaders of the party in the New England states opposed to the war, had grown every day more and more intemperate, while the great mass of the population of those districts, on the contrary, was becoming better reconciled to it. Under a mistaken idea of the real sentiments of the people, it was suggested that a convention, to consist of delegates from the different states composing New England, should meet at Hartford, in Connecticut. Its object, according to rumour, was no less than a discussion of the propriety of a dismemberment of the union. Whatever were the views of its projectors, the proposal was not received with much favour. Deputies from only three states, representing scarcely a third of New England, convened; and a short session terminated in the adoption of a declamatory address on subjects now nearly forgotten, and a remonstrance or memorial to the congress of the United States, enumerating some objections to the federal constitution. This extraordinary paper was submitted to the legislatures of the several states for their approbation, and was rejected by them all. In the legislature of Pennsylvania, it was referred to a committee; and a noble and eloquent report on the subject was drawn up by a member of the opposition,* in which the causes of complaint set forth in it were clearly refuted, the constitution of the union was ably vindicated, and the conduct of the memorialists severely censured. Let it be the warm prayer of every American, that the confederacy of the states, a fabric reared by the hands of sages and cemented by the blood of patriots, may be eternal. How much bloodshed has it not saved already, and how much will it not save in future? Let us place before our eyes the eternal wars of the Grecian states; and learn from them, that independent powers immediately adjacent to each other are natural enemies. What strength does not this glorious union give to each individual state! and what consequence does it confer on each individual citizen, who is thereby made the member of a great nation, instead of being one of a petty tribe! Let us hope that no unhappy jealousies, no irreconcilable interests, may arise to break in sunder the bonds by which we are united!

Another important matter was brought before congress during the present session. The destruction of the public buildings of Washington by the British afforded an opportunity to the opponents of that place as the seat of government, to

* Mr Biddle, now President of the Bank of the United States.

advocate the selection of another site ; and serious apprehensions were entertained that their views would prevail. But these fears, and the subject which gave rise to them, were soon put to rest. Veneration for the great father of our republic exercised a successful influence ; and the city of Washington is now destined for ages, and it is hoped for ever, to be the metropolis of the United States.

Our finances at this critical moment appeared to revive, under the indefatigable industry and great abilities of Mr Dallas, whom the President selected to fill the post of secretary of the treasury. His plans were characterized by the greatest boldness, but were unfolded in so luminous a manner as to carry conviction to every mind. He may be said to have plucked up the sinking credit of the nation by the locks. At the same time, the duties of the secretary of war, in addition to his other avocations, were discharged by Mr Monroe. In undertaking this office, he exhibited no small courage ; for it had become a forlorn hope of popularity : he was happily rewarded by the most fortunate success in all his measures, and by the applause of the whole country.

Meanwhile, the public attention was awakened by the alarming aspect of affairs to the southward.

General Jackson, after concluding the treaty recounted in a former chapter with the main body of the Creeks, residing in Alabama and Georgia, had transferred his head quarters to Mobile. Here, he received certain information that three British ships of war had arrived at Pensacola, in West Florida, then a possession belonging to the Spanish nation, with whom we were at peace, and had landed three hundred soldiers, and a large quantity of ammunition and guns for arming the Indians, with the view of making an assault upon Fort Bowyer, a battery situated on Mobile Point and commanding the entrance to Mobile Bay. He also learnt that the fleet of admiral Cochrane had been reinforced at Bermuda, and that thirteen ships of the line, with transports having ten thousand troops on board, for the purpose of invading some of the southern states, were daily expected. On the receipt of this intelligence, he immediately wrote to the governor of Tennessee, calling for the whole quota of militia from that state.

The three vessels at Pensacola, having been joined by another vessel, and having taken the troops on board, sailed from thence, and appeared, on the 15th of September, off Mobile Point. The naval force, mounting in all ninety guns, was commanded by captain Percy : the land troops, consisting of one hundred and ten marines, two hundred Creeks headed by captain Woodbine, and twenty artillerists, with a battery of one twelve-pounder and a howitzer, were under the command of the infamous colonel Nicholls. On the same day, at four o'clock in the afternoon, the troops having been landed, the attack commenced by a bombardment from the vessels, and a cannonade from the two pieces of artillery, which had been planted at a small distance from, and in the rear of, the fort. Fort Bowyer mounted twenty pieces of cannon, and was commanded by major Lawrence, of the Second regiment of infantry, with one hundred and twenty men under him. With this disproportionate force, he soon drove the enemy's troops from their position on shore, by discharges of grape and canister; and, after a cannonade of three hours, compelled the vessels to retire, with great loss. Captain Percy's ship, carrying twenty-two thirty-two-pounders, was driven on shore within six hundred yards of the battery, where she suffered so severely, that those on board were obliged to set her on fire. Of her crew, originally one hundred and seventy, only twenty effected their escape. The other ships, besides being considerably injured, lost eighty-five men in killed and wounded, and returned to Pensacola to repair their damage; while the troops retreated to the same place by land. They were again welcomed by the governor, in direct violation of the treaty between Spain and the United States.

General Jackson, now a major-general in the army, and commander of the southwestern military district, of the United States, having in vain remonstrated with the governor of Pensacola on his reprehensible conduct in harbouring and assisting our enemies, determined to seek redress, without waiting for authority from the American government. Having received a reinforcement of two thousand Tennessee militia and some Choctaw Indians, he advanced to Pensacola. On the 6th of November, he reached the neighbourhood of that post, and immediately sent major Pierre with a flag to the governor. This officer, however, was fired upon from the fort, and obliged to return, without communicating the object of his mission. Jackson then reconnoitered the fort, and finding it defended both by British and Spaniards, made arrangements for storming the town the next day. The troops were put in motion at daylight. They had encamped to the west of the town during the night; and in order to induce the enemy to suppose that the attack would be made from that quarter, the general caused part of the mounted men to show themselves on the west, whilst with the great body of the troops he passed undiscovered, in the rear of the fort, to the east of the town. His whole force became visible when a mile distant, and advanced firmly to the town, although

Y

there were seven British armed vessels on their left, a strong
fort ready to assail them on the right. and batteries of heavy
cannon in front.   On entering the town, a battery of two can-
nons, loaded with ball and grape, was opened on the central
column, composed of regulars, and a shower of musketry poured
from the houses and gardens.   This battery was soon carried,
and the musketry were silenced.   The governor now made
his appearance with a flag, and offering to surrender the town
and fort unconditionally, begged for mercy.   This was granted,
and protection given to the persons and property of the inhabitants.   The commandant of the fort, nevertheless, kept the
Americans out of possession until midnight ; and evacuated it
just as they were preparing to make a furious assault.   On the
8th, the British withdrew with their shipping; and Jackson,
having accomplished his purpose, set out, on the 9th, on his return to Mobile.

By the 1st of September it was reduced to a certainty, that,
notwithstanding the negotiations pending between the United
States and Great Britain at Ghent, formidable preparations were
making for an invasion of Louisiana.   Governor Claiborne
therefore ordered the two divisions of the militia of that state,
the first under general Villeré and the second under general
Thomas, to hold themselves in readiness to march at a moment's warning.   He also issued an animating address, calling
on the inhabitants to turn out *en masse*. for the defence of their
families and homes.   On the 16th of September, a number of
the citizens convened, in order, in co-operation with the civil
authorities, to devise measures for the defence of the country.
Edward Livingston, Esq , lately deceased, was chosen president of the meeting ; and, after an eloquent speech, he proposed
a spirited resolution, going to repel the calumnious insinuation
that the citizens of New Orleans were disaffected to the American government, and manifesting, as far as language could do,
their determination to oppose the enemy.   This resolution was
adopted by the meeting unanimously , and, when made public,
was received with demonstrations of universal applause.

Thus far, the war had been felt in this portion of the union
only in its effects on commercial and agricultural property.
In consequence of the suppression of trade and the low price
of all kinds of produce, the people had suffered much.   The
banks had stopped payment, and distresses of every kind had
begun to be felt.   The great mass of the planters of Louisiana,
(at least those of French origin) of an amiable and gentle disposition, had paid but little attention to the war ; and, outside
of the city of New Orleans, the militia could scarcely be said

to be organized, much less disciplined or armed. Nothing short of an actual invasion could rouse them. In the city the case was different. From the commencement of the war, as if sensible of the feeble help which they could expect from the general government, the inhabitants had manifested the greatest alacrity in qualifying themselves for taking the field against an invader. Every man, capable of bearing arms, had become a soldier, and perhaps in no other city of the country were there such frequent and elegant displays of well disciplined and well dressed volunteer companies. The aptitude of Frenchmen for the profession of arms was now shown to have been inherited by their descendants, and not a few of the natives of France, men who had served in her armies, were intermingled with them. The free people of colour, a numerous class, were permitted, as a privilege, to form volunteer companies and wear uniform : some of these were natives, but the greater part were refugees from the island of St Domingo. The dissensions, hitherto of frequent occurrence, between what were termed the American and French inhabitants, were healed by a union of dislike to the English and of hearty determination to frustrate their designs.

The chief dependence of the inhabitants of New Orleans for safety, was in the nature of the surrounding country, and its exceeding difficulty of access to an enemy invading by sea. In front is a shallow coast, and the principal entrance is a river, which, after crossing the bar, is narrow, deep and rapid, and of a course so winding that it was easy to fortify it. To the west are impassable swamps, and on the east, the low marshy coasts can be approached only through a shallow lake. The most natural defence of such a country, would be gun-boats, or vessels drawing little water and capable of being easily transferred from place to place. Great uneasiness, however, prevailed, on account of the inadequacy of the means for opposing the powerful invading force which was expected. Louisiana, like other parts of the union, had been left by the administration (which had neither money nor men to send) to rely chiefly on itself. It was certainly, as it respected men, arms and military works, in a most defenceless condition. The legislature had been convened, and was in session ; but instead of the active provision of means of resistance, much of its time was spent in idle discussion.

In times of general alarm and danger, nothing is of so much importance, as a man at the head of affairs possessed of firmness and decision of character. Happily, at this critical juncture, there was found such an one in general Jackson. This officer hastened his departure from Mobile, on hearing of the danger of New Orleans, and arrived there on the 2d of December. His presence was instantly felt in the confidence which it inspired, and the unanimity and alacrity with which all seconded every disposition and measure which he directed. He visited in person the points at which it was necessary to erect works. All the inlets, or bayous, from the Atchafalaya river to the Chef Menteur pass or channel, were ordered to be obstructed. The banks of the Mississippi were fortified by his direction, in such a manner as to prevent any of the enemy's vessels from ascending; and a battery was erected on the Chef Menteur, so as to oppose the passage of the enemy in that direction. He then called on the legislature to furnish him the means of expediting the different works which he had marked out—requisitions which met with prompt compliance. About one thousand regulars were stationed at New Orleans, which, together with the Tennessee militia under generals Coffee and Cariol, were distributed at the most vulnerable points. In anticipation of the approaching danger, military supplies had been forwarded by the Ohio river; and the governors of Tennessee and Kentucky had been called upon for a considerable force, to be sent with all possible expedition to Louisiana.

On the 9th of December, certain intelligence was received that the British fleet, consisting of at least sixty sail, was off the coast to the east of the Mississippi. Commodore Patterson, commander of the naval station, immediately despatched a flotilla of five gun-boats, under the command of lieutenant Thomas Ap Catesby Jones, to watch the motions of the enemy. They were discovered in such force off Cat Island, at the entrance of Lake Borgne, that the lieutenant determined to make sail for the passes into Lake Pontchartrain, in order to oppose the entrance of the British. The Sea Horse, sailing-master Johnson, after a gallant resistance, was captured in the Bay of St Louis. On the 14th, the gun-boats, while becalmed, were attacked by nearly forty barges, carrying twelve hundred men, and, after a contest of an hour with so overwhelming a force, they surrendered. The loss of the Americans was forty killed and wounded: among the latter lieutenant Spidden, who lost an arm, and lieutenants Jones and M'Keever. The loss of the enemy was estimated at three hundred men.

The destruction of the gun-boats now placed it in the power of the enemy to choose his point of attack, and, at the same time, in a great measure deprived the Americans of the means of watching his motions. The commander-in-chief ordered the

battalion of men of colour, under major Lacoste, together with
the Feliciana dragoons, to take post on the Chef Menteur, in
order to cover the Gentilly road, which leads from thence to the
city, and also to defend the passage from Lake Borgne into
Lake Pontchartrain ; while captain Newman, of the artillery,
who commanded the fort at the Rigolets, the second and only
other channel between these two lakes, was ordered to defend
that place to the last extremity. Other measures were rapidly
adopted. Colonel Fortier, one of the principal merchants of
city, who had the superintendence of the volunteers composed
of the men of colour, formed a second battalion. which was
placed under the command of major Daquin. By means of
bounties, a number of persons were induced to serve on board
the schooner Caroline and the brig Louisiana ; and thus the
places of the sailors captured by the British were supplied.
On the 18th, the commander-in-chief reviewed the city regiments, and was particularly gratified with the appearance of
the uniform companies commanded by major Planche. The
battalion of the latter, with a company of light artillery under
lieutenant Wagner, was ordered to Fort St John, for the protection of the bayou of that name, through which access could be
gained from Lake Pontchartrain into the upper part of the city
of New Orleans, or across to the Mississippi. An embargo for
three days was decreed by the legislature , a number of persons
confined in the prisons were liberated on condition of serving
in the ranks ; and at length the commander-in-chief conceived
it indispensable, for the safety of the country, to proclaim martial law, a measure which perhaps was justifiable in the circumstances. About this time Lafitte and his Baratarians—a
horde of smugglers and pirates, who had carried on their illegal
operations from an almost inaccessible island in the lake of that
name—availed themselves of the amnesty and pardon offered
them by governor Claiborne on condition that they would come
forward and aid in the defence of the country ; and joined the
American forces.

All the principal bayous which communicate with Lake
Pontchartrain, and intersect the narrow strip of land between
the Mississippi and the swamps, had been obstructed. There
was, however, a channel connected with Lake Borgne, called
the Bayou Bienvenu, and having its head near the plantation
of general Villeré, seven miles below the city. Although it
was not believed that this pass, which was known to few except fishermen, afforded much facility for the approach of an
invading army, general Jackson gave orders that it should be
obstructed and guarded. A small force was accordingly station-

Y⁷

ed near its entrance into the lake, at the cabins of some fishermen who, as afterwards appeared, were in the employment of the British; but its obstruction was neglected or forgotten. On the 22d, guided by these fishermen, a division of the enemy under general Keane, which had been transported thither in boats, came suddenly upon the American guard, and took them prisoners. By four o'clock in the morning of the 23d, they reached the commencement of Villeré's canal, near the head of the bayou. There they disembarked and rested some hours; after which, again proceeding, by two o'clock, P. M. they reached the bank of the Mississippi. General Villeré's house was immediately surrounded, as was also that of his neighbour, colonel La Ronde; but this officer, as well as major Villeré, was so fortunate as to effect his escape, and hastened to head quarters, to communicate intelligence of the approach of the enemy.

The commander-in-chief, on receiving this information, instantly resolved on the only course to be pursued, which was, without the loss of a moment's time, to attack the enemy. In one hour's time, Coffee's riflemen, stationed above the city, were at the place of rendezvous, the battalion of major Plauche had arrived from the bayou, and the regulars and city volunteers were ready to march. By six o'clock in the evening, the different corps were united on Rodrigue's canal, six miles below the city. The schooner Caroline, captain Henley, bearing the broad pendant of commodore Patterson, at the same time dropped down the river; and orders were given to lieutenant-commandant Thompson to follow with the Louisiana. General Coffee's command, together with captain Beale's riflemen, was placed on the extreme left, towards the woods; the city volunteers and the men of colour, under Plauche and Daquin, both commanded by colonel Ross, were stationed in the centre; and to the right, the two regiments of regulars, the Seventh and Fourty-fourth; while the artillery and marines, under colonel M'Rea, occupied the road. The whole force scarcely exceeded two thousand men. The British troops, which amounted to three thousand men, on their arrival at the Mississippi, instead of pushing directly towards the city, had bivouacked, with their right resting on a wood and their left on the river, in the full conviction that the most difficult part of the enterprise was already achieved. Coffee was ordered to turn their right and attack them in the rear; while general Jackson in person, with the main body of the troops, assailed them in front and on their left: a fire from the Caroline was to be the signal of attack. At half past seven o'clock, night having already set in, the action commenced by a raking broadside from the schooner, which was directed by the light of the enemy's fires, and afforded the first intimation of the approach of the Americans. Coffee's men, with their usual impetuosity, now rushed to the attack, and entered the British camp; while the troops in front and on the right, under the immediate command of general Jackson, advanced with equal ardour.

The enemy were taken by surprise, and although they soon extinguished their fires and formed, yet order was not restored before several hundreds of them had been killed or wounded. A thick fog, which arose shortly afterward, and a misunderstanding of instructions by one of the principal officers, producing some confusion in the American ranks, Jackson called off his troops, and lay on the field that night. At four of the following morning, he fell back to a position about two miles nearer the city, where the swamp and the Mississippi approached nearest to each other, and where, therefore, his line of defence would be the shortest and most tenable. In his front was a mill-race which was supplied with water from the river. The American loss in this battle was twenty-four killed, among whom was colonel Lauderdale of Tennessee, a brave soldier, who fell much lamented; one hundred and fifteen wounded; and seventy-four prisoners, of whom were many of the principal inhabitants of the city. That of the British was estimated at four hundred in killed, wounded and missing. If it was the object of the American general to teach his adversaries caution, and thus retard their advance, he fully succeeded; for during four days, they kept within their intrenchments, contenting themselves with active preparatory occupations. They were probably influenced somewhat to suspend the immediate execution of their intended movement on New Orleans, by the false accounts given by their prisoners, who stated that the American force amounted to fifteen thousand men.

Meanwhile general Jackson set to work immediately to fortify his position. This he effected by the construction of a simple breastwork, extending from the swamp to the river, with a ditch (the mill-race above mentioned) in front. To expedite these works, and to supply the place of earth, of which there was great scarcity owing to the swampy character of the ground, an extraordinary expedient was adopted. Bales of cotton, brought from New Orleans, were placed upon the line, and covered with earth; and of such materials was the rampart formed. As the enemy were still annoyed by the Caroline and the Louisiana, the latter having joined the former, and both being prevented from escaping up the river by a strong wind, batteries were constructed to attack them. From these, on the 27th, hot shot were thrown, by which the Caroline was set on fire. She blew up, about an hour after she had been abandoned by her crew. The Louisiana next sustained the fire of their batteries, until she was in imminent danger of sharing the fate of the Caroline. In losing her, the whole co-operative naval force would have been lost; but her commander, lieutenant Thompson, after encountering many obstacles, finally succeeded in extricating her from her perilous situation, and anchoring her on the right flank of general Jackson's position. After the destruction of the Caroline, sir Edward Packenham, the British commander-in-chief, having landed the main body of his army and a sufficient train of artillery, superintended, in person, the arrangements for attacking the American intrenchments. On the 28th, he advanced up the levee, as the narrow strip between the river and the swamp is called, with the intention of driving Jackson into the city; and at the distance of half a mile commenced the attack with rockets, bombs and cannon. When he came within reach, the Louisiana, and the batteries on the American works, opened a fire on him which was very destructive. At the end of seven hours, during which he made no attempt at a nearer approach to the American line, the British general relinquished the attack, and retired. The loss of the Americans was seven killed and eight wounded, among the former colonel Henderson of Tennessee; that of the British was computed at a total of one hundred and twenty.

On the morning of the 1st of January 1815, sir Edward Packenham was discovered to have constructed batteries near the American works, and at daylight commenced a heavy fire from them, which was well returned by Jackson. A bold attempt was, at the same time, made to turn the left of the Americans; but in this the enemy were completely repulsed. About three o'clock in the afternoon, the fire of the British was silenced; and, abandoning the batteries, their army returned to the camp. The loss of the Americans, on this occasion, was eleven killed and twenty-three wounded. On the 4th, general Jackson was joined by two thousand five hundred Kentuckians, under general Adair; and on the 6th, the British were reinforced by general Lambert, at the head of a reserve of four thousand men. The British force now amounted to little short of fifteen thousand of the finest troops; that of the Americans to about six thousand, chiefly untried militia, a considerable portion unarmed, and from the haste of their departure, badly provided with clothing. To supply those who were without weapons, all the private arms which the inhabitants of New Orleans possessed, were collected ; and the ladies occupied themselves continually in making clothing for those who were in want of it. The mayor of the city, Mr Girod, was particularly active at this trying moment.

The British general now prepared for a serious attempt on the American works. With great labour he had completed, on the 7th, a water communication from the swamp to the Mississippi, by widening and deepening the canal on which the troops had originally effected their disembarkation. He was thus enabled to transport a number of his boats to the river. It was his intention to make a simultaneous attack on the main force of general Jackson on the left bank, and, crossing the river, on the troops and fortifications which defended the right bank. The works of the American general on the left bank of the river, were by this time completed. His front was a breastwork of about a mile long, extending from the river into the swamp, till it became impassable, and for the last two hundred yards taking a turn to the left. The whole was defended by upwards of three thousand infantry and artillerists. The ditch contained five feet water ; and the ground in front, having been flooded by water introduced from the river and by frequent rains, was slippery and muddy. Eight distinct batteries were judiciously disposed, mounting in all twelve guns of different calibres. On the opposite side of the river, there was a strong battery of fifteen guns, and the intrenchments which had been erected were occupied by general Morgan, with some Louisiana militia, and a strong detachment of Kentucky troops.

On the memorable morning of the 8th of January, general Packenham, having detached colonel Thornton with at least five hundred men, to attack the works on the right bank of the river, moved with his whole force, in two columns commanded by major-generals Gibbs and Keane. The right and principal division, under the former of these officers, was to attack the centre of the works. The British deliberately advanced to the assault in solid columns, over the even plain in front of the American intrenchments, the men carrying, besides their muskets, fascines made of sugar cane, and some of them ladders. A dead silence prevailed until they approached within reach of the batteries, when an incessant and destructive cannonade commenced. Notwithstanding this, they continued to advance in tolerable order, closing up their ranks as fast as they were opened by the fire of the Americans, until they came within reach of the musquetry and rifles, when such dreadful havock was produced, that they were instantly thrown into the utmost

confusion. Never was there so tremendous a fire as that
kept up from the American lines. It was a continued stream;
those behind, loading for the men in front, and enabling them to
fire with scarcely an intermission. The British columns were
literally swept away: hundreds fell at every discharge. Broken,
dispersed, disheartened, they retreated. The most active efforts
were made to rally them. General Packenham was killed in
front of his troops, animating them by his presence and example;
and probably not less than a thousand men, dead and wounded,
were lying beside him Generals Gibbs and Keane succeeded
in bringing them up again; but the second approach was more
fatal than the first. The continued roll of the American fire re-
sembled peals of thunder; it was such as no troops could withstand. The advancing columns again broke; a few platoons
reaching the edge of the ditch, only to meet certain destruction.
An unavailing attempt was made to lead them to the attack a
third time by their officers, whose gallantry, on this occasion,
deserved a better fate, in a better cause. Generals Gibbs and
Keane were carried from the field, the latter severely, the former mortally wounded. The narrow field of strife between
the British and the American lines was strewed with dead.
So dreadful a carnage, considering the length of time and the
numbers engaged, has seldom been recorded : two thousand,
at the lowest estimate, pressed the earth, besides such of the
wounded as were not able to escape. The loss of the Americans did not exceed seven killed, and six wounded. Military
annals do not furnish a more extraordinary instance of disparity
in the slain, between the victors and vanquished. The decided advantage of the Americans, which may be acknowledged without detracting from their praise, gave to the conduct
of the enemy more of the character of madness than of valour.
By the fall of general Packenham, the command devolved on
general Lambert, who was the only general officer left upon the
field, and to whom had been consigned the charge of the reserve. He met the discomfited troops in their flight, and, being
unable to restore the fortune of day, withdrew them from the
reach of the guns, and finally from the field of battle.

  In the meantime, the detachment under colonel Thornton
succeeded in landing on the right bank of the river, and immediately attacked the intrenchments of general Morgan. The
American right. being outflanked, abandoned its position. The
left maintained its ground for some time; but, finding itself
deserted by the right and outnumbered by the enemy, spiked
its guns, and also retired. In the course of the contest, colonel
Thornton was severely wounded, and the command of the Bri-

tish devolved on colonel Gubbins. As soon as these disasters were made known to general Jackson, he prepared to throw reinforcements across the river, to dislodge the enemy. This measure was rendered unnecessary, however, by their voluntary retreat across the river, in obedience to the order of general Lambert.

On the 9th, general Lambert determined to relinquish the hopeless enterprise; and immediately commenced the necessary preparations, which were conducted with great secrecy. It was not until the night of the 18th, however, that the British camp was entirely evacuated. From the nature of the country, and the redoubts which the enemy had erected to cover their retreat, it was deemed unadvisable to pursue them. They left eight of their wounded, and fourteen pieces of artillery, behind them. Returning by the same route along which so short a time before they had advanced with hope and confidence, they reached the fleet without annoyance. Their loss in this fatal expedition was immense. Besides their generals and a number of valuable officers, their force was diminished by at least three thousand men. It was undertaken too at a time when peace, unknown to them, had been actually concluded; and its successful issue therefore could have led to no permanent results.

Commodore Patterson despatched five boats, under Mr Shields, purser on the New Orleans station, in order to annoy the retreat of the British fleet. This active and spirited officer succeeded in capturing several boats and taking a number of prisoners.

The British fleet on the coast was not inactive during these operations. It was intended that a squadron should enter the Mississippi, and, reducing the works at Fort St Philip, ascend the river, and co-operate in the attack on New Orleans. The bombardment of the fort commenced on the 11th of January, and was continued with more or less activity for eight days. At the end of this time, the enemy, finding they had made no serious impression, dropped down the river, and put to sea. The fort was garrisoned and bravely maintained by three hundred and sixty-six men under the command of major Overton.

Great rejoicing took place throughout the United States, and especially in New Orleans, in consequence of these events; and every honour was bestowed upon the commander-in-chief. It is to be regretted, however, that some unpleasant occurrences (the merit of which it is not within the plan of this work to discuss) tended to alloy the brilliancy of success. Whether these are to be ascribed to the *use*, or *abuse* of martial law, we will leave to others to determine.

While these bloody affairs transpired on the Mississippi, admiral Cockburn was pursuing a more lucrative and less dangerous warfare along the coast of the Carolinas and Georgia. He took possession of Cumberland island, and menacing Charleston and Savannah, sent out detachments which met with various success; but his chief and more interesting occupation was plundering the inhabitants of the products of the soil, and of their merchandize and household furniture. The letters of some of his officers to their companions, which were intercepted, displayed the spirit of petty and dishonourable cupidity and plunder by which these gentlemen were actuated. The most usual topics of these epistles were the amount and species of plunder which they procured; and desks, looking glasses, bureaus and cotton bales were exultingly enumerated, as if they had been the ultimate and glorious end of war.

The momentous intelligence of the defeat of the British at New Orleans, had scarcely ceased to operate upon the feelings of the people of the United States, when they received the welcome news of peace. If the declaration of war gave rise, at the time, to partial rejoicing, the announcement of its termination was celebrated with a pleasure that was universal. Peace was proclaimed by the president on the 18th of February 1815; and not long afterwards, a day of thanksgiving to the Almighty was set apart throughout the nation, by the same authority, for its blessed restoration.

The treaty was concluded on the 24th of December 1814, at Ghent, by lord Gambier, Henry Goulburn and William Adams, on the part of Great Britain; and by John Quincy Adams, James A. Bayard, Henry Clay, Jonathan Russel and Albert Gallatin, on behalf of the United States. It stipulated a mutual restoration of all places and possessions taken during the war, or which might be taken after the signing of the treaty. It further declared that all captures at sea should be relinquished, if made twelve days thereafter, in all parts of the American coast from the twenty-third to the fiftieth degree of north latitude, as far east as thirty-six degrees of longitude west from Greenwich; thirty days thereafter, in all other parts of the Atlantic north of the equator; the same time, for the British and Irish Channels, the Gulf of Mexico, and the West Indies; forty days, for the North Seas, the Baltic, and all parts of the Mediterranean; sixty days, for the Atlantic Ocean, south of the equator, as far as the Cape of Good Hope; ninety days, for every other part of the world south of the equator; and one hundred and twenty days, for all other parts without exception. It was further agreed that the parties should mutually put a stop to Indian hostilities, and use their best endeavours to extinguish the traffic in slaves.   But much the greater part of the treaty related to the adjustment of the boundaries between the British possessions and those of the United States, which had been imperfectly adjusted by the treaty of 1783.   The subjects of impressment, of paper blockade and of orders in council, and the rights of the neutral flag, were passed over without notice.

Thus terminated an eventful war of two years and eight months, or, as it is commonly called, three years.   It is related of the wise Franklin, that, hearing some one term our first war with Great Britain, *the war of independence,* he reproved him : " Sir," said he, " you mean of the revolution ; the war of independence is yet to come."   That war is now over ; and every hope on the part of Great Britain to bring us back to the state of colonies, has fled for ever.   By the seizure, during peace, of a thousand of our merchantmen and of seven thousand of our fellow citizens, she drove us into a war with her ; whereby two thousand of her merchantmen were lost, and many millions added to the sum of her already immense national debt. Still more : the frequent captures of her public vessels, by the ships of our small but gallant navy, have established the painful truth, that she has an equal on the ocean.   We have at last induced her to treat us with respect; and, into whatever portion of the globe his fortune may lead him, an American may now own his country with pride.   We have no wish to be otherwise than on terms of friendship with Great Britain.   We have a common origin, a common language, institutions nearly similar, and, to use the elegant language of Milton, we draw light from the same fountain.   Should she ever need a friend, notwithstanding the past, she will find a sincere one in the United States of North America.

To us the war is pregnant with important lessons.   We have acquired a knowledge of our weakness and of our strength.   We have been taught that our best policy is honourable peace, and the preference, in our intercourse with all nations, of justice to profit.   We have been taught, and the lesson is worth the sum we paid for the war, that we are weak in conquest, but sufficiently strong for defence.

THE END.

z

CPSIA information can be obtained
at www.ICGtesting.com
Printed in the USA
BVHW041417150421
605033BV00009B/830